THE
PRO FOOTBALL
HALL OF FAME
50TH ANNIVERSARY
BOOK

THE PRO FOOTBALL HALL OF FAME 50TH ANNIVERSARY BOOK

WHERE GREATNESS LIVES

Edited by JOE HORRIGAN and JOHN THORN

GRAND CENTRAL PUBLISHING

New York • Boston

Grand Central Publishing
Hachette Book Group
237 Park Avenue
New York, NY 10017

www.HachetteBookGroup.com

Printed in the United States of America

WOR

Design by BTDNYC

First Edition: July 2012

10 9 8 7 6 5 4 3 2 1

Grand Central Publishing is a division of Hachette Book Group, Inc.
The Grand Central Publishing name and logo is a trademark of Hachette Book Group, Inc.

The Hachette Speakers Bureau provides a wide range of authors for speaking events. To find out more, go to www.hachettespeakersbureau.com or call (866) 376-6591.

The publisher is not responsible for websites (or their content) that are not owned by the publisher.

LIBRARY OF CONGRESS CATALOGING-IN-PUBLICATION DATA

The Pro Football Hall of Fame 50th anniversary book : where greatness lives/edited by John Thorn and Joe Horrigan.

    p. cm.

  Includes index.

  ISBN 978-0-446-58396-1

1. Pro Football Hall of Fame (U.S.) 2. Football—United States—History. 3. Football players—United States—Biography. I. Thorn, John, 1947– II. Horrigan, Joe.

GV959.5.P76 2012

796.332'64—dc23

                    2011041519

ACKNOWLEDGMENTS

WARREN MOON

Upon seeing his bronzed bust for the first time, Hall of Fame quarterback Warren Moon leaned back and gazed approvingly. Stepping to the podium, he then turned his attention to the thousands of friends, family members, teammates, and fans who had assembled to share in his special day. "Thank you very much," he began, followed by an emotional, "Wow."

VINCE LOMBARDI CALLED THE Packer Sweep his number-one play "because it requires eleven men to play as one for it to succeed, and that's what team means." Well, like the Packer Sweep, this book is the product of many individuals working together as a team with one common goal—producing a quality book that celebrates pro football and the fiftieth anniversary of America's premier sports museum and showplace, the Pro Football Hall of Fame.

But before we pay tribute to those who were directly involved in the creation of this book, it is important to acknowledge—although far too many to list individually—the past and present members of the Hall of Fame staff, Board of Trustees, and the thousands of volunteers, all of whom collectively have made the Pro Football Hall of Fame a genuine success story. This book is a testament to their hard work and dedication.

Specific to the book, we certainly have many to thank. Let's begin with Steve Perry, president and executive director of the Hall of Fame. Without his support and encouragement the project simply would not have happened. It is his leadership and vision that is setting the course for the Hall of Fame's next fifty years.

Many thanks to Saleem Choudhry, researcher for the Hall of Fame, who was immensely helpful on a number of levels, including guiding us through the thousands of photos from which our final selections were made. Pete Fierle, manager of digital media/communications for the Hall of Fame, and researcher Jon Kendle scoured the archives to unearth the hundreds of quotes featured throughout. Additionally, Pete (who also contributed an essay), Saleem, and Jon proofed our copy, preventing factual errors from ruining otherwise good stories.

Jason Aikens, collections curator, and Christy Davis, registrar, also worked diligently to help us select not only the obvious artifacts of historical significance, but some that were just plain interesting. They then worked with photographer Shaun Wood of Studio 7 to bring the artifacts to life on film.

Chris Schilling, communications assistant at the Hall of Fame, transcribed interviews of Hall of Famers and frequently picked up the slack in the office to allow others to commit the time necessary to focus on this worthwhile project.

Beth Tondreau gave us a splendidly integrated design, no easy matter for a book comprised of so many distinct features. At Grand Central Publishing, Rick Wolff was our trusted editor and constant ally. Carolyn Kurek, Thomas Whatley, Nick Small, and Meredith Haggerty were stars behind the scenes, keeping us on track to our appointed hour of publication.

With such unified effort, this has been a Packer Sweep, indeed.

CONTENTS

The 1960s

THE MAN WHO MADE THE DECADE

The 1970s

DEFENSE WINS CHAMPIONSHIPS

The 1980s

THE NFL'S GREATEST DECADE?

The 1990s

CONSTRUCTING A WINNER

The 2000s

PROSPERING IN THE AGE OF THE SALARY CAP

The Eleven Greatest Moments

FOREWORD

HOWIE LONG

HOWIE LONG

In action at left, against the Denver Broncos in 1992, and during induction speech above.

IN 2000 I WAS ACCORDED THE HIGHEST SINGLE HONOR a pro football player can achieve when I was elected to the Pro Football Hall of Fame. Was Hall of Fame election something I dreamed of as a youngster? No. That came later. Was it something I worked hard to achieve? Oh, absolutely yes. But even now, more than a decade later, I'm still coming to grips with the magnitude of the tribute. To know that more than 23,000 men have played pro football, yet fewer than 300 have been elected to the Hall of Fame, is simply overwhelming.

When I reflect on my "road to Canton," I realize that so much of my personal success was nurtured by others. People like my high school coach Dick Corbin, who convinced a then-lanky 6'3", 220-pound sophomore—who'd never played any organized sports—to try out for the football team. I've always wondered if Coach Corbin was as surprised as I was by how well I took to the sport. Playing gave me a sense of belonging, a focus, and helped build my confidence. At that point in my life I was a troubled kid searching for something to grab hold of, and football provided that. This was the start of a journey that would end in Canton.

Following high school I earned an athletic scholarship to Villanova. Villanova is a terrific school, and was the right place for a very raw seventeen-year-old to develop both as a person and as a football player. But because of the level of competition I was never really challenged, and pro scouts were reluctant to sign off on a small-school guy, regardless of my upside. That changed, however, after I earned MVP honors in the postseason Blue-Gray Game. Suddenly there were scouts by the planeload. Still, some scouts doubted my ability to compete at the next level. One man who didn't was Oakland Raiders defensive line coach Earl Leggett, who had been dispatched to scout me. Earl believed in me and successfully lobbied the Raiders

HOWIE LONG UNIFORM
See page 189.

brain trust to select me in the second round of the 1981 draft. In training camp Earl made me his personal project. More than anyone, he is responsible for Howie Long the football player.

As a rookie, my goal was simply to make the team. My second year I wanted to be a starter. Then my third year I wanted to make the Pro Bowl, all of which I accomplished. In 1984, before the start of my fourth season, I was asked if I had any other personal goals. I remember replying without hesitation that I wanted to be a Hall of Famer. You see, as a young player with the Oakland Raiders, I had the luxury of being surrounded by great players: Hall of Famers Art Shell, Gene Upshaw, Fred Biletnikoff, Ted Hendricks, Jim Otto—on and on. Thinking in those terms was part of the makeup of the organization, so answering the question in that way wasn't bravado on my part— it was just me dreaming of living up to the standard that had been set by so many of those great players before me.

But, as we all know, setting a goal is the easy part; the willingness to put in the hard work and long hours to achieve that goal is what makes a difference—an attribute characteristic of every member of

ERNIE NEVERS' TRUNK
See page 34.

the Hall of Fame. That said, at the time I really had no idea just how high the Hall of Fame bar was already set. Nonetheless, that was my goal.

Now, when I visit Canton and the Hall of Fame and see my bronze bust, well, it's hard to explain. I feel a tremendous sense of pride and accomplishment, but it is tempered by a huge dose of humility as I look around and see the likenesses of players like Deacon Jones, Joe Montana, Walter Payton, and Dick Butkus. To be in the Hall of Fame is so special. And as I continue to learn more about the history of the game and its pioneers, like George Halas, Art Rooney, Red Grange, and Don Hutson, I realize how much they contributed and how important it is to preserve their legacy and the history of the game that has benefited so many of us.

The Pro Football Hall of Fame serves as the game's shrine and rightfully calls itself "America's premier sports museum." Within the walls of the Hall of Fame and the pages of this book one can truly gain an appreciation for the men who not only made pro football America's most popular sport but also, as I said in my enshrinement speech in 2000, made it "America's passion."

The Pro Football Hall of Fame 50th Anniversary Book brings to life some amazing stories that today border on the unbelievable. Stories like how a team called the Duluth Eskimos went on a 29-game, 17,000-mile barnstorming tour in 1926. And I'm still blown away by the fact that Hall of Fame fullback Ernie Nevers played in all but 29 minutes of that grueling schedule. Throughout the book there are examples of individual triumphs, team successes, and milestone moments brought to life by the written text and powerful images. When I looked at the image of a pair of high-top shoes alongside a blue-and-white Number 19 Baltimore Colts jersey, I knew immediately they could belong to only one man: Johnny Unitas. Likewise the Number 32 Cleveland Browns jersey featured in the book needs no explanation. Legends like Unitas and Jim Brown are bigger than the game.

This book is filled with unique artifacts and photos from every era, some never before published. *The Pro Football Hall of Fame 50th Anniversary Book* is an incredible tribute to the sport of professional football and the institution that for 50 years has preserved its remarkable story—a sport, a game, and an institution of which I'm incredibly proud to be a part.

Until you can come visit the Hall, for the first time or your next time, enjoy the pages to follow.

HOWIE LONG
2000 Hall of Fame Inductee

JOHNNY UNITAS UNIFORM
See page 110.

JIM BROWN UNIFORM
See page 138.

INTRODUCTION
Why Canton?

JOHN THORN

Let's begin by supplying the short answer to this question.

THE PRO FOOTBALL HALL OF FAME is located in Canton, Ohio, for three primary reasons. First, the American Professional Football Association, later renamed the National Football League, was founded in Canton on September 17, 1920, in Ralph Hay's Hupmobile showroom. Second, the Canton Bulldogs were an early pro football power, even before the days of the NFL; they were also the first two-time champion of the NFL in 1922 and 1923. The great Jim Thorpe played his first pro football season with the Bulldogs, starting in 1915. Third, Canton citizens early in the 1960s launched a determined and well-organized campaign to earn the site designation for their city.

But "why Canton?" becomes a question of interest only after we have already tacitly accepted certain other ideas, none of which were broadly held in the early years of the National Football League: that professional football is an institution that matters to America; that its history and heroes are worthy of celebration and study; and that its artifacts might attract visitors to a landmark repository, again and again. These beliefs underlie the mission statement of the Pro Football Hall of Fame, now celebrating its fiftieth anniversary: to honor, preserve, educate, and promote.

The Hall of Fame honors individuals who have made outstanding contributions to professional football. It preserves the game's historic documents and regalia. It educates the public regarding the origin, development, and growth of professional football as an important part of American culture. It promotes the positive values of the sport:

Previous page:

CANTON'S FIRST PRO TEAM

In the early 1900s pro football began to decline in the Pittsburgh area and its center shifted from Pennsylvania to Ohio. In 1905, the amateur Canton A.C., later known as the Bulldogs, became a professional team.

teamwork, tenacity, and striving for excellence, to name just a few. As a national shrine that incorporates local enthusiasms, a Hall of Fame becomes a stadium of stadiums, a cathedral for fans journeying to Canton from rival congregations.

The Pro Football Hall of Fame was not the first such institution proposed for a sport. Baseball was the first, dedicating its hall at Cooperstown, New York, in 1939. (It was modeled on the Hall of Fame for Great Americans, created on the New York University campus in 1900.) But while the first mention of a pantheon for baseball's greats earned some media coverage as early as 1907, the first proposal for a Football Hall of Fame came only three years later. On December 11, 1910, in an article titled "An All American Team of All Time," published in the *Canton Repository* and elsewhere, Tommy Clark wrote:

> Even though the football season of 1910 is now a thing of the past and all the big elevens have selected their leaders for next season and the experts have chosen their all star teams, an All American of All Americans will no doubt prove interesting to the followers of the strenuous gridiron game. The eleven is composed of men who have been awarded conspicuous places in the theoretical football hall of fame.

The veteran football writer was talking about the college game, of course, and in populating his hall of fame he was going back only twenty-one years, to Walter Camp's naming of the first All-America team in 1889. Of his illustrious eleven—consisting of men from Yale, Harvard, Princeton, Columbia, Chicago, and Michigan—few would be recognizable to the fan of today. Yet for the student of pro football history, one name leaps from the page: Pudge Heffelfinger, right guard for Yale and ringer for the Allegheny Athletic Association (AAA) in an ostensibly amateur contest in 1892. He is the first man for whom we have an indisputable record of having been paid to play the game.

One might think that the location of a Hall of Fame thus might attach to nearby Pittsburgh, or to New Haven, home of Pudge's collegiate exploits. But Heffelfinger's role was relatively unknown at the time when various localities competed for the right to host a Pro Football Hall of Fame. Not until some years after the hall was up and running in Canton did its first director, Dick McCann, discover a page torn from an account ledger of the AAA that included the line, "Game performance bonus to W. Heffelfinger for playing (cash) $500."

Before Canton won the NFL designation, the first and most compelling claim for a physical site for a pro football hall had come from Latrobe, Pennsylvania. In *Pro Football: Its Ups and Downs*, an anecdotal history self-published in 1934, Harry March wrote that on September 3, 1895, John Brallier had been paid "$10 and cakes [expenses]" to play quarterback for the Latrobe YMCA against a visiting club from Jeannette. Brallier himself believed that he was the first professional, and his claim was supported by many books over the ensuing decades, all of them repeating March's claim.

It was upon this basis that community leaders in Latrobe, beginning in 1947, petitioned the NFL for authorization to locate a Hall of Fame in their fair city. But Latrobe was looking for the league to provide major financial support, so despite the club owners' halfhearted approval, its effort never broke ground.

On September 12, 1949, came the news that the National Football Shrine and Hall of Fame, Inc., an organization created to form a College Football Hall of Fame, had selected as its location Rutgers University, site of the first intercollegiate game in 1869. Rutgers was chosen over Cazenovia, New York, erroneously offered as the birthplace of Gerrit Smith Miller, who had founded the Oneida Football Club, which played either rugby or soccer in Boston in 1862. Nothing much came of this either.

Above:

THE CHECKERBOARD FIELD (1906 GAME ACTION)

In an attempt to "open up" the game and reduce its "brutality," football rules were modified in 1906 to allow the forward pass. The new rule stipulated, however, that a forward pass could not cross the line of scrimmage within five yards of either side of the center. This was consistent with a 1903 rule stating that the first player to receive the ball from center also could not cross the line of scrimmage within that same space. If the ball carrier was the recipient of a handoff, lateral, or backward pass, he could cross the line at any point. To assist game officials, the field was marked off in five-yard grids. Some historians believe that the term "gridiron" was a result.

CHICAGO BEARS FOOTBALL CLUB
233 WEST MADISON STREET
CHICAGO 6, ILLINOIS

GEORGE S. HALAS
PRESIDENT

January 4, 1960

Mr. H. H. Timken, Jr.
Canton 6, Ohio

RECEIVED
JAN 7 1960
CANTON, OHIO

Dear Mr. Timken:

I received your letter of December 30 and am very much
in favor of Canton, Ohio, being established as the site of
the Professional Football Hall of Fame. How well I do
remember the organizational meeting we had of our league,
which was held in Ralph Hays' automobile showroom in 1920,
and made Jim Thorpe our first president.

Due to the fact that I have to be in New York on January 12
and 13, for a long promised appointment inaugurating the
National Football League Enterprises, I am sorry I will
not be able to accept your invitation for the dinner meeting
at the Congress Lake Country Club on Tuesday evening,
January 12. I have spoken to Chuck Mather and he will be
able to attend and speak for me.

Many thanks for your kind invitation and with best wishes for
the New Year, I am

Sincerely yours,

Geo. S. Halas

GSH:o

GEORGE HALAS LETTER

Just one month after Canton threw its hat into the ring and more than a year before being granted official site designation, Chicago Bears owner George Halas wrote to H. H. Timken indicating his support for Canton as the future home of the Pro Football Hall of Fame.
PHOTO: W. R. TIMKEN

Opposite page:

SITE

HALL OF FAME

CONSTRUCTION PHOTOS

1963 AERIAL

Canton won site approval for the Pro Football Hall of Fame in April 1961. Ground-breaking ceremonies were held on August 11, 1962, and the original two-building museum opened on September 7, 1963.

In 1950 the Helms Foundation in Los Angeles named a Hall of Fame board, consisting of seven Los Angeles sports editors, to select twenty-five "of the greatest professional footballers of all time," whose photographs would be placed at the Helms Hall. But in truth, this pale effort still left the door open—by decade's end there was still no institution or physical structure comparable to the Baseball Hall of Fame.

Then, on December 6, 1959, the *Canton Repository* and its editor Clayton Horn challenged its readers with the headline "PRO FOOTBALL NEEDS A HALL OF FAME AND LOGICAL SITE IS HERE." At Horn's behest, sportswriter Chuck Such crafted the story. On the following day Such received a call from Henry H. Timken Jr., the chairman of the board at Canton's largest industry, the Timken Roller Bearing Company. He offered his support, and assigned the company's recreation director, Earl Schreiber, to the project. "He thought the Hall of Fame here was a great idea," Such recalled. "He brought in Earl Schreiber and Bill Umstattd [president of Timken]. He said, 'I want us to give this every resource it needs.' There was one provision. This wouldn't be a Timken Hall of Fame. This would be Canton's Hall of Fame. He pledged as much as $250,000 there."

W. R. "Tim" Timken Jr., former U.S. ambassador to Germany, and retired Chairman of the Board and CEO of The Timken Company, is the nephew of the man whose financial guarantee won the NFL over to Canton's side. He is also a longtime member of the Hall's Board of Trustees. In a previously unpublished interview with the Hall of Fame's Don Smith, he told the backstory of Canton's bid:

"Henry Timken, my uncle, and my father together really decided they needed to change the image of Canton. As you may recall, Canton had the image of being the crime capital layoff city for gangsters out of Detroit and Cleveland...It was a pretty wide-open town and they were determined to change that image. [With a new mayor and police chief] they went on and won the *Look* All American Award and it all fit together from a community development point of view. As a result they were willing to put the resources and efforts in there, and I think that from a community point of view they needed some name recognition as well as financial backing to clear the hurdles that Pete Rozelle had set up. And so again they were willing to do that, and I don't think that Henry was the greatest football fan by any means. And from my recollection I don't remember Bill Umstattd being a football fan. They really did look at it as a betterment-to-the-community project coming together at the right time.

"If I recall the criteria, the city had to have historical significance from a professional football point of view. It had to have a financial backing to make it happen in the beginning. And then the site had to be located in an area where a lot of people could access it, not stuck out in the middle of some remote farm somewhere.

"I think that when they write the history of the Pro Football Hall of Fame, they have to conclude that the people on the board did an excellent job of deciding what this institution should be, how fast it should grow, what its policies should be, and it's been a remarkable success. There has been nothing else that has been as self-funding and self-perpetuating, and it has to be that all of those early board members—before my time on the board—had a great deal of wisdom and foresight and had an understanding of how to run a little business. I think that continues today, and from my point of view that's really the most important obligation of the board going forward, to be able to make as great of a success of it as the people in the past did.

"It really is a great history about football and how it started. I will always think back to the time when I was a kid, and that would have been in the '50s, I went to prep school in the East and I had to take the train from Canton, getting on about two in the morning and getting down to New York to Penn Station. And then I had to go over to Grand Central Station and catch another train to go up to New England. I would always have to get a cab to take over to the other place. New York cabdrivers inevitably, with this little kid sitting in

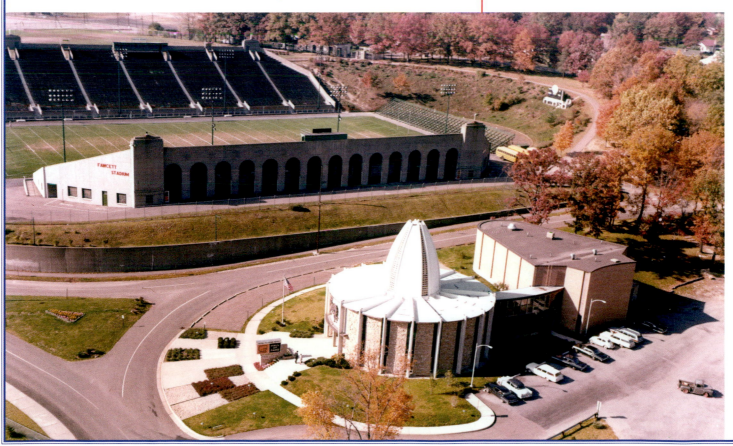

CLASS OF 2011
(L to R) Marshall Faulk, Chris Hanburger, Richard Dent, Shannon Sharpe, Jon Richter (representing his father, Les Richter), Deion Sanders. (Not pictured, 2011 enshrinee Ed Sabol.)

"It never ends. If you play the game to win one Super Bowl or two Super Bowls and then be satisfied, you are playing for the wrong reason. No matter how much you win, you want to win more.**"**

—**Emmitt Smith**

the backseat, they would say, 'Hey kid, where you from?' And I would say, 'I'm from Canton, Ohio.' And almost always you'd get back this, 'Canton, Ohio? That's where those gangs and crooks are, right?' It seemed like every New York cabdriver knew the bad parts of Canton. I can guarantee you today that if I were in New York and I got a cab and the driver said, 'Where are you from?' and you say, 'Canton, Ohio,' he'd say, 'Ah, Pro Football Hall of Fame.' And as far as I'm concerned that shows that the idea to put the Pro Football Hall of Fame in Canton worked. It worked for Canton, and obviously it worked for the Hall of Fame as an institution, for the league in fulfilling what people were looking for, and for all of those people who were enshrined here. I'm just overwhelmed with what's been created here and I think that getting the story down is an important one, because of all of those folks who stepped up to make bold decisions."

The fiftieth anniversary of the Pro Football Hall of Fame represents a triumph for the city, for the league, and for football fans everywhere. The Hall of Fame today reaches outside Canton through a variety of initiatives from traveling exhibits, artifacts on loan, youth and educational outreach programs, and a dynamic website. On December 10, 2010, the largest expansion/renovation project in the Hall of Fame's history was announced. The "Future 50 Project" is a $27 million project that will be completed to coincide with the conclusion of the Pro Football Hall of Fame's fiftieth anniversary year in 2013.

19TH CENTURY NOSE GUARDS

See page 8.

TIKI BARBER'S AND
TOM BRADY'S JERSEYS

See pages 241 & 239.

SUPER BOWL XLIII RING

See page 255.

Following spread:

EMMITT SMITH

RED GRANGE

THE
PRO FOOTBALL
HALL OF FAME
50TH ANNIVERSARY
BOOK

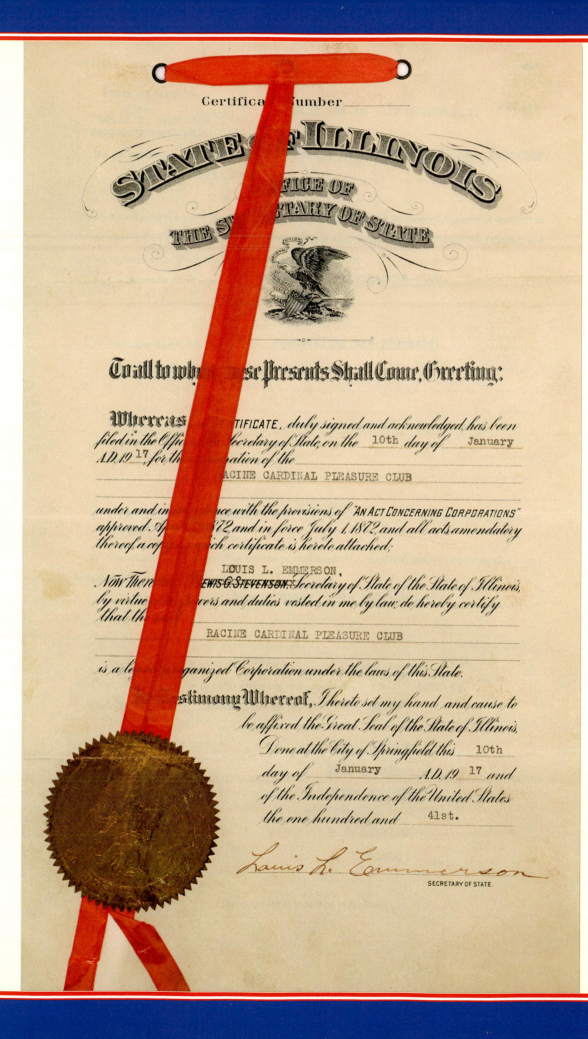

Certificate Number _____

STATE OF ILLINOIS

OFFICE OF
THE SECRETARY OF STATE

To all to whom these Presents Shall Come, Greeting:

Whereas, a CERTIFICATE, duly signed and acknowledged, has been filed in the Office of the Secretary of State, on the 10th day of January A.D. 19 17, for the organization of the

RACINE CARDINAL PLEASURE CLUB

under and in accordance with the provisions of "An Act Concerning Corporations" approved April 18, 1872, and in force July 1, 1872, and all acts amendatory thereof, a copy of which certificate is hereto attached;

LOUIS L. EMMERSON,

Now Therefore, I, LEWIS G. STEVENSON, Secretary of State of the State of Illinois, by virtue of the powers and duties vested in me by law, do hereby certify that the

RACINE CARDINAL PLEASURE CLUB

is a legally organized Corporation under the laws of this State.

In Testimony Whereof, I hereto set my hand and cause to be affixed the Great Seal of the State of Illinois, Done at the City of Springfield this 10th day of January A.D. 19 17 and of the Independence of the United States the one hundred and 41st.

Louis L. Emmerson

SECRETARY OF STATE.

1892–1919

"LET OLD JIM RUN"

BOB CARROLL

Opposite:

THE 1917 ARTICLES OF
INCORPORATION FOR
THE RACINE CARDINALS,
THE OLDEST CONTINUOUSLY
OPERATING TEAM IN THE NFL

The Arizona Cardinals, the oldest continuous professional football franchise, began as an amateur team in Chicago in 1898, known as the Morgan Athletic Club. Eventually the Morgan A.C. developed into a strong pro team known as the Racine Cardinals, a name that reflected both the color of their jerseys and the location of their playing field (Racine Avenue and 61st Street). In 1917 the Cardinals lost just two games and were recognized as city champions. In 1920 they became one of ten charter members of the NFL. That same year the team dropped "Racine" from its name in favor of "Chicago." In 1960 the Chicago Cardinals moved to St. Louis, and then in 1988 to Phoenix.

Bob Carroll was the leading historian of professional football, with a special love for its cradle days in Pennsylvania and Ohio well before the creation of the NFL. An author and encyclopedist, he was the founder and driving force behind the Professional Football Researchers Association, created in 1979 and still going strong. Bob died in 2009, but the editors of this volume could think of no better person to open this book's chronology with a peek into pro football's most distant past.

Bob's writings on the early game are unparalleled in their mastery of detail and do not lend themselves to condensation. We might have elected to provide from his collected writings the story of the rivalry between Canton and Massillon, going back to the early 1890s. Or we could have profiled, with Bob's words, the first documented professional football player (Pudge Heffelfinger), or the man whom the NFL long thought to be that figure (John Brallier). We might have looked to Bob for a story about the pro game's first owner (William C. Temple), or its first African American player (Charles Follis). Bob also wrote with great affection about such pioneer spirits as Sport Donnelly, Dave Berry, Peggy Parratt, Jack Cusack, and Blondy Wallace.

But in the end we settled upon Bob's great portrait of pro football's indispensable man, the one who made the game so popular that by 1920 the idea of a national league for professional football began to seem possible: Jim Thorpe. Here is how he came to play with the Canton Bulldogs.

DURING THE SUMMER OF 1914, members of the Massillon Chamber of Commerce asked Canton manager Jack Cusack to come over for a secret meeting to discuss a proposed new Massillon Tigers football team. From Cusack's point of view, a game against a strong Massillon

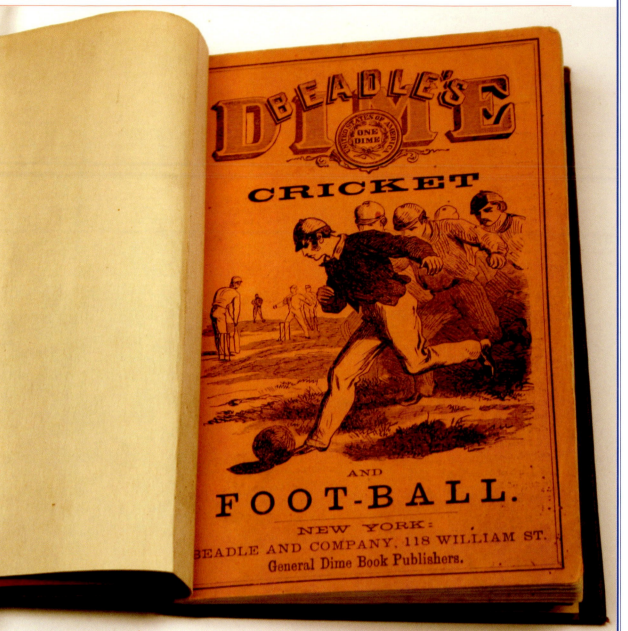

BEADLE'S DIME LIBRARY, 1866

In 1866, Beadle and Company, the originators of the "Dime Novel," broke away from its usual theme of romance or adventure novels and published this book on "Cricket and Foot-Ball." This sports guide, one of several Beadle issued in the decade, was the first book published in the United States on football. Although the football described in this rare book is really the European version of the game, it is from that game that American football evolved.

team—with its historic Canton rivalry—was bound to bring fans flocking to Canton's League (Lakeside) Park. But, much as he loved the idea in the abstract, he had a large reservation about one of the particulars.

"Where will you get your players?" he asked.

Simple, he was told. Massillon's team backers would offer George "Peggy" Parratt's top Akron players more money to perform for the new Tigers. Cusack didn't bother to mention the secret agreement among Ohio team managers to refrain from raiding other teams. He had a more cogent argument than that. Raids by Massillon would start a bidding war, raise players' salaries for all teams, and destroy the fragile profit margin he and a few other managers had established.

The Massillon people were unimpressed. Cusack played his ace. He would refuse to play any Massillon team built by raiding Akron. At first they didn't believe him, but finally he convinced them he wasn't bluffing. With no Canton-Massillon game, both teams would be hurt financially. But Massillon's wounds would be fatal. Plans for a new "Tigers" were put on hold.

But by the time the 1915 season rolled around, the situation had changed drastically. And as a result, Massillon raided Parratt with never a peep out of Canton. Cusack then took his share of weakened Akron, and the Youngstown Patricians, hoping to move up in class, applied the coup de grâce by gathering up Parratt's few remaining stars. Predictably, Massillon followed with a new round of expensive ringers. And Cusack responded with perhaps the single most important pro football action ever taken up till then: he hired Jim Thorpe. Over the remainder of the decade, escalation piled on escalation until all of it eventually necessitated the long-talked-about creation of a pro football league. Historically, the National Football League "began" in 1920, but its "beginnings" were in 1915.

No single team emerged as the class of the Midwest in that year. Canton lost an early game to the Detroit Heralds. Detroit lost to Evanston. Evanston beat the Fort Wayne Friars but lost to Wabash, which in turn lost to Fort Wayne. Toledo beat Columbus but lost to Dayton and Massillon. Dayton lost to Columbus. Columbus lost to Canton but topped Massillon. Two teams went undefeated.

Canton and Massillon scheduled each other for November games, the second and last Sundays. Neither team had a clear-cut claim to the Ohio League championship, but bragging rights for Stark County and the long history of bitter rivalry were at stake. That was plenty.

Cusack knew that the Tigers would "beef up" for the games. He decided to go them one better. Jim Thorpe was coaching the backs at Indiana University. Cusack sent Bill Gardner, once a Thorpe teammate at Carlisle, over to Bloomington with an offer that Jim (or any other footballer in his right mind) couldn't refuse—$250 a game.

MASSILLON TIGERS PROGRAM AND FAN RIBBON

The Massillon Tigers were titans of professional football in the early 1900s. The team took the sport by storm as an amateur squad in 1903 that went undefeated (with the help of a few hired pros) to capture the Ohio amateur title. The following year the Tigers played openly as a professional team and won the Ohio independent championship. Along the way, yearly matchups with neighboring Canton had become one of the game's biggest rivalries. A healthy debate could be waged as to whom the rivalry was more important, the players or the fans.

PRO FOOTBALL'S BIRTH CERTIFICATE

Due to growing competition between amateur sports clubs in the 1890s, football teams began to recruit established collegiate players to bolster their rosters for the big games. Players were known to bounce around from one team to another with no obvious ties to the team or community. Yet no proof of professionalism was offered or uncovered until decades later, when the Pro Football Hall of Fame unearthed an accounting ledger sheet belonging to the Allegheny Athletic Association (AAA). Dated November 12, 1892, the AAA expense sheet lists "game performance bonus to W. Heffelfinger for playing (cash) $500.00." This is the earliest evidence of a player being paid, making William "Pudge" Heffelfinger the first known professional football player. The document is considered "pro football's birth certificate."

Expense Accounting Allegheny Athletic Assoc. — Football Club —

Game of Oct. 29, 1892 — AAA vs. Washington, D.C.
balance carried over (account) $432.20
guarantee's gross profit (check) $258.00
team traveling expenses (cash) $221.85
net profit $36.15
total balance $468.35

Game of Nov. 12, 1892 — AAA vs. Pittsburg A.C.
balance carried over (account) $468.35
game receipts gross profit (cash) $1,683.50
visitors guarantee expense (check) $428.00
park rental expense (check) $50.00
Donnelly, Malley, Heffelfinger expense (cash) $75.00
Schlosser hotel bill for above (check) $9.00
game performance bonus to W. Heffelfinger for playing (cash) $500.00
total expenses $1,062.00
net profit $621.00
total balance $1,089.85

Game of Nov. 19, 1892 — AAA vs. W.J. College
balance carried over (account) $1,089.85
game receipts gross profit (cash) $746.00
visitors guarantee expense (check) $238.00
park rental expense (check) $50.00
payment B. Donnelly for playing (cash) $250.00
total expenses $538.00
net profit $208.00
total balance $1,297.00
This above accounting is hereby certified as correct by the below signed team manager:

WILLIAM "PUDGE" HEFFELFINGER

Pro football was born on November 12, 1892, when William "Pudge" Heffelfinger, a former star guard at Yale, accepted $500 to play for the Allegheny Athletic Association in its game against its chief rival, the Pittsburgh Athletic Club. By accepting the AAA's very generous payment—the equivalent of some $12,000 today—Heffelfinger became the game's first known professional.

Later generations tend to remember that Thorpe was a great kicker and little else about his playing ability. There is much more. Physically, he was perfect for his time. At 6'1" and 195 to 205 pounds he was bigger than most linemen of his day. He was extremely strong. His favorite running trick in an open field was to lower his shoulder and charge straight at a defender. Then, at the moment of impact, he would lift and "peel back" the defender. A generation later, "Bronko" Nagurski used the same style. Yet Thorpe was also a dash man on the Carlisle track team, and his speed on a football field enabled him to break away for long runs. He was an evasive runner, but probably not so much so as "Red" Grange. However, his combination of power and speed made him a more versatile runner than either Nagurski or Grange.

Knute Rockne was a popular after-dinner speaker in the 1920s. He told hundreds of football stories, but one of his favorites was the one in which he managed to tackle Jim Thorpe for a loss. "You shouldn't do that, Sonny," said Thorpe. "All these people came to watch old Jim run." On the next play, Rockne—determined to make an even more spectacular tackle—crashed in on Thorpe, only to be leveled by his shoulder. By the time Rock got to his feet, Thorpe was 40 yards downfield for a touchdown. He came trotting back to the still-dazed Rockne. "That's good, Sonny, you let old Jim run."

The story always brought gales of laughter, and got the same reaction when Steve Owen, the New York Giants coach, told it with himself as "Sonny." Dozens of other "Sonnys" told the same story with equal results. The point is not whether Owen or Rockne or Whoever was the real Sonny, or even if there was ever a real Sonny. The appreciative audiences recognized the more important truth—no one "let" Jim run, but when he was of a mind to do it, no one could stop him.

Passing was not a major weapon in the Thorpe arsenal, but he was usually his team's best thrower. According to some accounts he could throw long better than most. He was also a good receiver, although he had few opportunities to exhibit that skill.

On defense, he was considered a very rough player, but not a dirty one. When he had a runner cornered, his favorite tactic was to launch his body in what amounted to a cross-body block, a technique calculated to produce a fumble.

As a punter he was thought of as one of the best. His ability to placekick and drop-kick remained long after his other skills eroded. When nearing forty he could still give pregame exhibitions in which he would stand at the 50-yard line and drop-kick over the goalposts at one end of the field then turn and drop-kick over the posts at the other end.

He was quite durable. Although he was the main target for every opponent—and they often used extralegal tactics—he was forced out of only two games by injury before 1921. Others might rival him in

JOHN BRALLIER AND LATROBE

Quarterback John Brallier of the Latrobe (Pennsylvania) YMCA football team was the first to acknowledge openly that he was paid to play football. By his own account, Brallier accepted $10 and expenses in 1895 to play for the YMCA team against the neighboring Jeannette Athletic Club. Two years later the Latrobe Athletic Club became the first team to play an entire season with only professional players.

TURN-OF-THE-CENTURY FOOTBALL HEAD HARNESS

This well-ventilated leather helmet was typical of the style worn in the early 1900s. The *Spalding Athletic Guide* of 1900 describes the helmet as "brown canvas, nicely padded but very light and cool to wear."

NOSE GUARD

First introduced in the 1890s, the nose guard was designed to protect players from injuries to the nose and mouth. Made of hard rubber, it was held in place by a headband and a "bit" that the player would bite down on. The well-intended piece of equipment was relatively short-lived as it proved to cause more injuries than it prevented.

FOOTBALL, CIRCA 1890

"We have spared no expense in making this ball more perfect than ever, and offer this season the finest football ever produced. Each ball is thoroughly tested, packed in a separate box and sealed, so that our customers are guaranteed a perfect ball inside when same is received with seal unbroken" (Spalding Athletic Guide, 1890).

TURN-OF-THE-CENTURY GAME ACTION

Everyone seems to be looking for the ball in this photo of a typical turn-of-the-century football game. No one is in pass coverage, nor needed to be, since the forward pass was not made legal until 1906. Note the variation of head protection ranging from nothing, to hard-rubber nose protectors, to flat-top canvas-and-leather helmets.

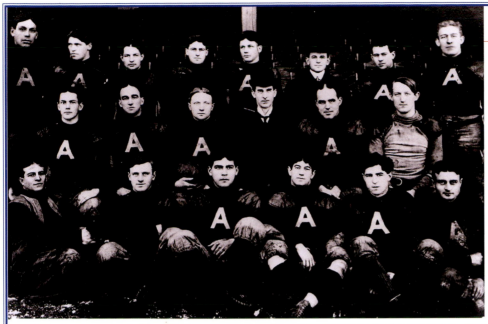

CONNIE MACK'S PHILADELPHIA ATHLETICS FOOTBALL TEAM

Baseball's Philadelphia Athletics and Philadelphia Phillies both fielded pro football teams in 1902. The A's football team was managed by legendary baseball manager Connie Mack and included pitcher Rube Waddell. A third team, the Pittsburgh Pros, featuring baseball's famed pitcher Christy Mathewson, joined the two Philadelphia squads and formed a loosely structured league they called the National Football League. All three teams claimed the mythical 1902 championship, but it was finally agreed that the Pros were most deserving. The A's made history when on November 21, 1902, they defeated the Kanaweola A.C. 39–0 in football's first night game, played at Elmira, New York.

PRO FOOTBALL'S FIRST INDOOR GAME (OVERALL-STYLE UNIFORM WORN BY HARRY MASON)

Pro football made its indoor debut on December 28, 1902, when a team billed as "New York" played the Syracuse Athletic Club at New York's Madison Square Garden. The game was the first of a five-team, four-game "Indoor Football Tournament" designed to fill the otherwise empty arena during New York's busy holiday season. The "New York" team was actually comprised of players from two strong Philadelphia teams, the Athletics and the Phillies, and was the favorite to win the tournament. The other participants were the New York Knickerbockers, the Warlow (Whitestone, Long Island) A.C., and the Orange (New Jersey) A.C. Taking a page from the "New York" playbook, Syracuse bolstered its team by adding several players from the powerful Watertown (New York) Red and Blacks, including fullback Harry Mason, who wore this uniform. The bolstered Syracuse A.C. eliminated "New York" in the first round and went on to win the tournament.

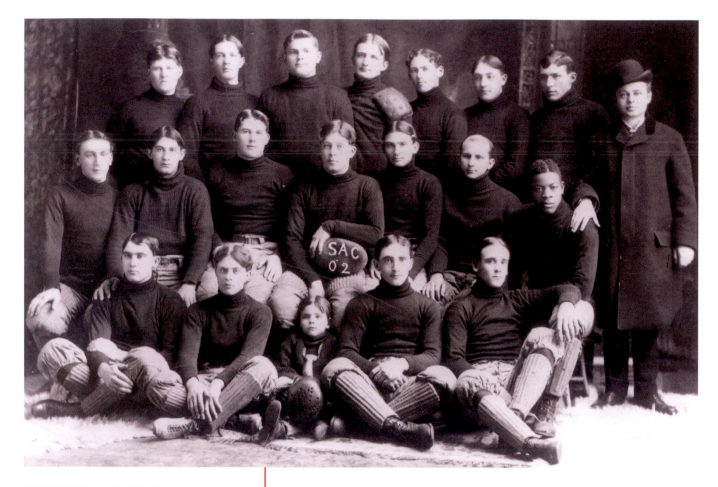

PRO FOOTBALL'S FIRST
AFRICAN AMERICAN PLAYER

Charles Follis, known as "the Black Cyclone," was the first African American to play professional football. Follis played for the Shelby (Ohio) Athletic Club in 1902–06. Although he was likely a pro from the start, the earliest definitive evidence of his "professionalism" came in the form of a September 16, 1904, sports story in the *Shelby Daily Globe* that reported, "Charles Follis has signed for the season." An occasional teammate of Follis was Branch Rickey, who in 1947 broke major league baseball's "color barrier" by signing Jackie Robinson to a contract with the Brooklyn Dodgers. Rickey sometimes played for Shelby during the 1902–03 seasons while attending nearby Ohio Wesleyan University.

individual skills. There were other feared runners, strong blockers, rugged defenders, accurate kickers, and good passers. But no one combined all of these to the same degree of perfection. He was much criticized for loafing in practice. Some said he was never as good as he could have been. The fact was that, until his later years when he seldom had competent teammates, his teams won nearly all their games.

Nevertheless, despite Thorpe's awesome reputation, Cusack's $250-per-game offer seemed outlandish to Canton fans, at least $150 over what the highest-paid players were receiving. Even the most loyal Cantonites thought Cusack had lost his mind and would soon lose his shirt, but when 6,000 showed up for the first Canton-Massillon game and 8,000 for the second, the Canton manager realized a tidy profit.

More than the big money he received was involved in Big Jim's appeal. Thorpe was not just a great football player; he was the quintessential American athlete: twice All-America at Carlisle, winner of two gold medals in the 1912 Olympics, professional baseball player with the New York Giants. There has never been anything like him.

In the 1912 Olympics held in Sweden, Thorpe won both the pentathlon and decathlon while compiling 8,412 of a possible 10,000 points. King Gustav presented the two gold medals, proclaiming, "You are the greatest athlete in the world."

Thorpe modestly responded, "Thanks, King."

Within a year it was learned that Thorpe had played professional baseball for Rocky Mount, North Carolina, of the Eastern Carolina League in 1909 and 1910, earning $60 a month. Many student-athletes played summer baseball in those days, but normally under pseudonyms to protect their amateur status. At the time, the strict rules of the Olympics made a professional in one sport a professional in all sports. The International Olympic Committee removed his name from its records and demanded that Thorpe send back his medals. It was said Thorpe mourned the loss of the medals until his dying day. In 1982, twenty-nine years after his death, the Olympic Committee responded to numerous pleas and petitions and returned the medals to his family.

After leaving Carlisle in the spring of 1913, Thorpe signed to play baseball with the New York Giants. For two seasons and part of a third, he was a seldom-used outfielder with a batting average that hovered around .200. Giants manager John McGraw insisted that Thorpe couldn't hit a curveball, but part of Thorpe's troubles stemmed from the fact that he and McGraw did not care for each other. The intense, dictatorial McGraw was the exact opposite of the easygoing Native American.

After spending a season and a half in the minors, Thorpe returned to the majors in 1917 and stayed until 1919. In his final major league year, he hit .327 in 62 games for New York and Boston of the National League. With Akron of the International League in 1920, he hit .360, with 16 home runs. In 1921, he played for Toledo of the American Association, batted .358, and had 112 RBI. After one more season, he retired from baseball.

But football was his game. When Thorpe turned to professional football in 1915, he put the sport on the front pages because he was bigger than the game itself.

Although Thorpe's gate appeal brought out a big crowd, his first game as a pro was a failure on the field. The Bulldogs' coach, Harry Hazlett, decided to keep Thorpe on the bench at the opening of the game, held at Massillon's Driving Park. Hazlett's stratagem was either

1906 HELMET

In the early days of pro football it was not uncommon for an amateur to play football on a Saturday for his college, then travel to a nearby town or city to play pro football on Sunday under an assumed name. This 1906 version of the helmet not only offered "full-face" protection, it also provided protection from discovery.

IT WAS A TOUGH GAME

These unidentified "gridiron warriors" appear to be suggesting in a comical way that football was a pretty tough business.

THE 1906 CANTON-MASSILLON GAME (CROPPED FROM 1906 CANTON-MASSILLON GAME PANORAMA SHOT)

The competition between the Canton Bulldogs and neighboring Massillon Tigers was one of pro football's earliest and fiercest rivalries. The two teams met twice in 1906, with each winning at home. Massillon's Hospital Grounds Field, depicted here, was the site of the second game. Charges by both teams accusing the other of attempts to fix the outcome of the matchups dimmed enthusiasm for pro football throughout the state. Canton was unable to produce a serious pro team again until 1912, and Massillon didn't field a major team until 1915.

because the great Indian had not practiced with the team or because he resented Thorpe's high pay. Whatever the reason, the Tigers led 3–0 on a field goal by Gus Dorais when Thorpe entered the game with a minute left in the first quarter. Then Bulldogs quarterback Don Hamilton, presumably on orders from Coach Hazlett, called Thorpe's number only intermittently. Thorpe ended the game back on the bench. Meanwhile, Dorais drop-kicked two more field goals and set up a touchdown with a pass. Massillon 16, Canton 0.

Cusack was angry. With the second Massillon game scheduled for two weeks later, he replaced Hazlett as coach with Thorpe. Quarterback Hamilton quit the team in a huff and a new signal caller was imported from Indiana.

Cusack left the Sunday before the Massillon rematch and Thanksgiving Day open date. In theory, open dates would keep his stars from being injured, but most of them simply played for another team on those days. Massillon, in the meantime, went to Toledo the Sunday after the first Canton game to take on the tough Maroons. Despite

CONTRACT   October 19, 1910

Party of the First Part Ben Clarke agrees to Coach team backed by Party of the Second Part John Davis till such a time as his services are no longer required. Party of the First Part agrees to devote two nights a week to practice and to do all in his power to make a winning team having complete charge of all men trying out under him.   And when he possibly can to be with team on Sundays either morning or afternoon. Whereby Party of Se Part agrees to pay Party Of First Part stipulated sum of two dollars a week and a jersey for his services. It is understood that Party Of the Second Part can at any time after two weeks Coaching release said Coach providing he does not live up to terms of this Contract. Also that said compensation is to be paid after second practice of each week.

                                    Signed

BEN CLARKE'S 1910 COACHING CONTRACT

The 1910 contract terms for the coach of a local Canton pro football team were pretty straightforward: practice twice a week, do what he could to have a winning team, and show up on Sunday. For this Ben Clarke got a whopping $2 a week and a jersey.

BOXMAN

The official name for the member of the chain crew who handles the down marker is the "boxman." This is because the down marker was originally a four-sided box on a metal rod that was rotated toward the field after each play to confirm the down.

1911 COLUMBUS PANHANDLES FOOTBALL

This football from the Columbus Panhandles' 1911 season was given to lineman Oscar Kuehner, who went on to play thirteen seasons with the team, including two (1920–21) as a member of the NFL. The logo on the football reflects the fact that most of the Columbus players worked for the Panhandle Division of the Pennsylvania Railroad, sponsors of the team.

JIM THORPE'S 1912 OLYMPIC BLAZER

Jim Thorpe was the first big-name athlete to play pro football. A football All-America at the Carlisle Indian School, he gained his greatest fame after winning the decathlon and pentathlon events in the 1912 Summer Olympics. Thorpe was later stripped of his Olympic records and medals when it was learned that he had played minor league baseball in 1909–10. In 1984, after years of petitioning, the Olympic Committee agreed that the disqualification was an unfair interpretation of the Olympic rules of that time and voted to restore his records and return his medals to his family. A charter member of the Pro Football Hall of Fame, Thorpe began his twelve-year pro football career in 1915 as a member of the Canton Bulldogs and in 1920 served as the NFL's first president.

making 17 first downs to the Maroons' one, the Tigers found themselves in a scoreless tie as the final gun approached. Then Dorais kicked a field goal from the 28-yard line to send the Tigers home with a victory.

New Bulldogs coach Thorpe was unavailable to practice with his team on Thanksgiving Day. He was back in Indiana earning another $250 with Clare Rhode's Pine Village team in his second pro game. Rhode kept him off the bench and in the game, and Jim scored two touchdowns.

In addition to turning the Bulldog reins over to Thorpe, Cusack moved to shore up his line. He imported tackles Earl Abell of Colgate and Bob Butler of Wisconsin, both legitimate All-Americas. Then, as an afterthought, he brought in a third tackle, Charlie Smith from Michigan State. Smith, one of the few early black pros, would play only one game in a Canton uniform, but he would be at the center of one of the most riotous endings ever to take place on a football field.

A standing-room-only crowd that ringed the field at League Park was equally split between Bulldog and Tiger fans. Thorpe lived up to his reputation, running well and leading the Canton defense. In the opening quarter, he drop-kicked a 21-yard field goal to put Canton in front. He added a third-quarter placekick from 37 yards out to make the score 6–0.

Cusack's only criticism of Thorpe as a coach was that the Indian was sometimes reluctant to replace a player on the field. Before the game, he and Big Jim agreed that Cusack would control Canton substitutions from the Bulldog bench. As the game entered the final quarter, Massillon began gaining freely through Abell, the Colgate All-America. Cusack sent in Charlie Smith at tackle. When Abell reached the sideline, he was near collapse from a heavy cold.

Smith played well and the Bulldogs held the Tigers in check until the very end. Suddenly, Dorais shot a pass to Maury "Windy" Briggs, formerly of Ohio State. Briggs raced down the sideline toward the goal line as the crowd surged closer. At the two-yard line, he disappeared into a wall of spectators. Suddenly, the ball came bounding out onto the field and Smith, the replacement tackle, fell on the fumble, apparently preserving the Canton victory.

But Briggs was apoplectic. He had *not* fumbled, he screamed. Indeed a Canton fan—a uniformed policeman, no less—had kicked the ball out of his hands. Briggs wasn't helping his case, because everyone knew that Canton had no uniformed policemen at that time. Nevertheless, the halfback continued to describe the alleged football-kicking cop right down to the brass buttons on his blue coat.

By now the crowd was all over the field and the game was effectively over. But what was the score? If Briggs's story was believed,

it was a 6–6 tie. If he was lying (or crazy), Canton had the win. At stake were the championship of Stark County, an argument for the "Ohio League championship," and—most important—more than a thousand dollars in bets. However, the referee knew he'd have 4,000 people after his hide no matter what his decision.

The ref was no fool. He agreed to render a sealed decision, not to be revealed until 12:30 that night, by which time he would be far away on a train bound for home. That night, at thirty minutes after midnight, the envelope was opened at Canton's Courtland Hotel. Although couched in statesmanlike language, the basic message was, "No buttons, no policeman, no kicker, no touchdown. Canton, 6–0."

There was a coda to the story. About ten years later, Cusack met a man who claimed that he had indeed kicked the ball out of Briggs's hands because he'd bet $30, his whole week's pay, on Canton. Cusack believed the fellow. Who wouldn't believe the open-faced streetcar conductor in his blue coat with shiny brass buttons?

THERE WAS NO MAJORITY opinion favoring any single team for the Ohio League title. Massillon people insisted they'd won, not merely tied, the final meeting with Canton, blithely assuming that their team would have made the extra point after Briggs's touchdown. The Columbus Panhandles claimed a share of the title based on their victory over Massillon. But the Toledo Maroons had whipped the 'Handles, and the

1914 CANTON VS. COLUMBUS

Major professional football returned to Canton in 1912 in the form of the Canton Professionals. Competitive immediately, by 1914 the team was making a serious bid for the so-called Ohio League championship. Canton won their first six games, including this one, a 40–10 win over the Columbus Panhandles, and finished with a 9–1–0 record. But because the Akron Indians coasted to an easy 21–0 win over Canton in the season finale, the title went to Akron.

JIM THORPE SIGNS WITH THE CANTON BULLDOGS

In 1915, Canton Bulldogs owner Jack Cusack hit the jackpot when he signed former Carlisle Indian School All-America Jim Thorpe to a $250-per-game contract. Thorpe, the first big-name athlete to play pro football, was an exceptional talent and major gate attraction. His outstanding play not only enabled Canton to lay claim to unofficial world championships in 1916, 1917, and 1919, but also once again made Ohio the focus of the pro football world. In this photo, Thorpe (left) shakes hands with Charlie Brickley, star of the Massillon Tigers.

Dayton Gym-Cadets had topped the Maroons but lost to Columbus. And on and on.

One point emerged from all the arguing. At season's end, the Canton Bulldogs had Jim Thorpe. With Big Jim in the lineup, Canton would be favored to beat any other team in Ohio. So, for what Thorpe could do more than what he actually accomplished, he gave Canton the strongest claim to the state crown.

In the long run, what was most important about the 1915 season was not who won or lost games but who played and how much it had cost. After years of careful "independent" football dominated by local sandlotters, the game moved into a new stage where college-trained players would lead the way. The influx of better-prepared players meant a major increase in the quality of football played.

However, the progress of pro football also brought a great increase in the cost of doing business, as player salaries jumped. Those teams willing to pay for superior players usually prospered on the field if not in their ledger books; those that refused to spend money on talent and attempted to continue with lower-paid sandlotters usually dropped to second-class status—and third-class incomes. One anonymous Massillon official revealed that it had taken between $1,500 and $2,000 to bring in the Tigers lineup that opposed Canton in the final game. In the future, now that a full-scale bidding war had opened, the cost could only go up.

LEO LYONS LIKED TO talk about the time he took his Rochester Jeffersons team to Canton in 1917 and got walloped 49–0. According to Lyons, as he was walking off the field, he found himself beside Jim Thorpe. "You know, Jim," he said, "someday this game will draw like professional baseball. We should form a league."

The way Leo told it, although he didn't exactly say so, you got the idea that no one had ever thought of a pro football league before that moment. You might even draw the conclusion that there never would have been a National Football League had Leo not come up with his brainstorm.

Leo managed the Jeffersons from before World War I until they went belly up as NFL members in 1925. Then he hung around league meetings year after year until the owners finally named him unofficial league historian to give him a reason for being there. Until he died in 1976, Leo used his position to promote himself as one of the more important founders of the league. Thanks to interviews with him, one popular history of pro football devotes five pages to the Rochester Jeffersons—a team that won three league games in its six league seasons—while allowing some of the stronger teams only a paragraph or two. And one respected pro football encyclopedia places the founding of the league in 1919 at a preseason meeting in Canton that Leo remembered attending. Of course there was no such 1919 meeting; the league wasn't founded that year and it's likely that Leo didn't get back to Canton until 1921.

And just for the record, the Canton newspapers identified the team that Canton slaughtered in 1917 not as Leo's Jeffersons but as a service team—the Syracuse 47th Infantry—and the actual score was 41–0. Nevertheless, it's quite possible that Lyons mused about forming a league while he watched his team—whatever his team was that day—get its butt kicked in Canton. After all, that idea had been all over the sports pages the previous spring.

NEW HAVEN INDIANS VS. EUREKA

These two Connecticut football teams—likely amateur—drew a few curious onlookers, some of whom are standing under the makeshift goalpost. Note the swollen size of the football tucked under the ball carrier's arm.

The hot rumor had been that the major baseball owners were ready to jump in and form a pro football counterpart to their diamond leagues. There was never anything to it. As soon as Connie Mack of Philadelphia and Barney Dreyfuss of Pittsburgh pointed out the losses they'd suffered when they fielded football teams back in 1902, the other baseball owners dropped the idea like a Teflon pop fly.

THORPE'S HEROICS AS PLAYER-COACH had allowed Canton to claim pro football championships in 1916 and 1917, and to think of itself as the pro football center of the world. He had help, of course. Fellow Indian Pete Calac punched holes through rival lines nearly as well as Jim. Earle "Greasy" Neale showed himself a clever end before the war. Bulldog quarterback Milt Ghee threw 17 touchdown passes during the

KNUTE ROCKNE'S
MASSILLON TIGERS HELMET

During pro football's pre-NFL years, it was not uncommon for players to jump from team to team, often under assumed names to hide their identity. One such player was a young Notre Dame assistant coach, Knute Rockne, a relatively well-known ringer with the 1919 Massillon (Ohio) Tigers. Apparently Massillon wasn't the only team for which he played. A former member of the Columbus Panhandles once claimed that Rockne played against his team six times in one season— each time with a different team. Rockne wore this helmet as a member of the 1919 Massillon Tigers.

Opposite:

1917 MASSILLON VS. CANTON
POSTER AND GAME FOOTBALL

The Canton Bulldogs were the dominant pro team in 1917. Canton's big matchup was with their long-standing crosstown rival, the Massillon Tigers. The Tigers, hell-bent on beating Canton, brought in Harvard All-America Charlie Brickley for the game. It didn't help, as Canton won 14–3.

1917 season. Any number of outstanding linemen blocked and tackled in the best of football tradition. But Thorpe was the one who made it all work. He was the nonpareil.

Bulldog fans breathed a great deal easier when Thorpe wrote from Boston, where he was playing major league baseball for the National League Braves, to say he'd return to the Bulldogs for the 1919 football season after having missed the 1918 campaign. He'd been convinced by the fans' enthusiasm and a part interest in the team.

But the great Indian was past thirty, a dangerous age for an athlete. Not many played football after exiting their twenties. Additionally, everyone had heard those stories about his drinking. The cynics, including many who'd been flattered to lift a glass along with Thorpe, speculated about Jim's spending a year away from football but nary a day away from a bottle.

But even Thorpe at his best needed allies. Could Calac still smash through opponents' lines after he had suffered serious war injuries? Had Ghee switched his allegiance to some team out in Illinois? Was Neale likely to continue slipping away from his college coaching to be a Bulldog on Sundays? Who would block? Who would tackle?

The Bulldogs' new management was an unknown quantity too. Jack Cusack, the local promoter who originally brought Thorpe to Ohio and surrounded him with a capable supporting cast, departed after the 1917 season to seek his fortune in the Oklahoma oil fields. Control of the Bulldogs fell to Ralph E. Hay, a successful Canton auto dealer. Hay sported an ambiguous reputation as a "great hustler," but whether he and Thorpe could mold a team to equal those turned out by Cusack remained to be seen.

The Massillon Tigers were Canton's nearest rival both geographically and athletically. A craving for victories over the Bulldogs had been a longtime compulsion in Stark County's second city, only seven miles west of Canton and a third its size. Several years of frustration had only increased the desire among Massillon fans, but Jack Donahue and Jack Whalen, the Tigers' backers since 1915, took a $4,700 red-ink bath in 1917. How long would they accept such financial losses in the name of civic pique?

Akron, less than twenty miles north in Summit County but with double Canton's population, hadn't seriously challenged for the pro crown since 1914, when sports entrepreneur Peggy Parratt fielded teams in the Rubber City. Prospects for 1919 were hopeful but confused. Yet only one year later, from this cauldron of uncertainty the NFL was forged.

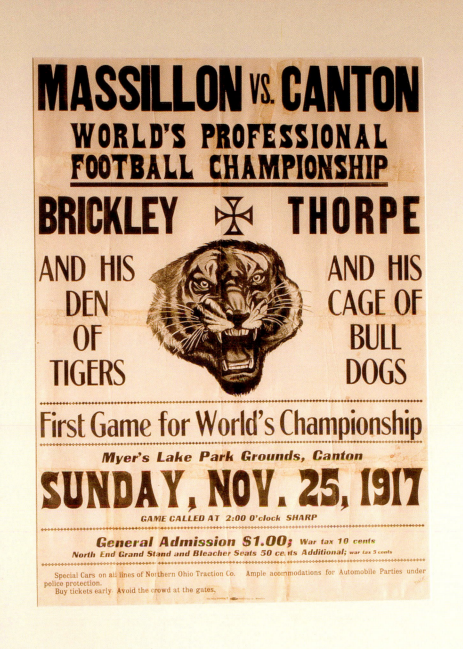

MASSILLON VS. CANTON
WORLD'S PROFESSIONAL
FOOTBALL CHAMPIONSHIP

BRICKLEY ✠ THORPE

AND HIS
DEN
OF
TIGERS

AND HIS
CAGE OF
BULL
DOGS

First Game for World's Championship

Myer's Lake Park Grounds, Canton

SUNDAY, NOV. 25, 1917

GAME CALLED AT 2:00 O'clock SHARP

General Admission $1.00; War tax 10 cents
North End Grand Stand and Bleacher Seats 50 cents Additional; war tax 5 cents

Special Cars on all lines of Northern Ohio Traction Co. Ample acommodations for Automobile Parties under police protection.
Buy tickets early. Avoid the crowd at the gates.

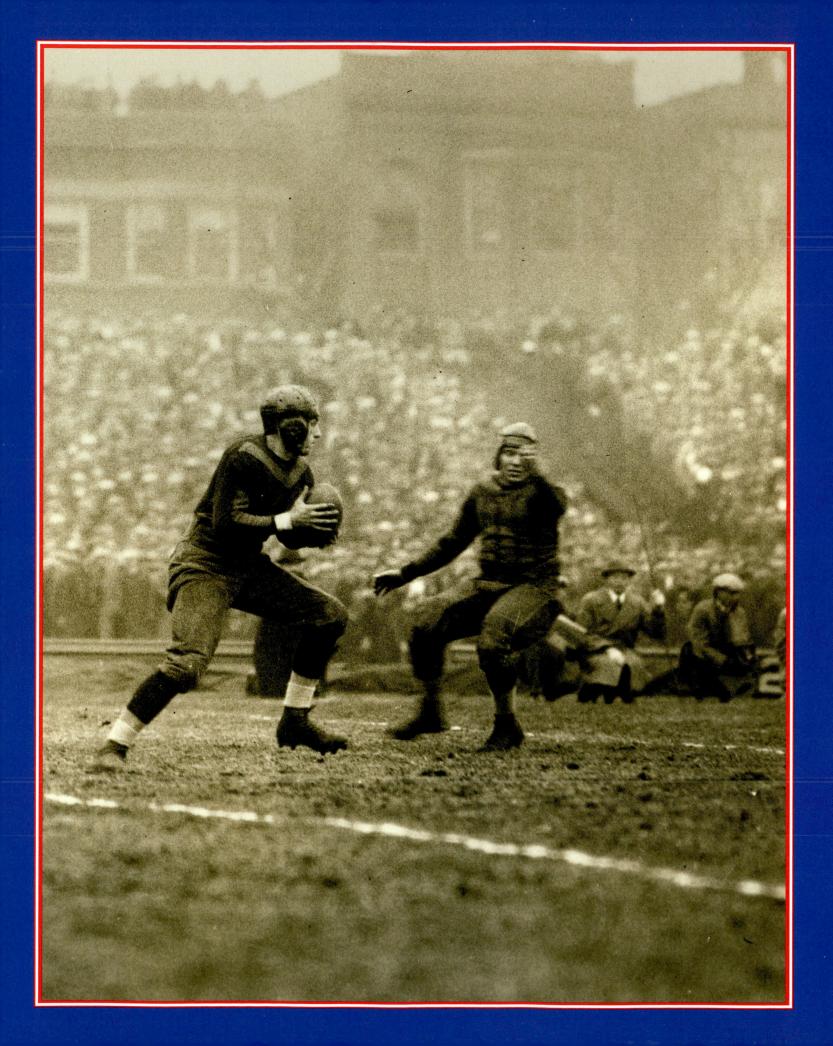

The 1920s
CASH, CARRY, AND GALLOP

JOE HORRIGAN

Opposite (detail) and below (full frame):

RED GRANGE ACTION PHOTO FROM
BEARS-CARDINALS DEBUT GAME

On Thanksgiving Day 1925, former Illinois halfback Red Grange played his first pro game with the Chicago Bears. A sellout crowd of 36,000 fans filled Cubs Park (later to be renamed Wrigley Field) to witness Grange in his pro debut, facing the Chicago Cardinals. Ten days later more than 70,000 packed New York's Polo Grounds to see Red and the Bears take on the New York Giants. After completing the final games of the 1925 NFL season, Grange and company set out on a cross-country "barnstorming tour" arranged by Grange's manager, C. C. (Cash and Carry) Pyle.

PHOTO: DUTCH STERNAMAN COLLECTION

The decade of the 1920s was dubbed the "Golden Age of Sports." In postwar America a newfound sense of prosperity and innovation blossomed. Americans had more leisure time, a few more bucks to spend, and, after the prior decade's wave of death and destruction, a yearning for distractions.

BASEBALL, TENNIS, GOLF, SWIMMING, boxing, and college football all flourished during the decade, and each sport had its star. There was Babe Ruth in baseball. Tennis fans cheered "Big Bill" Tilden. Golf enthusiasts celebrated Bobby Jones. Swimming had Johnny Weissmuller. Boxing boasted Jack Dempsey, and Harold "Red" Grange of Illinois was the favorite of college football devotees.

A burgeoning industry of newspapers, magazines, radio, and movies all played a role in boosting the profile of sport and its giants. And, oh yes, as sporting interests grew, opportunistic promoters found creative ways to capitalize.

Even though professional football had been around since the 1890s and was growing in popularity, it hadn't ascended to the level of public acceptance and excitement of college football. In fact, pro football was widely regarded as an affront to the amateur version played on college campuses across the country. Critics alleged—and to a degree were right—that the pro game lacked organization, stability, and credibility. But even so, by the start of the 1920s the play-for-pay model had earned the right to stake its claim as an emerging alternative to college football.

To that end, on September 17, 1920, a group of football "moguls," as they were called, representing ten unaligned professional teams from four states, met in Canton, Ohio, and formed the American Professional Football Association (APFA). Two years later the APFA was renamed the National Football League.

FRANK NIED   A. F. RANNEY

AKRON PROFESSIONAL FOOTBALL TEAM
LEAGUE PARK

OFFICE
21 N. SUMMIT STREET
BELL MAIN 1786

CARROLL AND BEAVER STREETS
AKRON, OHIO

E. W. TOBIN, COACH
C. COPLEY, CAPTAIN

MINUTES OF MEETING — SEPTEMBER 17th—1920.

Meeting called to order at 8:15 P.M., by
Chairman, Mr. Hay. Teams represented were, Canton Bulldogs,
Cleveland Indians, Dayton Triangles, Akron Professionals,
Massillon Tigers, Rochester, N.Y., Rock Island, Ill.,
Muncie, Ind., Staley A.C. Decatur, Ill., Racine Cardinals,
Wisconsin, and Hammond, Ind.

Minutes of previous meeting were given in a resume
by the Chairman.

Old Business.

Massillon withdrew from professional football for
the season of 1920.

New Business.

It was moved and seconded that a permanent organization be formed to be known as American Professional Football
Association. Motion carried.

Moved and seconded that officers be now elected,
consisting of President, Vice President, Secretary and
Treasurer. Carried.

Mr. Jim Thorpe was unanimously elected President,
Mr. Stan Cofall, Vice President, and Mr. A. F. Ranney,
Secretary and Treasurer.

Moved and seconded that a fee of $100.00 be charged
for membership in the Association. Carried.

Moved and seconded that the president appoint a

Above and opposite:

A LEAGUE IS BORN

On September 17, 1920, representatives of ten professional teams from four states met in Canton, Ohio, and formed the American Professional Football Association (APFA). Ralph Hay, owner of the Canton Bulldogs, hosted the meeting in his Jordan and Hupmobile automobile showroom. Two years later the APFA was renamed the National Football League. Teams represented at the meeting included the Akron Pros, Cleveland Tigers, and Dayton Triangles from Ohio; the Muncie Flyers and Hammond Pros from Indiana; the Racine Cardinals, Decatur Staleys, and Rock Island Independents from Illinois; and the Rochester Jeffersons from New York State. Although listed as present, Massillon was represented by Canton's Hay, who informed the group that the Tigers did not intend to field a team. Four other teams—the Buffalo All-Americans, Chicago Tigers, Columbus Panhandles, and Detroit Heralds—joined the league later that year. These are the NFL's organizational meeting minutes.

FRANK NIED

A. F. RANNEY

AKRON PROFESSIONAL FOOTBALL TEAM
LEAGUE PARK
OFFICE
21 N. SUMMIT STREET
BELL MAIN 1786

CARROLL AND BEAVER STREETS
AKRON. OHIO

E. W. TOBIN, COACH
C. COPLEY, CAPTAIN

committee to work in conjunction with a lawyer to draft
a Constitution, bylaws and rules for the Association.
Carried.

Mr. Thorpe appointed Mr. A. A. Young of Hammond,
Chairman, and Messrs. Cofall, Flanigan and Storch associates.

Moved and seconded that all Clubs mail to the Secretary
by January 1, 1921, a list of all players used by them this
season, the Secretary to furnish all Clubs with duplicate copy
of same, so that each Club would have first choice in services
for 1921 of his team of this season. Carried.

Moved and seconded that all members have printed upon
their stationery, "Member of American Professional Football
Association". Carried,

Mr. Marshall of the Brunswick-Balke Collender Company,
Tire Division, presented a silver loving cup to be given the
team, awarded the championship by the Association. Any team
winning the cup three times should be adjudged the owner.

It was moved and seconded that a vote of thanks be
extended by the Secretary to Mr. Marshall.

The meeting was adjourned.

Next meeting to be called by the President some time in January
1921.

A H Ranney

> "Baseball has become successful because of the excellent way in which it is organized, and I can honestly say that I believe the National Football League is just as strongly entrenched as any league in baseball. The fly-by-night birds are now on the outside looking in, and we intend to keep them there."
>
> —Joe Carr

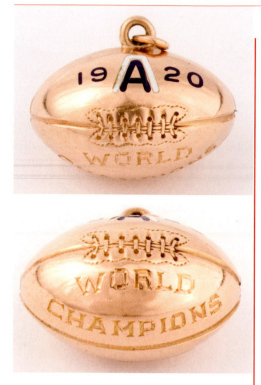

1920 AKRON PROS CHAMPIONSHIP WATCH FOB

The Akron Pros were charter members of the NFL and the league's first champions. Each member of the 1920 championship team was presented an inscribed gold football-shaped watch fob commemorating the championship season. This one belonged to tackle Karl "Pike" Johnson. In addition to their place in history as the NFL's first champions, the Pros are remembered as one of only two teams in the league in 1920 to have an African American player. Further, in 1921 Akron named its African American halfback, Fritz Pollard, its head coach. He thus became the first and only black head coach in the NFL until Art Shell in 1989.

> "It was evident in my first year at Akron, back in 1919, that they didn't want blacks in there getting that money. And here I was, playing and coaching and pulling down the highest salary in pro football."
>
> —Fritz Pollard

Brief newspaper accounts of the meeting reported that the APFA was organized with the stated purpose of "raising the standards of professional football." Chief among the league's founding tenets was the desire for teams to address the problems of players' high salary demands, players being induced to jump from one team to another, and the signing of players while still enrolled in college. Ironically, it would be the violation of the latter two of those organizational canons that ultimately contributed more to the league's early success than any of the founding fathers' rules and good intentions.

Throughout the first half of the decade the NFL struggled as it sought to enhance its image as an honest-to-goodness major league. Franchises came and went with all too much regularity. The league needed marquee teams in major markets and big-name stars in big cities whose aura could enhance the entire league.

In 1925, the biggest name in college football was Illinois halfback Red Grange, who at twenty-two was already a sports legend. Even before the start of his final season at Illinois, rumors circulated that the "Galloping Ghost," as he was known, had already been approached with lucrative offers from pro teams. Some even suggested he'd signed a contract. On November 21, after he had played in his final collegiate game, Grange announced he was turning pro and joining the Chicago Bears. Although this didn't come as a complete surprise, it was headline news across the country and a major coup for the pro game.

Joining Grange at his signing announcement were George Halas and Edward "Dutch" Sternaman, co-owners of the Bears, and Charles C. Pyle, a man identified as Grange's manager. These three had been working on the deal for weeks, if not months. Although the contract violated the NFL's prohibition of signing players while still enrolled in college, league officials made no attempt to quash the deal. After all, in Grange, the Bears and the NFL had the big-name player they desperately wanted.

Pyle, better known as C.C., or "Cash and Carry," was one of those opportunistic sports promoters who surfaced during the decade. Among other interests, he owned a movie theater in Champaign, Illinois, that was frequented by members of the Illinois football team. It was there that he first connected with Grange. As the story goes, after spotting Grange in his theater, Pyle dispatched an usher to invite the Illinois star to join him in his office at the conclusion of the movie. Assuming it was just another well-wisher wanting to make his acquaintance, Grange respectfully reported. After the obligatory niceties, Pyle jumped right to the heart of the matter and revealed his plan to the young football star of how he could earn $100,000 or more in just one winter.

Pyle's plan called for Grange to turn pro immediately after his college football season was over. He would join the Chicago Bears for the remainder of their season and then embark on a barnstorming tour that would begin in Florida.

Dazzled and overwhelmed by the prospect of such a big payday, Grange agreed to allow Pyle to proceed on his behalf. Not wanting to jeopardize Grange's football eligibility, the two decided that there would be no contract or money exchanged between them until after the Illinois football season was over. Grange would then sign a contract naming dealmaker Pyle his manager for two years.

Pyle's first contact with the Bears came in the form of a letter to Sternaman dated August 9, 1925. In the letter Pyle requested a meeting to "discuss a tour that I am interested in arranging for Red Grange this winter or as soon as his season with Illinois is over." While the letter establishes Pyle's first contact with the Bears—which was, as some suspected, even before the start of Grange's final season at Illinois—it gave no indication that Grange had any idea of what Pyle was up to.

COLUMBUS PANHANDLES

Organized in the early 1900s, the Columbus Panhandles were one of pro football's most colorful teams. Members of the NFL from 1920 until 1926 (the last four seasons of which they were known as the Tigers), the team featured as many as six brothers of the Nesser family—Al, Ted, Phil, John, Fred, and Frank. A seventh brother, Ray, played a few games in the team's pre-NFL years. In at least one game during the 1921 season, Ted's son Charlie joined the squad, marking the first and only time in NFL history that a father and son played on the same team at the same time.

PROBABLE LINE-UP

WASHINGTON			Position	CANTON		
No.	Weight	College		No.	Weight	College
17 Patterson	165	U. S. Navy	L. E.	1 Higgins	170	Penn State
14 Smeach	195	Georgetown	L. T.	18 Henry	235	W. & J.
11 McDonald	197	Boston Tech	L. G.	2 Osburn	175	Penn State
16 Crouch	187	Davidson	C.	6 Feeney	170	Notre Dame
10 Gormley	225	Georgetown	R. G.	23 Griffith	180	Penn State
15 Litkus	187	Shenandoah	R. T.	11 West	182	Colgate
24 Kaplan	166	Lehigh	R. E.	12 Carroll	185	W. & J.
3 Walson	174	Univ. of Maryland	Q.	4 Kempton	142	Yale
1 Sullivan	170	N. C. State	L. H. B.	19 Way	159	Penn State
4 Leighty	168	Georgetown	R. H. B.	13 Griggs	196	Texas
6 Hudson	170	N. C. State	F.	5 Smith	175	Center

Subs for Canton: (24) Robb; (3) Morrow, Pitt; (14) Speck; (16) Kellison, W. Va.; (22) Steele, Harvard; (7) "Horsey" Edwards, Coach.

NUMBER, ETC., OF WASHINGTON PLAYERS

No.		Weight	Position	College
(1)	Sullivan	170	Full-Back	North Carolina State
(2)	Bleir	160	Half-Back	Army
(3)	Walson	174	Half-Back	Univ. of Maryland
(4)	Leighty	158	Half-Back	Georgetown
(5)	Robb	176	Quarter-Back	Penn State
(6)	Hudson	170	Half-Back	North Carolina State
(7)	McCarthy	172	End	Lehigh
(8)	Letzkus	164	End	Westminster
(9)	Van Meter	212	Guard	Univ. of Nebraska
(10)	Gormley	225	Tackle	Georgetown
(11)	McDonald	197	Guard	Boston Tech
(12)	Ahearn	200	Guard	Georgetown
(14)	Smeach	195	Tackle	Georgetown
(15)	Litkus	187	Center	Shenandoah
(16)	Crouch	187	Center	Davidson
(17)	Patterson	165	End	Navy
(18)	M. Turner	188	Guard	North Carolina State
(19)	Beyers	171	Half-Back	Gonzaga
(21)	Gerardi	165	End	Vigilants and Rex
(22)	Dowrick	172	Half-Back	Georgetown
(23)	Coster	174	Center	Univ. of Maryland
(24)	Caplan	166	End	Lehigh
(25)	Unitas	181	Tackle	Johns Hopkins
(26)	Morrissey	179	Half-Back	Georgetown
(27)	Livers	175	Half-Back	Georgetown
(28)	B. Turner	195	Tackle	New Haven Pros
(30)	Bilcher	191	Half-Back	Georgia Tech

A GOOD ARGUMENT

After watching the Army-Navy football game the foreign delegates to the Arms Conference are likely to figure that we don't need any weapons but those we were born with.

"JOHNNY" BLEIR

He kicked a mean football, this boy,
He used both of his feets,
And every time the ball came down
The thing was full of cleats.

SEASON 1921

WASHINGTON FOOTBALL CLUB

MEMBER OF AMERICAN PROFESSIONAL FOOTBALL ASS'N.

WASHINGTON
vs.
CANTON
[BULL-DOGS]

SUNDAY, NOVEMBER 27—3 P·M.

AMERICAN LEAGUE PARK

15 MINUTE QUARTERS

Referee, GUYON (Carlyle).   Timekeeper, APPLE (Michigan)
Umpire, METZLER (Springfield)   Headlinesman, TOWERS (Eastern)

MINIATURE FOOTBALL GAME

The Democrat and Republican Pages will play four 3 minute quarters between the halves Sunday. Each team averages about 105 pounds.

CANTON BULLDOGS VS. WASHINGTON SENATORS 1921 GAME PROGRAM

The Washington Senators were members of the NFL for just one season (1921). Although they played a full schedule, only three games were against league members and two of those were against the Canton Bulldogs. This rare November 27, 1921, game program is from the Senators' inaugural NFL game against the Bulldogs. Anxious to win, the Senators, before the game but after the program was printed, signed three former Bulldogs players—Joe Guyon, Johnny Gilroy, and Pete Calac. Also, the referee listed on the program is "Guyon" from Carlyle, who was undoubtedly related to the recently signed Joe Guyon, also of Carlyle. Despite their efforts, the Senators fell to the Canton crew 15–0.

DETROIT TIGERS SEASON TICKETS

Like other early-day NFL teams, the 1921 Detroit Tigers borrowed a baseball team name in the hope of generating interest and support. The Tigers were Detroit's second entry in the NFL in as many years. Although the team created an attractive season-ticket booklet, their win-loss record was an ugly 1–5–1.

GREEN BAY
PACKERS
VS. CHICAGO
BEARS
HANDBILL

The rivalry between the Green Bay Packers and Chicago Bears goes back to 1921 when the Packers joined the NFL. Chicago (then known as the Staleys) defeated the Packers 20–0 in their first meeting on November 27, 1921. Since that time the two have faced each other more than any other teams in NFL history.

"Imagine…
when I started with the Bears we had fifteen [players]. You were hired to play a football game and you played it— all sixty minutes of it."
—George Trafton

ALL AMERICAN
FOOTBALL
Chicago Bears vs. Green Bay Packers

Sunday AT **Cubs** Park 2:15 P. M.

NOVEMBER 22nd

In their last meeting, the early part of October, the Green Bay Packers defeated the Chicago Bears at Green Bay by the score of 14 to 10.

The Cardinal Game on Thanksgiving Day Will Start at 11 A. M.

RALPH SCOTT, Wisconsin, Tackle for Chicago Bears

JACK HARRIS, 1924 Wisconsin Captain

The Packers have a powerful team, including the following stars:

"CUB" BUCK	Wisconsin	"CURLEY" LAMBEAU	Notre Dame
JACK HARRIS	Wisconsin	FRED LARSEN	Notre Dame
"MOOSE" GARDNER	Wisconsin	JACK VEGARA	Notre Dame
LEWELLEN	Nebraska	MATHYS	Indiana

TICKETS ON SALE AT SPALDING'S, 211 SO. STATE STREET, AND CUBS PARK

TICKETS ON SALE NOW FOR CARDINAL-BEAR GAME THANKSGIVING DAY

Game shall be played regardless of weather conditions.

[Said in 1926]

" My earning days in athletics are at an end, and while sports have been my livelihood, I have really played for the love of competition. "

—Jim Thorpe

OORANG INDIANS

One of pro football's most unusual teams was the Oorang Indians. Granted an NFL franchise in 1922, the team was coached by Jim Thorpe and was composed entirely of Native Americans. The concept of an "all-Indian" team came from Walter Lingo, owner of the Oorang Dog Kennels in LaRue, Ohio. Since the tiny community of LaRue had no playing field, the team operated as a traveling team and lasted only two seasons. Thorpe stands at the center of the back row. Joe Guyon is in the front, left.

" I was a marked man. I made up my mind to give up football and avoid any possible injury that would hurt my chances in baseball. "

—Joe Guyon

CANTON BULLDOGS CHAMPIONSHIP ARTIFACTS

The Canton Bulldogs were the NFL's first two-time champions, with back-to-back titles in 1922 and 1923. Although undefeated in both seasons, they were tied three times, twice in 1922 and once in 1923. This jersey was worn by Bulldogs quarterback Wolcott "Wooky" Roberts and the helmet was worn by Hall of Fame tackle Pete "Fats" Henry during the Bulldogs' championship seasons.

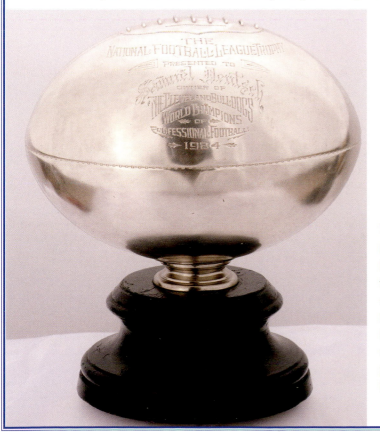

1924 CLEVELAND BULLDOGS NFL CHAMPIONSHIP TROPHY

Fifty miles to the north of Canton, Sam Deutsch, owner of the Cleveland Indians, a good but not great team, was looking for a quick remedy to his team's on-field mediocrity. Taking advantage of the Bulldogs' financial straits, Deutsch offered $2,500 for the failing franchise. Stunned Canton loyalists mounted an unsuccessful effort to block the sale, but in the end Bulldogs management accepted Deutsch's offer. Deutsch immediately suspended operations of the Canton franchise and added the best Canton players to his Cleveland franchise, which he renamed the Cleveland Bulldogs. Deutsch's new and improved team went on to win the NFL's 1924 championship.

**POTTSVILLE MAROONS
SIDELINE JACKET**

With two weeks remaining in the 1925 season, the league-leading Pottsville Maroons were expelled from the NFL for violating the "territorial rights" of the neighboring Frankford Yellow Jackets. The Chicago Cardinals, who had earlier lost to the Maroons, finished the season with the best record and were declared league champions. The Maroons, conditionally reinstated in 1926, felt they should have gotten the honor based upon their league-leading record at the time of their suspension. The disappointed team created sideline jackets that reflected their conviction.

The Bears ownership let Pyle know they were interested. A series of back-and-forth correspondence and meetings followed until a final agreement was hammered out. By all accounts, the Pyle-Grange arrangement came only after the cagey promoter was sure he had a deal with the Bears. What better team for the Illinois star to make his pro debut with than the Bears, owned by two former Illinois players, Halas and Sternaman?

For his part, Grange always maintained that he signed nothing until the morning of November 21. "In the morning, [Grange] met with Pyle, Dutch and me in my room at the Morrison Hotel," Halas wrote in his autobiography, *Halas by Halas*. "Red signed a contract making Pyle his manager."

Interestingly, Halas said nothing of Grange signing a contract with the Bears. That's because he didn't. Grange's deal was with Pyle, not the Bears. So one could argue that the Bears didn't violate the league rule not to sign players still enrolled in college; Pyle did. In the end, however, it was just semantics; Grange was a pro and playing for the Bears.

Not everyone was pleased with Red's decision. Many high-profile college coaches, including Illinois coach Bob Zuppke, publicly criticized the former college football sensation. Even Grange's father expressed displeasure, telling the *Chicago Herald and Examiner* that he attempted to talk his son out of turning pro right up to an hour before he signed his contract with Pyle. "I'd rather that my boy had agreed to something that would have enabled him to stay in school if that were possible," Lyle Grange said. "I want to say here and now though, that I want my boy to have nothing to do with that Pyle, and you can go as strong as you like about that."

Disregarding his father's advice, Grange signed with Pyle and made his pro debut on Thanksgiving Day, just five days after he had closed out his college career. Playing in front of a sellout crowd of 36,000 fans, the largest gathering for a pro football game to date, Grange was held to just 36 yards rushing. However, a respectable 56 yards on punt returns and an interception near the Bears goal line that stopped the Chicago Cardinals' most serious scoring threat was enough to please most in attendance. The game ended in a scoreless tie. More importantly, though, Grange and the Bears scored a touchdown at the box office.

The game contract, which was rewritten after Grange was added to the lineup, provided that the first $14,000 net after deduction of war tax and park rental was to be divided equally between the Bears

"We were scum. Pros were dirt. Why, I would have been more popular with them *[college coaches]* **if I had signed up with the Al Capone gang around Chicago, rather than turning professional."**

—Harold "Red" Grange

and Cardinals. After that, Pyle and Grange took 35 percent of the net balance. The remaining 65 percent was again divided between the Cardinals and Bears. The Bears' take amounted to $15,364.04, while Grange and Pyle netted a hefty $9,007.43, which they divided 60/40—Grange scoring the larger share. Not too shabby, considering the average *annual* income in the United States in 1925 was $1,236.

"Gosh, kicking a football to Red Grange would be like grooving a baseball to Babe Ruth. It's something to be avoided whenever possible." *[Driscoll punted 23 times in the 1925 debut of Red Grange that resulted in a 0–0 tie.]*
—Paddy Driscoll

DAYTON TRIANGLES JERSEY AND HELMET, 1926

The Dayton Triangles had only two winning seasons during their ten years (1920–29) in the NFL. With a small home field and mostly homegrown talent, the Triangles were unable to attract top teams to Dayton and as a result played most of their games on the road. After winless seasons in 1928 and 1929, the franchise was sold and moved to Brooklyn, New York, where they played fourteen seasons as the Brooklyn Dodgers and one final season in 1944 as the Tigers. This helmet and jersey were worn by end Mack Hummon during the Triangles' 1–4–1 1926 season.

> **"Like the others, I too enjoyed the frivolity of our travels** *[the Red Grange barnstorming tour of 1925]*, **but you must have somebody who evidences leadership, who takes charge."**
> **—Ed Healey**

Three days after his pro debut, 28,000 fans returned to a snow-covered Cubs Park to watch Grange and the Bears defeat the Columbus Tigers 14–13. Though the attendance was down from his debut game, it should be noted that a good pre-Grange home attendance for the Bears would have been in the 6,000 to 8,000 range.

Five games remained on the Bears' 1925 schedule. On December 5 they were scheduled to travel to Philadelphia to play the Frankford Yellow Jackets. One day later it was off to New York to meet the Giants, followed by the Providence Steam Roller on the ninth in Boston. There was a final road game in Detroit on December 12 against the Panthers and a season-ending rematch with the Giants back home in Chicago on December 13.

Somehow over the years, this final leg of the Bears' regular season, in which all games but the season finale were on the road, has been misconstrued as a hastily scheduled exhibition "barnstorming tour." The truth is that the final five league games were scheduled by the Bears prior to Grange signing with Pyle.

What has confused historians somewhat is that even before Grange was "officially" added to the roster, the Bears ownership and Pyle went back to each of the previously scheduled opponents, told them of what was in the works, and insisted on changes to their existing game contracts. Not only was the revenue split renegotiated, but two of the opponents, Frankford and Providence, were required to abandon their small-capacity playing fields and secure "big league parks" if they wanted to remain on the schedule.

Eager to comply, the Yellow Jackets relocated from Frankford's Legion Field to Philadelphia's Shibe Park and the Steam Roller moved from the Cyclodrome, a bicycle racing stadium they called home, to Braves Field in nearby Boston. Since Detroit and New York had suitably large stadiums, they merely had to agree to accept new financial terms that provided a larger percentage going to the Bears and Pyle. The promise of a substantially larger gate was more than enough to motivate and compensate the home teams.

For Pyle, bigger stadiums with increased revenue potential alone weren't enough. Always the promoter, Pyle managed to organize and squeeze into the schedule three exhibition games against non-league "All-Star" aggregations in St. Louis on December 2, Washington, D.C.,

THE FRANKFORD YELLOW
JACKETS VS. NY GIANTS, 1926

The 1926 Frankford Yellow Jackets, seen
here in their October 17 game against the
New York Giants at the Polo Grounds, captured the NFL title in just their third year in
the league with a 14–1–2 record. Their 14
wins were not surpassed by an NFL team in
the regular season until 1984 when the
San Francisco 49ers posted a 15–1 record.

on December 8, and Pittsburgh on December 10. The result was a grueling eight games in twelve days, with varying results.

The exhibition game in St. Louis drew just 5,000 fans on a bitterly cold day. But three days later 25,000 fans came to Shibe Park and saw Grange score both of Chicago's touchdowns in their 14–7 win over the Yellow Jackets. The Shibe Park shift proved lucrative for all parties. Grange and Pyle walked away with $17,835.18, the Bears $23,260.01, and the Yellow Jackets $23,760.01. But it was the next day, December 6, that the Galloping Ghost and the Bears really hit the big time, not only for themselves, but for the New York Giants and pro football in general.

In 1925, the other big story in the NFL was that the league had finally secured a team in New York City. Local bookmaker (a legal profession at the time) Tim Mara had agreed to try his luck at running an NFL team in Gotham even though he'd never even attended a pro game.

For Mara this inaugural season in pro football was a struggle. Even though the upstart team was drawing decent crowds, his franchise was awash in red ink. But then, like the proverbial knight in shining armor, along came Grange.

"Getting a winner, or building a winner, isn't easy. It requires experience in the front office, long-range planning, shrewd promotion, careful appraisal of costs, and luck. Bad luck, with injuries or the weather, can ruin the most conscientious and forward-looking operation."

—Tim Mara

ERNIE NEVERS' ESKIMOS TRAVEL TRUNK AND GREATCOAT

In 1926, Stanford All-America Ernie Nevers signed a contract with the Duluth (Minnesota) Eskimos. Capitalizing on his national fame, the team was renamed Ernie Nevers' Eskimos and set out on a twenty-nine-game, 17,000-mile barnstorming tour. Nevers, a true iron man, played in all but twenty-nine minutes of the tour and the vagabond team posted a respectable 6–5–3 record. However, even Nevers wasn't enough to save the franchise. After a disappointing 1–8–0 record in 1927, the team ceased operations. Nevers missed the 1928 season due to injuries, but returned with the Chicago Cardinals in 1929. In a game against the Chicago Bears on November 28, 1929, he scored 40 points, an NFL record that stands to this day.

"I liked it the way I played it. You went the full sixty minutes. When I turned pro and joined the Duluth Eskimos in 1926, we barnstormed after the regular season. We went from September to January and from Maine to Texas to the Pacific Coast. In all we played twenty-nine games and we had only sixteen men on the squad. If the coach took a man out of the game for a substitution, he got mad. That's how much we loved it."

—Ernie Nevers

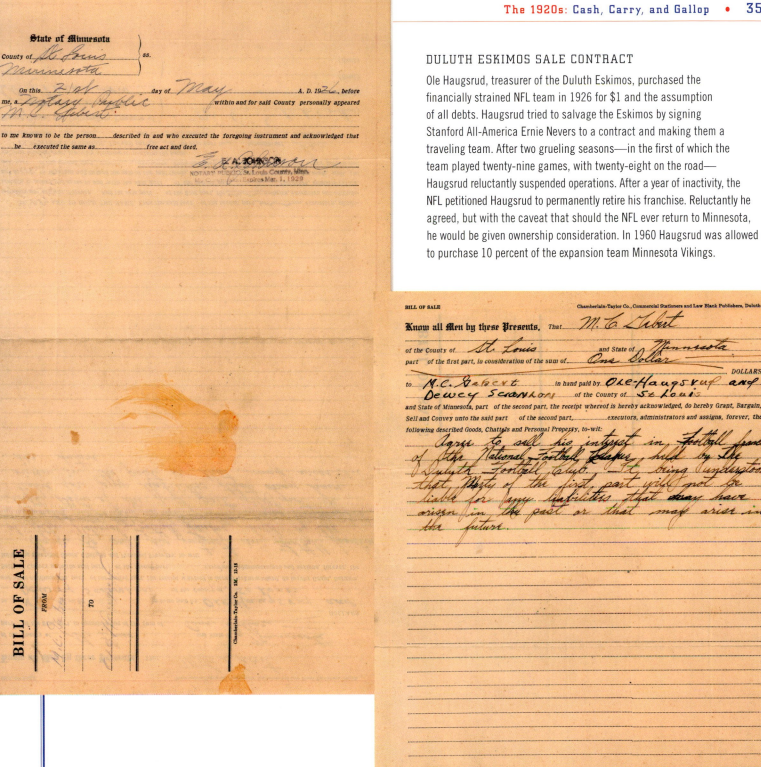

DULUTH ESKIMOS SALE CONTRACT

Ole Haugsrud, treasurer of the Duluth Eskimos, purchased the financially strained NFL team in 1926 for $1 and the assumption of all debts. Haugsrud tried to salvage the Eskimos by signing Stanford All-America Ernie Nevers to a contract and making them a traveling team. After two grueling seasons—in the first of which the team played twenty-nine games, with twenty-eight on the road—Haugsrud reluctantly suspended operations. After a year of inactivity, the NFL petitioned Haugsrud to permanently retire his franchise. Reluctantly he agreed, but with the caveat that should the NFL ever return to Minnesota, he would be given ownership consideration. In 1960 Haugsrud was allowed to purchase 10 percent of the expansion team Minnesota Vikings.

RED GRANGE'S HELMET

Following a loss to Red Grange's New York Yankees, a disappointed Cleveland Panthers running back named Guy "Zeke" Roberts decided to take a parting shot at Grange, "liberating" his helmet that sat unattended in the Yankees' bench area. Some six decades later Roberts jokingly told the Hall of Fame that he figured "the statute of limitations must be up by now" and the Hall of Fame was a better home for his ill-gotten souvenir.

The RACING ROMEO

"You'll win the race -- and the girl, yet. Cheer up!"

Could their love win out against a world of obstacles?

Although the Bears defeated the Giants 19–7, a record crowd, reported to be 70,000, filled New York's Polo Grounds. The gate receipts were not only enough to turn Mara's red ink black, but also enough to convince him that there was a future in the sport and that he shouldn't give up on his pro football venture, something he had been considering.

Famed writer Damon Runyon wrote in his *New York American* column, "There gathered at the Polo Grounds in Harlem yesterday afternoon the largest crowd that ever witnessed a football game on the Island of Manhattan, drawn by the publicity that has been given one individual—Red Grange, late of the University of Illinois." Another New York newspaper reported that Grange's "growing fame drew almost one hundred reporters, from papers from as far West as St. Louis, to the Polo Grounds to cover his playing and send out the news to millions." Never had an NFL team or one of its players received such attention.

While the game may have saved the Giants franchise and certainly provided the NFL with much-needed publicity, it came at a price for Grange. The Giants, like all of the Bears' previous opponents, seemed hell-bent on stopping the famed Galloping Ghost. But the Giants game may have been the nastiest. Grange called it "one of the most bruising battles I had ever been in." Among several hard blows he absorbed during the game, one in particular, a kick to his forearm, caused the most damage. Although he managed to play in the next three games, eventually the pain became too much to bear. According to Halas, Grange's injured arm "grew to twice its normal size" and had to be put into a splint. He spent the final two games of the season on the bench.

RACING ROMEO

Red Grange made his Hollywood debut in 1926 as "Red" Wade in *One Minute to Play*. A year later he played "Red" Walden in the film *A Racing Romeo*.

" I suppose some people think an interest in sports is frivolous, but not for myself. I've loved sports since I was old enough to cross a Chicago street by myself. I'm happy that I made pro football a career. It has been good to me in the material sense, but more important is that I have been associated with youth in all my years as a pro football coach and owner. **"**

—**George Halas**

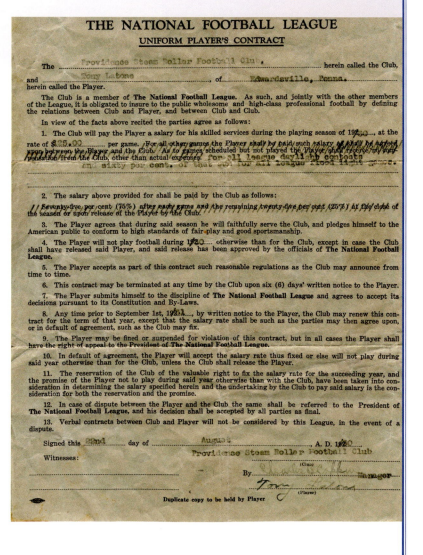

> "Courage is a mysterious quality, touching at times the strong and the weak, the rich and the poor, the wise and the fools in a bewildering method of selection."
>
> —Jimmy Conzelman

JIMMY CONZELMAN'S 1928 PROVIDENCE STEAM ROLLER MOST OUTSTANDING PLAYER TROPHY WITH CHAMPIONSHIP BANNER

The Providence Steam Roller, a successful independent pro team, joined the NFL in 1925. After two fairly successful seasons, the team got a significant boost when several players from the defunct Detroit Panthers joined the squad, including player-coach and future Hall of Famer Jimmy Conzelman. The Steam Roller won the 1928 NFL title and Conzelman was selected as the team's most outstanding player.

PROVIDENCE STEAM ROLLER NIGHT GAME

The Providence Steam Roller made NFL history on November 6, 1929, when they hosted the Chicago Cardinals in the league's first game played at night under lights. The game drew 6,000 fans and the interest of the local media. One newspaper reported that the ball, painted white for the game, "had the appearance of a large egg," and when it was passed there was a panicky feeling that the receiver "would be splattered with yellow yolk." While floodlights may not have had an immediate effect on the pro game, they did affect the Steam Roller players, as evidenced by fullback Tony Latone's 1930 contract that paid him $125 "for all league daylight games and sixty percent of that sum for all league floodlight games." According to team management, the reduction in pay was to "help pay for the installation costs of the floodlights."

PRO FOOTBALL'S NEW YORK
YANKEES AUTOGRAPHED
FOOTBALL

After a highly publicized debut season
with the Chicago Bears, Red Grange and his
manager, C. C. Pyle, attempted to secure an
NFL franchise in New York City. After being
turned down, Grange and Pyle organized the
rival American Football League and operated
the league's marquee team, the New York
Yankees. The AFL lasted just one season
before folding. The Yankees were conditionally
absorbed into the NFL for the 1927 season.
This AFL football is signed by Grange and
his Yankee teammates.

The December 13 season finale, a 9–3 loss to the Giants, was the
last of Grange's ten game appearances with the Bears. For the rest of
the Bears players, it was the end of a marathon twenty-game season.
But the fun wasn't over yet.

After a two-week rest and recovery period, Grange and the Bears
were back on the road as the stars of Pyle's barnstorming tour. Originally Pyle had intended, after the completion of the Bears' NFL season, to form his own "All-Star" team with Grange as his headliner,
but having a ready-made squad in the Bears was just too convenient.
Since the "tour" games would be exhibition games and didn't require
NFL opponents, Pyle, Halas, and Sternaman agreed to a single contract to simplify their relationship. The Bears owners maintained
their role as managers of the team, and for their services would receive 10 percent of the first $300,000 of net profits after expenses and
7.5 percent of anything over $300,000. The players, with the exception
of Grange, would receive their usual game salaries as provided in
their NFL game contracts.

While the deal certainly favored Pyle and Grange, it did put all
the expenses—including player salaries, travel, and accommodations—
in Pyle's column. The Bears owners had the potential of earning

*[Referring to playing football at
age thirty in 1926]*

❝I love the game. That's why I play it.
I might make more money in some
other line of endeavor, so it is not
the 'sugar' that keeps me at it.❞
—Guy Chamberlin

❝Some people say, 'Doesn't it make you feel bad to see your records broken?' And it doesn't—not in the slightest.
I get a kick out of it. I want the Packers to go unbeaten. Records are made to be broken. I'm not one to live in the
past—if records are being broken, it means we're going someplace.❞

—Earl "Curly" Lambeau

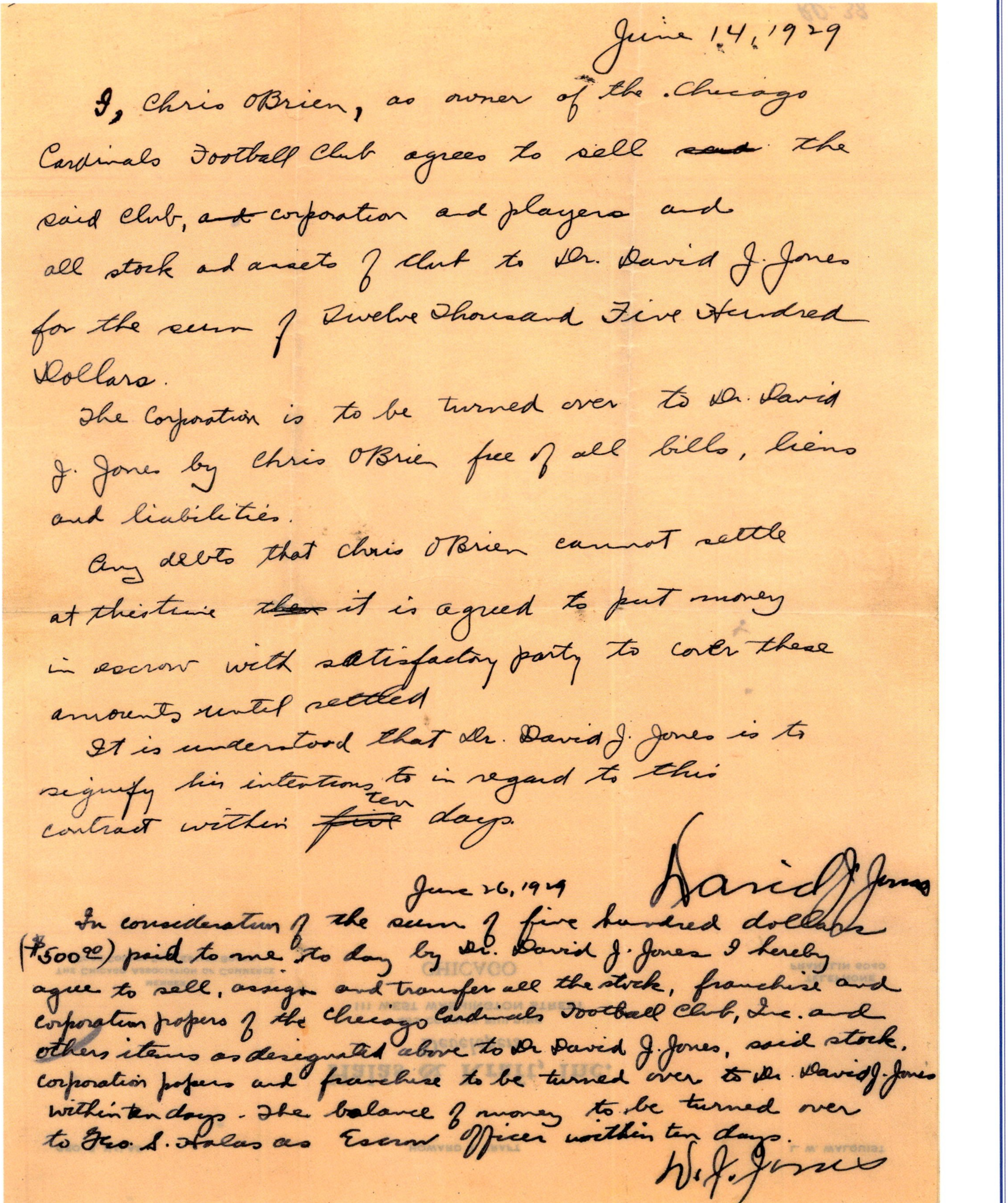

June 14, 1929

I, Chris OBrien, as owner of the Chicago Cardinals Football Club agrees to sell ~~and~~ the said Club, ~~and~~ corporation and players and all stock and assets of club to Dr. David J. Jones for the sum of Twelve Thousand Five Hundred Dollars.

The Corporation is to be turned over to Dr. David J. Jones by Chris OBrien free of all bills, liens and liabilities.

Any debts that Chris OBrien cannot settle at this time ~~then~~ it is agreed to put money in escrow with satisfactory party to cover these amounts until settled

It is understood that Dr. David J. Jones is to signify his intentions to in regard to this contract within ~~five~~ ten days.

June 26, 1929   David J. Jones

In consideration of the sum of five hundred dollars ($500ºº) paid to me to day by Dr. David J. Jones I hereby agree to sell, assign and transfer all the stock, franchise and corporation papers of the Chicago Cardinals Football Club, Inc. and others items as designated above to Dr David J. Jones, said stock, corporation papers and franchise to be turned over to Dr. David J. Jones within ten days. The balance of money to be turned over to Geo. S. Halas as Escrow officer within ten days.

W. J. Jones

"The biggest difference today is the talent and the patterns that have evolved. If I had the patterns and the receivers you see in the game today, it would have been terrific. I also regret never having the chance to play with the smaller ball. The big ball wasn't a passing ball. It was great for dropkicking."

—Benny Friedman

$30,000-plus over the course of the nine-game, five-week tour, and the simplified contract provided far less risk on their part. Just show up and play.

The tour began on Christmas Day in Coral Gables, Florida, where a 30,000-seat wooden stadium was constructed just two days before the game. Only 5,000 seats were needed. The Coral Gables disappointment was followed by games in Tampa and Jacksonville. A stop in New Orleans was followed by three games in California—Los Angeles, San Diego, and San Francisco—and a final two in Portland and Seattle.

Although most of the games drew less than expected, in Los Angeles, 75,000 fans filled the L.A. Coliseum to witness the Grange-led Bears defeat a team billed as the Los Angeles Tigers, 17–7. Two weeks

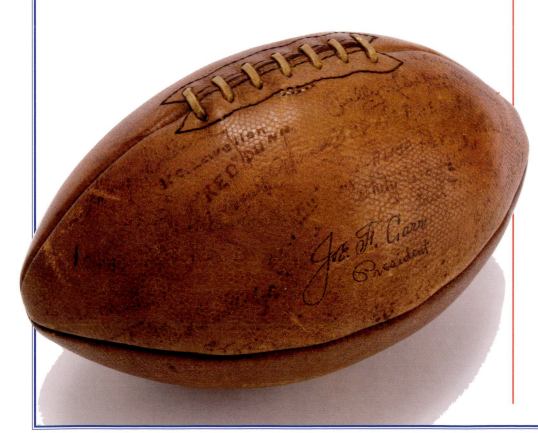

Opposite:

CHRIS O'BRIEN SALE CONTRACT OF CHICAGO CARDINALS

This one-page handwritten document, dated June 14, 1929, is the purchase agreement for the Chicago Cardinals between Dr. David Jones and longtime owner Chris O'Brien. The sale came just months before the New York stock market crash and the start of the Great Depression. After four tough years, Jones sold the franchise in 1933 to Charles Bidwill. The team, now known as the Arizona Cardinals, is still owned by the Bidwill family.

"The Canton Bulldogs was a grand team, but pro football has come a long way since then. The teams today are better drilled and coached. I believe any of them would have run away with us."

—Wilbur "Pete" Henry

AUTOGRAPHED 1929 GREEN BAY PACKERS CHAMPIONSHIP GAME BALL

The Green Bay Packers won their first NFL championship in 1929 after posting an impressive record of 12–0–1. This game ball was signed by each member of the championship team, which included four future Hall of Famers: Curly Lambeau, Johnny "Blood" McNally, Cal Hubbard, and Mike Michalske. The Packers then went on to win NFL titles in 1930 and 1931, becoming the first and only team to win three consecutive NFL championships, something they did again in 1965–67.

"I'm old and worn out. This [the 1934 NFL Championship] was probably my last game. God, I would have loved to swagger about and tell my grandchildren and all the folks out in Nebraska, 'Boys, I played on an undefeated team—the greatest team that ever played football."

—Link Lyman

"People say we weren't good enough to play the game today. Well, I was and a lot of other players were, too. We might have been smaller, but we played both ways. Send some of those 280-pound hulks out on a pass play today and see how they stack up. We could take them on."

—John "Blood" McNally

Opposite:

1928 CHICAGO BEARS SEASON
TICKET POSTER

Talk about a home-field advantage: the 1928 Chicago Bears played just three of their thirteen games on the road—and one away game was just across town to play the Chicago Cardinals. While no doubt advantageous, it was in fact a good deal for the smaller-market visiting teams as their lesser split of the larger Wrigley Field gate was greater than what they could generate at home.

later in San Francisco, 23,000 disappointed fans saw Grange carry the ball just seven times for 43 yards. Following the game, rumors surfaced that Pyle was behind on his payments to the players and that tensions between the Bears and Pyle were high. One San Francisco newspaper suggested that Grange's lack of carries and the manner in which he was used was the Bears' way of expressing their frustration with Pyle and perhaps a little "Grange fatigue."

"Grange, as everyone knows," reported the newspaper, "receives the lion's share of gate receipts, while the Chicago Bears receive a pittance for the effort. The Chicago Bears, it seems, do not warm up to the idea of playing second ukulele, and a dispute is said to have arisen between its chiefs and 'Cash and Carry' Pyle, manager of Grange."

Whether there was friction between the two entities or not, the tour ended with two lopsided wins for the Bears. In both games Grange's star shone brightly. It was a fitting end to a very long and personally trying season for the former college idol. "I'm glad I turned pro," he said, "but I'll be glad to quit."

For the Bears players, the signing of Grange provided each with an extra twelve paychecks. The team of Sternaman and Halas made out too, earning $45,000 in "salary and bonuses" each, while the team recorded a profit of $14,675.01.

NFL President Joe Carr, in his annual report to the owners, also offered his stamp of approval. "Attendance and publicity were augmented when Mr. Grange elected to become a professional," he reported. "Much discussion followed the entry of this most talked of athlete of modern times into our League. I am firmly convinced the net result has been in favor of our organization. Thousands upon thousands of people were attracted to their first game of professional football through a curiosity to see Grange in action, and many became profound advocates."

And in the end, "Cash and Carry" Pyle delivered on his promise to Grange. "Twice during the tour Pyle gave Red a check for $50,000," reported Halas. "When the final accounting was made of receipts and royalties, Red received another $100,000. Red came to the Bears famous. Ten weeks later he was rich."

CHICAGO BEARS

1928
Season Tickets
On Sale at
THE HUB
235 South State St.
Phone Wabash 3500

10 Games $20.

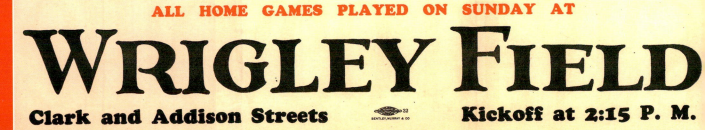

Assure Yourselves Good Seats For The Entire Season

1928 SCHEDULE
CHICAGO BEARS
FOOTBALL CLUB

Sept. 23—	At Cardinals, (Normal Park).
Sept. 30—	At Green Bay, Wisconsin.
Oct. 7—	Open
Oct. 14—	New York Giants (Bruce Caldwell)
Oct. 21—	Green Bay Packers
Oct. 28—	Detroit (Benny Friedman)
Nov. 4—	New York Yankees
Nov. 11—	Dayton Triangles
Nov. 18—	Pottsville Maroons
Nov. 25—	Detroit (Benny Friedman)
Nov. 29—	Chicago Cardinals
Dec. 2—	Philadelphia Yellow Jackets
Dec. 9—	Green Bay Packers
Dec. 15—	At Philadelphia, Pa.
Dec. 16—	Open

All games in black played at Wrigley Field

How To Order Season Tickets

In ordering please state:—

1. How many tickets you desire. Send $20 for each season box seat ordered.

2. Preference as to location: Lower or upper deck; high or low in respective decks.

3. The charge of $20 for a season box seat covers ten games and reserves for you the same seat at each game. Remittance must accompany each application.

4. Make all checks payable to Chicago Bears Football Club, Inc., and mail ℅ The Hub, 235 South State Street, Chicago, Illinois.

Season tickets will be mailed in time for first game.

All games will be played regardless of weather conditions.

Address all orders to
CHICAGO BEARS FOOTBALL CLUB
℅ THE HUB,
235 South State Street,
Chicago, Ill.

ALL HOME GAMES PLAYED ON SUNDAY AT

WRIGLEY FIELD

Clark and Addison Streets BENTLEY, MURRAY & CO 32 **Kickoff at 2:15 P. M.**

PROFESSIONAL
FOOTBALL PROFESSIONAL
FOOTBALL

BORCHERT'S FIELD

8th and Chambers - Milwaukee

BIG LEAGUE FOOTBALL
at
"NIGHT"
Under Giant Electric Flood Lights
Entire Stadium to be illuminated

Chicago Bears
*one of Americas most powerful professional club
with their two All American Stars*

"RED" | "BRONKO"
GRANGE | # NAGURSKI

The Famous "RED" | **The Big Train**
Illinois' Galloping Ghost | **from Minnesota**

vs.

Milwaukee (Badgers)

Made up of All American and All Western Stars

THURSDAY, OCTOBER 2; 8:00 P. M.

General Admission $1.00   **Reserved Seats $1.50**

Tickets on sale at Hotel Schroeder, J. Morgenroth's, Hugo Walter

NOTICE: America's leading professional clubs will show
here every week. Watch Newspapers for details.

The 1930s

SAVING THE NFL:
A CHAMPIONSHIP IS BORN

JOHN THORN

Opposite:

CHICAGO BEARS VS. MILWAUKEE
BADGERS HANDBILL

The 1930 Milwaukee Badgers, an independent pro team, scheduled exhibition games with NFL clubs in an effort to impress league owners and officials. Badgers owner O. C. Haderer was interested in purchasing the defunct Buffalo Bisons franchise, but was eventually turned down by the league.

Throughout its first decade the National Football League was a single entity, without subordinate divisions or conferences. In this the NFL modeled itself on the rise of professional baseball's league structure, going back to 1871, when the championship was decided by the best record in the league season. Baseball did not have a postseason championship contest until an upstart league in its third campaign, the American Association, challenged the National League to meet in a World Series in 1884.

IN THE NFL'S FIRST DECADE, the number of clubs in a given season ranged from a high of twenty-two in 1926 to a low of ten only three years later, with no requirement that clubs contending for the championship play an equal number of games. In 1928, for example, the Providence Steam Roller (8–1–2) was named the champion despite having played five fewer games than the Frankford Yellow Jackets (11–3–2). The NFL awarded its championship to the club with the highest winning percentage, disregarding ties—which were plentiful, as were the disputed titles.

But these were not the only issues threatening the continued existence of the NFL. After a brief flurry of prosperity in the wake of the Red Grange tour of 1925, which prompted the formation of a rival American Football League for the following season, pro football sank back into a morass of low-scoring thumb-twiddlers played largely by fly-by-night franchises in second-tier cities. In 1931, half of the league's teams averaged less than seven points per game.

A relaxing of the substitution rules for 1932, allowing a replaced player to return in a subsequent quarter, failed to boost scoring. In 1932, NFL games averaged only 16.4 points *for both teams*. Of the fourteen games played by the champion Chicago Bears that season,

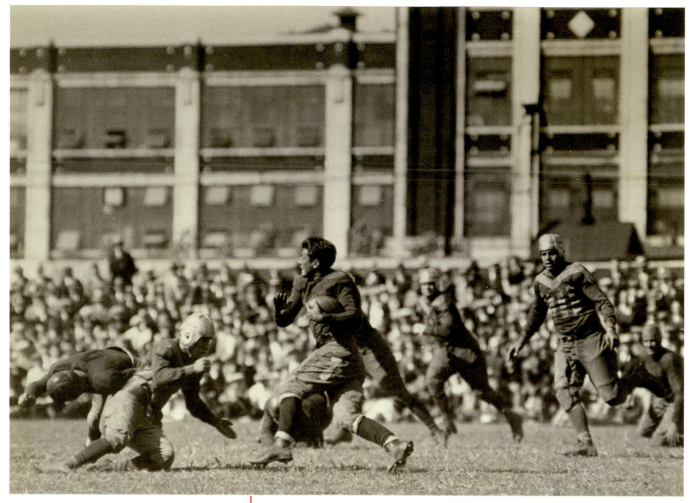

BROOKLYN DODGERS VS. CHICAGO BEARS, 1930

Following the 1929 season, Brooklyn businessman John Dyer purchased the Dayton Triangles franchise, moved it to Brooklyn, and renamed the team the Brooklyn Dodgers. The Dodgers finished 7–4–1 in 1930. All four of their losses were shutouts, and their one tied game was a scoreless contest against the Chicago Bears.

"Running is like driving a car. When you drive, you're looking quite a ways down the street. The things that are close you take care of automatically with reflex action."

—Earl "Dutch" Clark

six ended in ties. By this time the league had franchises in New York, Brooklyn, and Boston, and two in Chicago—as well as that hardy ex-urban outlier, Green Bay—but it also had clubs in Staten Island and Portsmouth, Ohio. Along the way, franchises had failed in major cities such as Philadelphia, St. Louis, Detroit, and Cleveland, not to mention Akron, Buffalo, Cincinnati, Kansas City, Louisville, Milwaukee, Minneapolis, Newark, Providence, and Toledo.

With the Depression settling in, it seemed that the prospects for professional football were growing dimmer with each passing year. The number of league clubs declined in each year between 1929 and 1932, until only eight teams lined up for play. Competitive imbalance left two-thirds of the NFL's clubs to play out the string before the frost was on the punkin. The league had neither parity nor a plan for achieving it: the first draft of collegiate players would not come until 1936.

What saved the NFL was a series of happy accidents in the season finales of 1932 and 1933; the first was a playoff game to break a tie for the pennant, while the next was the league's first championship game, the direct ancestor of our great national festival, the Super Bowl. Rules innovations born of desperation opened up the stodgy old game to the dormant capabilities of the forward pass; innovative play calling and increased scoring came to the rescue just as the lights were about to be shut off.

Coming into the 1932 season, the Green Bay Packers, who had won the last three championships, were once again counted as the favorite. However, a midseason tie with the Bears and upset losses to the New York Giants and Portsmouth Spartans left them on the outside looking in despite their record, going into the final weekend, of 10–2–1. Portsmouth had already completed its schedule at 6–1–4, but the 5–1–6 Bears still had one more game to play and, with a win over the defending champions, could pull into a tie.

On December 11 the punchless Bears struggled to a 0–0 tie with the Packers through three snowy quarters in Chicago. In the final period, however, the Bears put up nine points to create the NFL's first deadlocked season. Had the league compiled its standings then as it does now, and has since 1974—counting each tie as half a win and half a loss—the title would have gone to Green Bay, with ten-and-one-half "wins" to Chicago's nine and Portsmouth's eight. But in 1932 ties were nonevents.

The NFL had no policy for dealing with a season-ending tie for first place; in fact, the league didn't even handle scheduling—that was up to the teams themselves. The Bears and Spartans agreed to hold a showdown game at Chicago on December 18. But Sunday's snow showed no sign of letting up as the days wore on and paralyzing cold gripped the city. It would be impossible to host the game at Wrigley Field even for the hardiest fans.

This was not to be a postseason championship game, but an additional regular-season game that would be counted in the standings. Whichever team lost would slip to third place behind the Packers!

George Halas, recalling a charity game that the Bears and Cardinals had played only two years before, suggested that the contest be moved indoors to Chicago Stadium. The Spartans, hoping for a change in the weather, waited to commit but on Friday finally relented.

This indoor facility, built in 1929 to host civic events, hockey games, boxing matches, and circuses, was not meant for football, at 45 yards wide and 80 yards long. Rounded corners further cut into the athletes' space. With two

> **"Kicking is more than just the fellow who boots the ball. It's a close teamwork between three players. The center has to get the ball back just right, with the laces in the correct position. The holder must know how to catch the snap and how to place it down with the greatest speed and accuracy. Then, of course, it's up to the kicker to get it between the uprights. There's not much room for error anywhere along the line."**
>
> **—Ken Strong**

DUTCH CLARK

Dutch Clark was an all-league player with the Portsmouth Spartans (1931–32) and Detroit Lions (1934–38). A true triple-threat back, Clark consistently finished among the league leaders in rushing and once completed 53.5 percent of his passes in a season when the league average was just 36.5 percent. He led the league in scoring three times, kicked field goals and extra points, and is generally considered the last of the great dropkickers.

"You may say that a professional team lacks the spirit of a college team. Perhaps we do. But it's only the fervor and frenzy of a young boy playing for the glory of his college. There is little wasted effort on the professional field. We are more mature and less impulsive."

—Cliff Battles

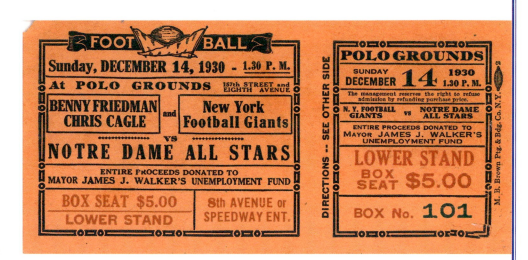

NOTRE DAME ALL-STARS VS. NEW YORK GIANTS, 1930

Mayor Jimmy Walker, looking to raise funds for New York's unemployment relief fund, asked New York Giants owner Tim Mara for his help. Mara agreed to host a charity game on December 14, 1930, against an All-Star team of former Notre Dame players, coached by Knute Rockne and featuring the legendary "Four Horsemen." The Giants handily beat the out-of-shape All-Stars 22–0, but the real winner was the relief fund, which received a check for $115,153. Sadly, it was the last game Rockne coached before his fatal plane crash on March 31, 1931.

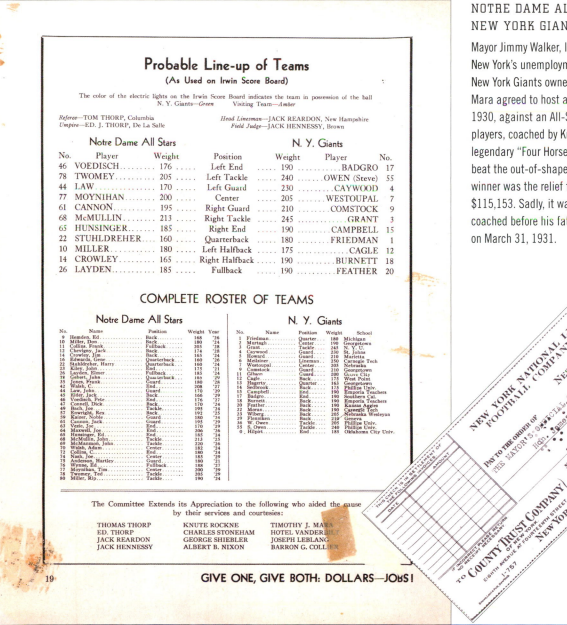

1931 JOE CARR LETTER

Although NFL franchises in the 1920s and 1930s were sold at what today sound like bargain-basement prices, what is sometimes overlooked is that teams also were required annually to deposit guarantee fees in the range of $1,500 to be drawn against by the league for fines or the settlement of financial disputes between member clubs. Following the 1930 season, Chicago Bears co-owner Dutch Sternaman filed a complaint with the league office regarding the college eligibility status of some opposing players his team had faced during the season. Carr in this letter responded that his means to investigate were "rather limited" and asked that Sternaman, unless he could deliver definitive evidence, withdraw his complaint, which he later did.

PHOTO: DUTCH STERNAMAN COLLECTION

BENNY FRIEDMAN'S BROOKLYN DODGERS

Michigan All-America quarterback Benny Friedman had Grange-like magic when he entered the NFL in 1927. Two years later, New York Giants owner Tim Mara purchased the failing Detroit franchise just to get Friedman for his Giants. Friedman led the league in touchdown passes for four consecutive years, 1927–30. Although a leg injury in 1931 slowed the triple-threat quarterback, he continued to be a major gate attraction through his final years (1932–34) with the Brooklyn Dodgers.

BOSTON BRAVES STATIONERY

A group headed by George Preston Marshall was awarded an NFL franchise for Boston in 1932. Because they played in the home park of the baseball Braves, they too were known as the Braves. A year later, the team, then solely owned by Marshall, relocated to Boston's Fenway Park and was renamed the Redskins. In 1937, citing a lack of strong support in Boston, Marshall moved the team to Washington, D.C., where it remains.

half-moon end zones, the normal playing surface of 100 yards would somehow have to be shoehorned into 60. Sports historian Bob Carroll observed:

> A circus was scheduled into the stadium a few days later so a six-inch layer of dirt covered the floor. Apparently the dirt was recycled from an earlier circus; several of the players who appeared in the game insisted that years later they still had the smell of elephant manure in their nostrils.

Here necessity proved the mother of invention, as it had for the 1930 exhibition game. The ball was kicked off from the 10-yard line. Only one set of goalposts was used, and that was placed at the goal line, not at the end line. When a team crossed midfield, it immediately was set back twenty yards. Because the twelve-foot-high hockey dasher boards surrounded the whole field only a few feet from the sidelines, the ball was moved in ten yards after each out-of-bounds play instead of starting the next play right at the edge, as was the normal practice. The offensive team sacrificed a down each time the ball was thus moved. College football, whose rules the NFL almost universally adopted, had legalized this use of "hash marks" a year earlier, but this was its first use in the pro game. Another special rule dictated that touchbacks were brought out to only the 10. Field goals were banned.

Portsmouth had been led all season by quarterback Dutch Clark, but he could not play in the playoff game because, anticipating a December 11 end to the NFL season, he had committed himself to coach basketball at his alma mater, Colorado College, which would permit no delay. Tailback Glenn Presnell picked up the slack, losing a certain touchdown on a fourth-and-goal play from the six-yard line when he slipped on the suspect turf.

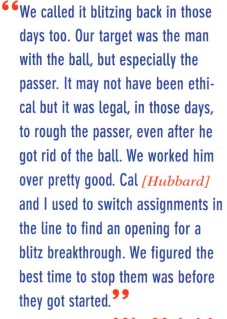

"We called it blitzing back in those days too. Our target was the man with the ball, but especially the passer. It may not have been ethical but it was legal, in those days, to rough the passer, even after he got rid of the ball. We worked him over pretty good. Cal *[Hubbard]* and I used to switch assignments in the line to find an opening for a blitz breakthrough. We figured the best time to stop them was before they got started."

—**Mike Michalske**

1932 INDOOR GAME

In 1932, the Chicago Bears and Portsmouth Spartans played an extra game to break a tie in the standings and determine the league champion. Due to frigid conditions, the game was moved indoors to Chicago Stadium and played on an 80-yard field encircled by a wooden wall. Rules changes were made to accommodate the mini-field, including moving the ball 10 yards in-bounds after out-of-bounds plays and placing the goalposts on the goal line. The game's lone touchdown came on a disputed pass play from Bronko Nagurski to Red Grange. The Spartans claimed Nagurski wasn't back five yards behind the line of scrimmage, as was then required for a pass to be legal. However, the play stood and the Bears won 9–0.

1932 PLAYOFF GAME PROGRAM

This rare and badly charred game program from the 1932 NFL playoff game between the Chicago Bears and the Portsmouth Spartans survived a fire in the Chicago Bears offices in 1962.

"I didn't like losing games and I didn't like losing money. But I'll tell you from the bottom of my heart: whatever I lost in money I was lucky to be able to lose it. I'd pay to lose it…to keep in this game. I love it that much."

—Art Rooney

The National Football League Franchise

Promotion of Good Fellowship   **Elevation of Football Standards**

To All to Whom These Presents Shall Come, Greeting:

The _Philadelphia National League Football Club_, having complied with the rules and regulations set forth in the Constitution and By-Laws of the National Football League, and being a member in good standing therein, are hereby granted the right to operate a professional football club in the city of _Philadelphia, Pa._

The above named club, by the acceptance of this franchise, pledges itself to the American Public to conform to high standards of fair play and sportsmanship, and to the promotion of the business and ethical interests of professional football.

Signed at _Columbus, Ohio_ this _1st_ day of _August_ 19_33_

Attest:

Joe F. Carr
Secretary

THE NATIONAL FOOTBALL LEAGUE,
By _Joe F. Carr._
President

© GOES 137

PHILADELPHIA EAGLES 1933 FRANCHISE CERTIFICATE

In 1933 the NFL added three new franchises: the Cincinnati Reds, Pittsburgh Pirates, and Philadelphia Eagles. While the Reds and Pirates borrowed the names of their baseball counterparts, the Eagles took their name and logo from the symbol of the National Recovery Act, an integral part of President Roosevelt's New Deal program. The Cincinnati franchise folded after eight games of the 1934 season. In 1940 the Pirates, founded by Art Rooney, were renamed the Steelers.

"The players today are bigger and faster than they were in my time, but some of the stars in my time would still be stars today. Red Grange and Cliff Battles were the best runners when I played. They could really break games open. They were a lot like Walter Payton today _[1981]_."

—Morris "Red" Badgro

"The experiences you gain on the football field can be carried over in many other aspects of life. Teamwork is something that's important in both professions. *[After football, Fortmann became a surgeon.]* A surgical team must work together. I learned a lot about teamwork playing football with the Bears."

—Dan Fortmann

"I've taken enough beatings for one man. Not that I couldn't take some more. It's not fat nor age that's driving me out. I scale at 253 today, which is just one pound more than I carried in the line at college. I've just had enough shoving and kicking around."

—Cal Hubbard

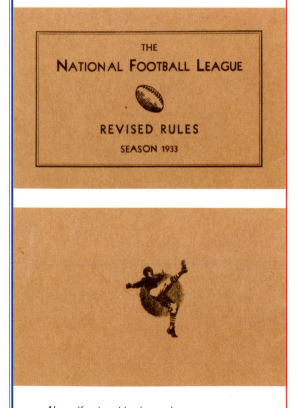

THE

NATIONAL FOOTBALL LEAGUE

REVISED RULES

SEASON 1933

*Above (front and back cover)
and opposite (interior):*
1933 NFL RULES BOOKLET

The Bears were led by the veteran Red Grange, no longer elusive after injuries to his knees but still a heady runner, and Bronko Nagurski, a 238-pound fullback who trampled would-be tacklers with his head down and his knees pumping, as well as a fearsome linebacker. Although the Spartans had the best of play through three quarters and might well have jumped out on top had field goals been permitted, the score was—yet again in this dismal season for scoring—tied at 0–0. The 12,000 fans who had left their hearths for this indoor novelty game began to wonder why.

Then Chicago halfback Dick Nesbitt intercepted an Ace Gutowsky pass and returned it ten yards before being knocked out of bounds at the Portsmouth seven. The ball was brought into the field ten yards, costing the Bears a down. On second down, Nagurski burst through the line for six yards. On his next try, he lost a yard. Fourth and two! Nagurski faked a plunge into the line, retreated a few steps, and fired a jump pass to Grange for the go-ahead touchdown.

NFL rules allowed a forward pass only if it was thrown five or more yards behind the line of scrimmage. The Spartans protested that Nagurski had not stepped back far enough. The officials disagreed. The Bears added the conversion and, a few moments later, a safety.

Who emerged as the champion of this struggling eight-team league was not the central fact about this game. At their meeting in Pittsburgh in February 1933, NFL owners adopted three rules changes inspired by the playoff confines: (1) the ball was to be moved ten yards in from the sideline after going out of bounds, without costing the offensive team a down, and hash marks were placed on the field; (2) goalposts were moved from the end line to the goal line to increase scoring; and (3) a forward pass was allowed from anywhere behind the line of scrimmage, since the previous rule had been observed largely in the breach.

These changes began to thaw the game from its defensive deep freeze, increasing scoring and cutting the number of ties in half. George Preston Marshall, owner of the Boston Braves (now the Washington Redskins), seeing that the playoff game of 1932 had won unprecedented coverage for the NFL, urged his fellow magnates to reorganize the league (restored to ten teams for 1933) into Eastern and Western divisions, with a postseason championship game.

2 IN ALL INSTANCES OTHER THAN IN THE EXCEPTIONS NOTED HEREIN THE RULES OF THE NATIONAL INTERCOLLEGIATE ATHLETIC ASSOCIATION ARE TO BE FOLLOWED.

KICK-OFF AND FREE KICK

1. The receiving team may line in any position beyond the ten yard restraining line.

2. It is permissible for the kicking team to use a natural tee made from the soil in the immediate vicinity of the point of kick-off.

FLYING BLOCK AND TACKLE

The flying block and flying tackle are permitted.

3 FORWARD PASS

The passer may pass the ball from any point behind the line of scrimmage.

TIME OUT

Officials **must** notify the captain of each team when time has been out three (3) times—and no penalty is to be imposed for additional time out unless such notice has been given.

DEAD BALL

In Rule 7—Section 7—Article (1a) of the Intercollegiate rules **omit** the words "when any portion of his person except his hands or feet touches the ground".

4 ### PERSONAL FOULS

Use of hands—in Rule 10—Section 2—Article 1—Item 2 of the Intercollegiate Rules, **omit** the words "players on defense may not strike the opponent on the head, neck, or face with the palms of their hands".

CLIPPING

The penalty for clipping shall be 25 yards—officials shall enforce this rule to the letter.

GOAL POSTS

The goal posts shall be placed on the goal-line instead of ten yards beyond.

Account the goal posts being placed on the goal-line the following rules become effective:

5
1. A ball kicked from the field of play, except one scoring a goal, which strikes the goal posts or cross-bar before being touched by a player of either side, shall become a dead ball and is to be ruled a touchback.

2. A ball kicked from behind the goal-line which strikes the goal posts or cross-bar and is recovered by the opponents in the end zone shall be ruled a touchdown. In the event it is recovered by a player of the kicking team, or rolls outside the side line extended, or beyond the end line in the end zone, it shall be ruled a safety. Should the ball strike the goal posts or cross-bar and continue into the field of play it shall be played as if it did not hit the goal posts.

3. A forward pass thrown from the field of play which strikes the goal posts or cross-bar before or after it has been touched by an eligible player and before it has touched

6 the ground shall be declared incomplete and ruled a touchback.

4. A forward pass thrown from behind the goal-line which strikes the goal posts or cross-bar shall be subject to recovery by the opposing team or any eligible player of the passing team before it strikes the ground. (The passer is included among the eligible men.) Should the ball be recovered by an opposing player within the end zone before it strikes the ground it shall be ruled a touchdown. If it is recovered by a member of the passer's team and not advanced into the field of play, or bounds beyond the side line extended, or beyond the end line, it shall be ruled a safety. Should the ball strike the goal posts or cross-bar and continue into the field of play it shall remain in play as though it had not touched any obstruction.

7 ### NOTICE TO OFFICIALS

1. Where only three officials are used the Umpire shall be the timekeeper unless another official is designated by the Referee. Where the fourth official is used the Field Judge shall be the timekeeper.

2. All officials must wear white trousers, white shirt, black tie and preferably black stockings.

3. All railroads sell reduced rate week-end round trip tickets. You are instructed to purchase such transportation.

APPROVED:
GEO. S. HALAS,   JOE F. CARR,
Chairman, Rules Committee.   President.

1933 NFL RULES BOOKLET

In 1933, the NFL for the first time instituted playing rules that differed from the Intercollegiate Football Rules Book. Chief among the differences was the NFL's legalization of the forward pass from anywhere behind the line of scrimmage. The new rules also called for the addition of in-bounds lines 10 yards from the sidelines, and the moving of the goalposts from the end line to the goal line.

BOSTON REDSKINS POSTER

The Washington Redskins franchise began in 1932 as the Boston Braves. In 1933 the team changed its name to the Redskins, and in 1937 it relocated to Washington, D.C.

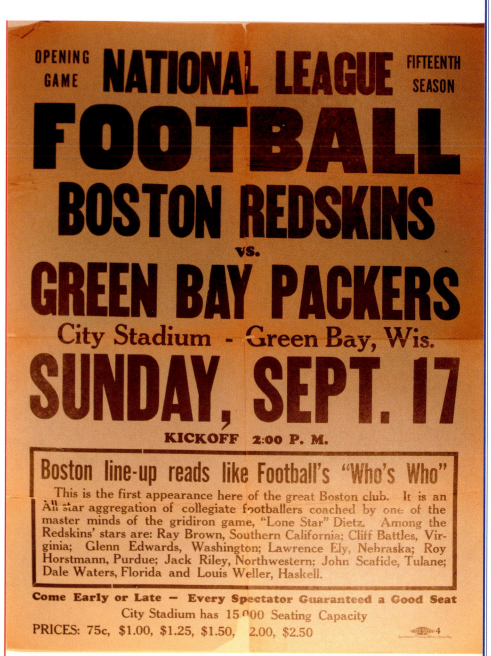

"I weighed 190 pounds as a senior in high school, 190 pounds at Notre Dame, 190 pounds playing for the Redskins. And 190 pounds now *[1976]*.**"**

—Wayne Millner

"I used my pride instead of my mind. I thought I was so big I couldn't be replaced. Nobody's that big, not in football, not in anything.**"**

—Joe Stydahar

Soon wide-sweeping runs and passes would provide the points that power, endurance, and off-tackle runs had not; the tricky blocking schemes of the single wing soon would seem dowdy compared to the passing plays possible out of the T formation. The forward pass itself was not new. It had entered the game with the collegiate rule changes of 1906, designed to blunt the impact of mass-momentum plays and reduce injury. Brad Robinson, playing for St. Louis University coach Eddie Cochems, is said to have thrown the first legal pass in a September 5, 1906, game against Carroll College at Waukesha, Wisconsin. Notre

GEORGE PRESTON MARSHALL, THE WASHINGTON REDSKINS' FLAMBOYANT FOUNDER

In 1932 George Preston Marshall was granted an NFL franchise for Boston. After they won the NFL title in 1936, Marshall decided to move the team to Washington, D.C. Flamboyant, controversial, and a master showman, Marshall sponsored progressive rule changes, pioneered gala halftime shows, and organized the first team marching band. A regular on his team's sideline, he was often seen in this full-length fur coat.

"I'm not any different than I ever was. Marshall's not as wild as he used to be *[they say]*. **Well, hell, Marshall was never wild. I sure have been accused of being anti-everything. Anti-Jewish, anti-Catholic. Oh, I don't know. Maybe I'm just anti-people."**

—George Preston Marshall

Dame quarterback Gus Dorais, who is sometimes credited with this innovation himself, entered football lore with his passing exploits against Army in 1913, completing 14 of his 17 heaves of the oblate spheroid, many to end Knute Rockne, in a 35–13 upset victory.

The 1933 Championship Game, between the defending titleist Bears and the New York Giants, building upon the new rules, pointed the way to the NFL's future. A razzle-dazzle display rarely if ever equaled since, it retains its status as one of the most exciting football games ever played.

> This *[1954]* team is better than the 1942 outfit. I shouldn't be making comparisons because the game has changed a lot in the last twelve years. We didn't go two ways *[offensive and defensive platoons]* then and the boys had to play a lot of football. I had Bill Dudley then and he did a lot of running for us. We've got to do a lot of passing now to keep up with the others.
> —Walt Kiesling

Opposite and above:

"HAIL TO THE REDSKINS" SHEET MUSIC

The lyrics to "Hail to the Redskins" were written by owner George Preston Marshall's actress wife, Corinne Griffith Marshall. Some of the original lyrics were later changed, as they were deemed insensitive. Among the changes, the phrase "for old Dixie" was changed to "for old D.C."

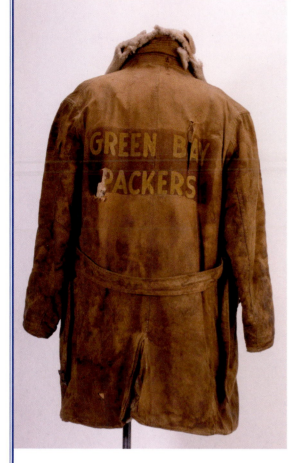

ARNIE HERBER'S WELL-WORN GREEN BAY PACKERS SIDELINE COAT

Green Bay Packers quarterback Arnie Herber was one of the game's great early-day passers. He led the league in passing in 1932, 1934, and 1936. With the arrival of Don Hutson in 1935, pro football had its first "famous" quarterback-receiver tandem. Although Herber retired in 1940, the New York Giants coaxed him back for two more seasons in 1944 and 1945, due to the NFL's manpower shortage during World War II.

1934 PITTSBURGH PIRATES

Art Rooney was granted an NFL franchise for Pittsburgh in 1933. He named his team the Pirates after the city's National League baseball club. The team never finished above .500 during the 1930s and, judging by their 1934 uniforms, surely would not have won any fashion awards. In 1940 Rooney renamed the team the Steelers. But even with a new name and better-looking uniforms, it wasn't until 1972 that the team won a playoff game.

> "It is still an individual thing, a question of running the pass pattern correctly. Pass patterns have probably changed less than anything else in football."
>
> —Don Hutson

Before the season, the Giants, who ran a single-wing offense as did every other NFL club except the Bears, brought in triple-threat quarterback Harry Newman from the University of Michigan. From the dissolved Staten Island Stapletons, they added sturdy halfback Ken Strong. The Giants finished the regular season 11–3, first in the new Eastern Division. Newman, center Mel Hein, and end Red Badgro were named first-team All-NFL. The daring Newman led the league in passes completed (53), passing yards (973), and touchdown passes (11), despite completing under 40 percent of his attempts. (The league average that year barely topped 35 percent; Sammy Baugh's standard of accuracy was still a few years off.) Newman also led his team in rushing.

The Bears went 10–2–1 and won the Western Division, led again by Grange and Nagurski and a T-formation backfield in which everyone was a threat to throw the ball. Halfback Keith Molesworth, for example, threw more passes than quarterback Carl Brumbaugh. Speedy left end Bill Hewitt, who had caught passes from Harry Newman at Michigan, threw three touchdown passes off end-around plays. The Bears and Giants split their regular-season contests and looked to be evenly matched for the championship game, played on December 17 before 26,000 fans at Wrigley Field.

Expectations of a high-powered offensive display were foiled at the outset as the teams retreated to caveman football, each running the ball three times and punting on its first two possessions. Despite the liberalized passing rule, in 1933 it still bordered on heresy to throw the ball inside your own 40-yard line. So teams would run and punt, run and punt—often kicking away on early downs—until a break came along.

At last it did. Keith Molesworth, the Bears' diminutive halfback, lofted a punt to Newman, who found a crack straight up the center and scooted to midfield. On third down, four yards to go, with the ball still at the left hash mark, the Giants lined up unbalanced to the right, with left tackle Len Grant standing to the right of center Hein. Next came a surprise the Giants had cooked up especially for this game: in a simultaneous shift, left end Badgro pulled back from the line, wingback Dale Burnett stepped up alongside right end Ray Flaherty, and Newman moved in behind center, just as a T quarterback would. Thus Burnett became the right end, Flaherty was no longer an eligible receiver, Badgro became a back, and the left end was…Hein! This

BRONKO NAGURSKI

Bronko Nagurski was the dominant football player of his time. When asked about his running style, he once explained, "Just before they got to me, I'd put my shoulder down and ram 'em in the stomach. I'd knock 'em out of the way and keep running." New York Giants coach Steve Owen's solution to stopping Nagurski was simple: "Shoot him before he leaves the dressing room."

> **"I always used my strength in football. I liked to meet guys head-on when I was carrying the ball. Then I'd drop my shoulder, and catch him with that, and then brush him off with my arm. It worked, most of the time."**
>
> **—Bronko Nagurski**

> **"That was something I never experienced, the sensation of Nagurski or Grange running up my back, so I guess I did a few things right when they carried the ball and I blocked for them. Nagurski let you know where you stood, though. We'd turn that corner and I could hear him back there yelling, 'C'mon, move, move.' I never looked back. He'd have left footprints on my back."**
>
> **—George Musso**

> "I just loved the game. I know a lot of players back then, and myself included, who would have played for nothing."

—Alphonse "Tuffy" Leemans

> "Football is a game played down in the dirt, and it always will be. There's no use getting fancy about it."

—Steve Owen

center-eligible play very nearly provided the game's first score, as Hein took a flip from Newman that traveled no more than six inches in the air and hid the ball under his jersey as he jogged downfield. But then he got nervous and began really to run. He was tackled short of the goal line, and instead Chicago broke out on top with a couple of Jack Manders field goals. In the second period Newman found Badgro for a 10-yard touchdown and the Giants led at the half, 7–6.

The game warmed up in the second half, as the Giants recorded another touchdown and Manders added a third field goal. Nagurski dusted off his jump pass from the indoor playoff and completed a touchdown to Bill Karr. The score was still 16–14, Bears, when the third quarter came to an end with the Giants on the Chicago eight-yard line. In this period alone, Newman completed 9 of 10 passes for 131 yards. To appreciate the magnitude of this aerial display, consider that for the entire season, fourteen games, he passed for only 69 yards per contest—and established a new pro record at that!

It was dawning upon those in attendance that this was a different sort of football.

On the first play of the final period, with the ball spotted at the right hash mark, the Giants lined up unbalanced to the right, a formation that seemed to indicate either a pass or an inside run. Yet at the snap, Strong looped behind Newman, took a short pitch, and motored toward the left end. The play was slow to develop, however, and the right side of the Bear line closed off the outside. About to swallow a loss, Strong heaved an overhand lateral back across the field. Newman juggled the ball, then scrambled right, dodging tacklers while giving up ground to the 15. As the Bears focused their energies on corralling Newman, Strong drifted unaccompanied into the left portion of the end zone and waved for the ball. Newman heaved it nearly 50 yards across the field to Strong, who stumbled into the end zone. This sandlot hocus-pocus was pure inspiration, though in later years it would find its way into the Giants' playbook (it never worked again). Strong provided the extra point, and the Giants went ahead 21–16.

The fans could scarcely believe what they were seeing.

[After Curly Lambeau signed him to a Packers contract]
> "What he didn't know at the time is that I wanted to play so badly that I would have signed for nothing."

—Clarke Hinkle

Then, with most of the final period left to play, the Giants turned conservative in an effort to protect their lead. Time wound down until Strong shanked a punt that gave the Bears the ball barely inside New York territory. With less than two minutes remaining, Brumbaugh took the snap, faked a handoff to Grange, then slapped the ball into Nagurski's belly. Bronko lowered his head, but instead of proceeding through the hole, he straightened up, leapt, and lobbed the ball to Hewitt some 10 yards downfield. Hewitt took two steps, with Burnett on his heels. But before he could be thrown down he lateraled to Karr, who raced into the end zone. After the kick, the Bears led 23–21 with one minute to play.

Strong returned the kickoff to the Giants' 40; a long field goal would win the game. Newman tried the center-eligible play that had bedeviled the Bears in the first period. It did not work.

THE NFL'S FIRST CHAMPIONSHIP GAME

Trailing the New York Giants 21–16 with just minutes to play in the 1933 NFL Championship Game, Chicago Bears fullback Bronko Nagurski and ends Bill Hewitt and Bill Karr combined on a game-winning "hook and lateral" play. First, Nagurski tossed a 14-yard jump pass to Hewitt (without a helmet), who then tossed a lateral pass to Karr—who ran the remaining 19 yards for a touchdown and a 23–21 Bears win. The 1933 Championship Game was the first official title game played between the newly created Eastern and Western divisions.

PROFESSIONAL FOOTBALL CHAMPIONS OF THE WORLD

CHICAGO BEARS

THE CHICAGO BEARS' UNUSUAL 1933 CHAMPIONSHIP GAME MEMENTO

Following their 23–21 victory over the New York Giants in the NFL's first official championship game, Chicago Bears owner George Halas presented each member of the 1933 squad with a custom-painted and inscribed bearskin commemorating the win.

"We played sixty minutes in those days. I don't think I would have liked to play just half the time as they do today."
—Mel Hein

Time for just one more desperation play. Returning to the single wing, Newman faked to Strong while Badgro and Flaherty ran patterns to the left side of the field. Then he flipped a little pass off to the right to halfback Burnett, who ran straight at Grange, playing some 20 yards off the line of scrimmage in a 1930s version of the "prevent" defense. Trailing alongside Burnett was Hein, undefended and ready to receive a lateral the moment Grange made a move for Burnett. But Red looked in Burnett's eyes, sensed his own dilemma, and, with the instincts of a truly exceptional player, made what George Halas in years to come would describe as "the greatest defensive play I ever saw." Grange tackled Burnett around the chest, pinning his arms so he could not flip the ball to Hein. He didn't even try to bring Burnett down; he was content to lock him in a bear hug as Hein pleaded for the ball and time ran out.

The Bears had won the first NFL Championship Game, but the real victor was the league itself, which had shown the nation the brand of ball the pros could play. The college coaches would derisively call it basketball, but soon they would imitate it. The future of football had been glimpsed on this day.

1934 NFL CHAMPIONSHIP TROPHY

The playing field at New York's Polo Grounds was a sheet of ice on December 9, 1934, when the New York Giants met the Chicago Bears in the NFL Championship Game. With both teams struggling for solid footing throughout the first half, it looked as though the Bears' 13–3 lead would hold. However, the Giants players changed their football cleats for sneakers "secured" from nearby Manhattan College at halftime. Wearing the rubber-soled shoes, the Giants exploded for 27 unanswered points in the second half and went on to a 30–13 victory. Today, the 1934 NFL Championship Game is known as the "Sneakers Game."

DETROIT LIONS 1935 CHAMPIONSHIP FOOTBALL AND SIDELINE JACKET

This autographed football was used in the 1935 NFL Championship Game in which the Detroit Lions defeated the New York Giants 26–7. The colorful Lions sideline jacket belonged to triple-threat quarterback Dutch Clark, who scored on an exciting 40-yard run in the first quarter.

PHILADELPHIA EAGLES 1936 CANCELED CHECK

This check, signed by De Benneville "Bert" Bell is "repayment in full" of a loan made to the Philadelphia Eagles by Chicago Bears owner George Halas. It is likely that the loan was to cover the $2,500 guarantee the Eagles were required to pay the Bears for their October 2 game in Philadelphia.

SUNDAY, OCT. 11, 1936　　　　CHICAGO BEARS vs. CHICAGO CARDINALS

Next Sunday, Oct. 18th
CHICAGO BEARS
VS.
PITTSBURGH PIRATES
With the League Leading Forward Passer
Ed. Matesic
Who Has Completed 18 Out of 34 Forward Passes
For An Average of 52 per cent
KICK-OFF — 2:15 P. M.
TICKETS ON SALE AT A. G. SPALDING & BROS. — 211 S. STATE STREET

1936 CHICAGO BEARS VS. PITTSBURGH PIRATES GAME PROGRAM

The forward pass was still evolving in 1936, as the promotional note on this game program suggests. After three games, Ed Matesic, the league's leading passer, had completed 18 of 34 passes.

THE BIRTH OF THE NFL DRAFT

The NFL draft was the creation of Philadelphia Eagles founder/owner and later NFL Commissioner Bert Bell. His idea was to have teams make their draft picks in inverse order of finish, with the goal of helping weaker teams improve. The first player chosen in the inaugural draft was Jay Berwanger, the Heisman Trophy–winning halfback from the University of Chicago. Although Berwanger opted not to play pro football, four future Hall of Fame players—Wayne Millner, Joe Stydahar, Dan Fortmann, and Tuffy Leemans—were selected that year in the nine-round draft.

"To be able to throw four touchdown passes in the last half and beat the Philadelphia Eagles, 28 to 21, is a thrill that hardly can be matched for me. This took place for me when I was thirty-five years old and had been in the National League since 1932. When you get old and past your prime, to have a good day—any kind of a good day—is a memorable thing in a player's life."

—Arnie Herber

"It *[a 1938 game between the Redskins and Bears]* was the toughest, meanest game I've ever played in my seven years in the pro league, but I think the Bears have got a few souvenirs, too.**"**

—Albert Glen "Turk" Edwards

WHIZZER WHITE— 1938'S LEADING RUSHER

Byron "Whizzer" White was a first-round draft pick of the Pittsburgh Pirates in 1938. An outstanding student who ultimately would become a Supreme Court justice, he decided to delay his enrollment at Oxford University as a Rhodes Scholar until 1939 so he could play a year of pro football. As a rookie, Whizzer led the league in rushing. After completing his studies at Oxford, White returned to play two seasons (1940–41) with the Detroit Lions, with whom he won another rushing crown.

"We broke even in 1938...in eight of the eleven games I played sixty minutes; in the other three I played about fifty-seven minutes. I had a good year, led the league in passing.**"**

—Clarence "Ace" Parker

1939 PRO ALL-STAR GAME PROGRAM

The predecessor to the NFL Pro Bowl was the short-lived Pro All-Star Game series that began in 1939 but ended in 1942, primarily due to World War II. The first three games were played in Los Angeles, but the fourth was moved to New York because of fears of a Japanese invasion of the West Coast. A fifth and final game was played in Philadelphia.

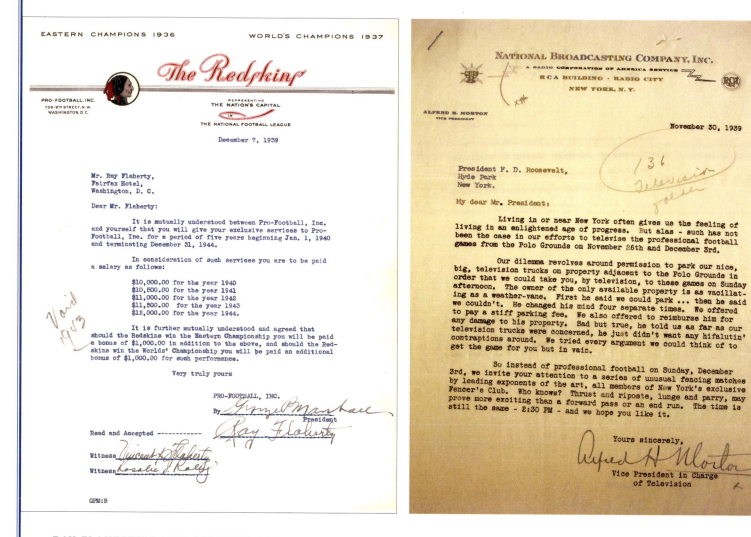

RAY FLAHERTY'S 1939 COACHING CONTRACT

Ray Flaherty began as coach of the Washington Redskins in 1936 when the team was still in Boston. He led the Redskins to two NFL championships and four divisional titles during his coaching tenure. Flaherty didn't complete this five-year contract extension (above), as he enlisted in the Navy in 1942 following a title win over the Chicago Bears. Upon his return from military service, Flaherty accepted the head coaching position with the New York Yankees of the rival All-America Football Conference, where he won division titles in each of his two seasons at the helm. He left the Yankees midway through the 1948 season and spent 1949 as coach of the AAFC Chicago Hornets.

A PRESIDENTIAL SNUB

Just one month after pro football made its television debut, an NBC executive sent this letter to President Franklin Roosevelt to explain why he would be unable to watch "professional football from the Polo Grounds." It seems the owner of the property next to the Polo Grounds, where NBC needed to park its broadcast truck, didn't want any "hifalutin' contraptions" on his property. As a result, the president would either have to buy a game ticket or watch "a series of unusual fencing matches" on his television.

" If I were still coaching I'd still be stressing fundamentals. You've got to block and tackle and play defense. It's a specialist's game now but it's still a game of fundamentals. That's how you win. "

—Ray Flaherty

THE NFL'S TELEVISION DEBUT

The National Broadcasting Company (NBC) made history on October 22, 1939, by televising an NFL game. The site was Brooklyn's Ebbets Field, where 13,050 football fans watched the football Dodgers defeat the Philadelphia Eagles 23–14. Since there were only about five hundred television sets in New York at the time, few actually watched the broadcast in their homes. Most who witnessed the game on television did so at the RCA Pavilion at the World's Fair in New York.

"Now's the time to quit. I want them to remember me as a good end. I've heard those boos from the grandstand before, and believe me, it's a lot more fun to quit with cheers ringing in your ears."

—Bill Hewitt

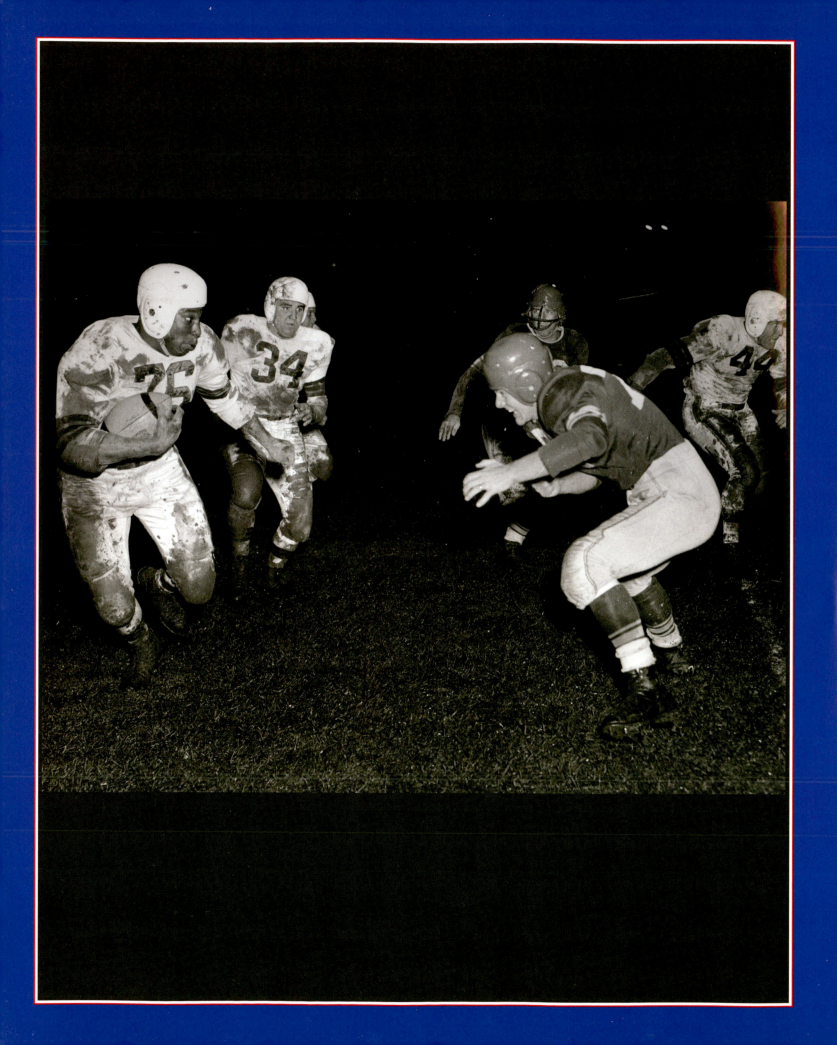

The 1940s
SMASHING THE COLOR BARRIER

JARRETT BELL

Kenny Washington. Woody Strode. Bill Willis. Marion Motley. *Linked together, these four stand higher in football history than the Four Horsemen or the Fearsome Foursome. They were the men who reintegrated pro football in 1946.*

YET IN MANY REGARDS, their courageous contributions in breaking pro football's color barrier—Washington and Strode with the NFL's Los Angeles Rams, Willis and Motley with the Cleveland Browns in the All-America Football Conference (AAFC)—were overshadowed.

Or ignored. Or forgotten. Or simply never known.

These four made their mark a year before Jackie Robinson shattered Major League Baseball's color barrier with the Brooklyn Dodgers, an event that is embedded in America's consciousness. Pro football, back then, wasn't even as popular as college football.

And while Robinson—who, incidentally, played in the same UCLA backfield with Washington and Strode—had a storyline containing the dramatic tension of a single man enduring the pressures of changing a social structure, the black football pioneers carried the weight of history in tandem efforts in two different leagues, with contrasting results.

Motley and Willis were Hall of Famers, key cogs on a team that won each of the four AAFC titles and continued to dominate after joining the NFL in 1950. Washington and Strode had little impact, with the latter lasting for only a single season. Still, for pro football to have evolved into the phenomenon that it has become—a national institution with a widespread appeal that transcends all social, cultural, and ethnic divisions—its debt is clear to Washington and Strode, Willis, and Motley.

Opposite:

MARION MOTLEY

Fullback Marion Motley was a twenty-six-year-old rookie in 1946 when Paul Brown signed him to a contract with the Cleveland Browns. Brown was very familiar with the powerful fullback, having coached him at the Great Lakes Naval Station during World War II. Years earlier, Brown, then the coach at Washington High School in Massillon, Ohio, coached against Marion, who played at crosstown rival McKinley High School in Canton.

SLINGIN' SAMMY BAUGH

In 1937, when quarterback Sammy Baugh signed with the Washington Redskins, pro football was largely a running game; the forward pass was used sparingly. By the time he retired in 1952, the forward pass was a primary offensive weapon. A major catalyst of the change, Baugh was one of the game's most accurate passers. During his career, "Slingin' Sammy" won a record-setting six NFL passing titles and earned first-team All-NFL honors seven times. Versatile, he was the first of only two players to lead the league in separate offensive, defensive, and special teams categories. In 1943 he led the league in passing, pass interceptions, and punting.

SAMMY BAUGH'S 1940 CONTRACT

From the day quarterback Sammy Baugh signed a contract with the Washington Redskins in 1937, he was one of the NFL's most celebrated players. Team owner George Preston Marshall used Baugh's celebrity status to help promote his young team. In 1940, in an effort to compensate his star properly, Marshall signed Baugh to a personal services contract. NFL rules, however, dictated that Baugh must also sign a standard player's contract. And so Baugh's "official" 1940 player's contract paid him just $1.

THE NATIONAL FOOTBALL LEAGUE
UNIFORM PLAYER'S CONTRACT

The PRO-FOOTBALL, INC. ....herein called the Club, and SAM BAUGH ...., of SWEETWATER, TEXAS .... herein called the Player.

The Club is a member of **The National Football League.** As such, and jointly with the other members of the League, it is obligated to insure to the public wholesome and high-class professional football by defining the relations between Club and Player, and between Club and Club.

In view of the facts above recited the parties agree as follows:

1. The Club will pay the Player a salary for his skilled services during the playing season of 19 40., at the rate of $1.00 ------------------ dollars for each regularly scheduled League game played. For all other games the Player shall be paid such salary as shall be agreed upon between the Player and the Club. As to games scheduled but not played, the Player shall receive no compensation from the Club other than actual expenses.

............Plus transportation to and from training camp. If team wins championship player agrees to play one game as directed as per terms of this contract. Player is not to receive compensation for exhibition games other than herein stipulated

2. The salary above provided for shall be paid by the Club as follows:

Seventy-five per cent (75%) after each game and the remaining twenty-five per cent (25%) at the close of the season or upon release of the Player by the Club.

3. The Player agrees that during said season he will faithfully serve the Club, and pledges himself to the American public to conform to high standards of fair play and good sportsmanship.

4. The Player will not play football during 19 40 otherwise than for the Club, except in case the Club shall have released said Player, and said release has been approved by the officials of **The National Football League.**

5. The Player will not participate in an exhibition game after the completion of the schedule of the Club and prior to August 1 of the following season, without the permission of the President of the League.

6. The Player accepts as part of this contract such reasonable regulations as the Club may announce from time to time.

7. This contract may be terminated at any time by the club giving notice in writing to the player within forty-eight (48) hours after the day of the last game in which he is to participate with his club.

8. The Player submits himself to the discipline of **The National Football League** and agrees to accept its decisions pursuant to its Constitution and By-Laws.

9. Any time prior to August 1st, 19 41., by written notice to the Player, the Club may renew this contract for the term of that year, except that the salary rate shall be such as the parties may then agree upon, or in default of agreement, such as the Club may fix.

10. The Player may be fined or suspended for violation of this contract, but in all cases the Player shall have the right of appeal to the President of **The National Football League.**

11. In default of agreement, the Player will accept the salary rate thus fixed or else will not play during said year otherwise than for the Club, unless the Club shall release the Player.

12. The reservation of the Club of the valuable right to fix the salary rate for the succeeding year, and the promise of the Player not to play during said year otherwise than with the Club, have been taken into consideration in determining the salary specified herein and the undertaking by the Club to pay said salary is the consideration for both the reservation and the promise.

13. In case of dispute between the Player and the Club the same shall be referred to the President of **The National Football League,** and his decision shall be accepted by all parties as final.

14. Verbal contracts between Club and Player will not be considered by this League, in the event of a dispute.

Signed this.............. day of ....September............................A. D. 19.....40

Witnesses:

....

....

PRO-FOOTBALL, INC.
(Club)
By Ray Flaherty (Coach)

Sam F Baugh
(Player)

Original copy to be held by Club Management

The NFL had growing pains during its early years that mirrored America's challenges. From the league's inception in 1920 through 1934, sixty-five different teams took the field in the NFL, including franchises that changed names or cities.

By the 1940s, much of the movement had subsided and a core of flagship franchises was well established. But after facing enormous obstacles to growing the league in the face of the Great Depression in the 1930s, the business climate during the following decade was further challenged by World War II.

With depleted rosters, a shrinking fan base, and the wartime priorities of the nation, the NFL's survival was not a given. Rams owner Dan Reeves suspended operations for a year in 1943. Art Rooney, who founded the Pittsburgh franchise in 1933, merged with Philadelphia for a year, 1943, forming a team known as the "Steagles." The next year, Rooney's team merged with the Chicago Cardinals and formed "Card-Pitt." Tough times demanded such creative measures in the name of survival.

This was also a time of extreme racial divisions. The Jim Crow South. Segregation. Unequal opportunities. Lynchings. It was a cruel irony that African Americans fought alongside whites in a world war in the name of democracy and freedom, only to come home to blatant discrimination and the lack of basic civil rights in their own country.

The NFL, slowly and ever so subtly, would soon find itself changing with America. Such a need was amplified on January 15, 1946, when Halley Harding, sports editor of the *Los Angeles Tribune*, addressed the Los Angeles Coliseum Commission in what historians have described as a riveting speech. Harding represented a group of African American newspapers that urged the commission to stipulate that the Rams not be permitted to use the colossal stadium, built and operated with public funds, if it maintained the status quo in the NFL and fielded an all-white team.

Harding's words were influential, if not pivotal. Reportedly he told the commission and Rams general manager Chile Walsh that California was a lot more liberal than America at large. This came about a month after the Rams had captured the NFL title on a brutally cold day in Cleveland—their hometown at the time—defeating the Washington Redskins 15–14 behind sensational rookie quarterback Bob Waterfield, the league's MVP.

> **"I was such a good blocker that the men they put in front of me—and some were stars who were supposed to be making a lot of tackles—they would have their coaches saying, 'Why ain't you making any tackles?' They'd say, 'That bum Turner is holding.' Well that wasn't true... I could handle anybody that they'd put in front of me."**
>
> **—Clyde "Bulldog" Turner**

SAMMY BAUGH'S SHOES

Although remembered mostly for his prolific passing, Washington Redskins quarterback Sammy Baugh was also a great defender and a fine punter. Baugh, who wore these shoes, led the NFL in punting four consecutive seasons, 1940–43. His 45.1-yard career average was the league's best for half a century, and his 51.4-yard average in 1940 is still an NFL record.

> **"Not too dang many funny things happened to me in football, on or off the field. I can't think of anything funny that ever happened on the field. When I walked on the field, I was serious. You've got to be. I wasn't a loner, I conversed with my teammates, but I was very serious about my job. We had a good group of boys. We had fun during practice. I think at that time we had more fun than they do today. We enjoyed it more."**
>
> **—Sammy Baugh**

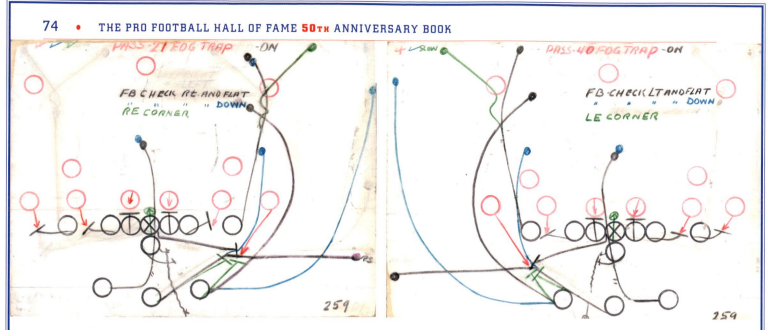

CLARK SHAUGHNESSY

Clark Shaughnessy is often described as the father of the modern T formation. As a part-time coach-consultant with the Chicago Bears in 1934, the former University of Chicago head coach helped refine the T formation that the Bears had been using to some degree since the early 1930s. By 1940 it was the Bears' standard offensive formation. These are two of Shaughnessy's many coaching diagrams that are part of the Hall of Fame's collection.

SID LUCKMAN AND THE T FORMATION

Sid Luckman was the game's first great T-formation quarterback. In the 1940 NFL Championship Game he showed how explosive the T formation could be. Although he passed just six times, completing four for 102 yards, he led the Bears to a lopsided 73–0 rout of the Washington Redskins. While not all teams had instant success behind the T attack, the Bears won four championships and just missed a fifth and Luckman was a major reason for the success. He was named first- or second-team All-NFL in 1940 through 1948 and league MVP in 1943.

> "Just when we think we have a certain rule edited so that it sounds logical and is fair to both the offensive and defensive teams, along comes a coach with a newfangled shift or play. Then we've got to change the rule in order to plug up the loophole."
>
> **—Hugh "Shorty" Ray**

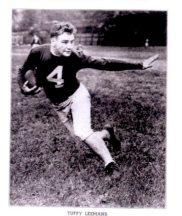

Price 10 Cents

NEW YORK GIANTS
vs.
BROOKLYN DODGERS

LEEMANS' DAY

TUFFY LEEMANS

POLO
GROUNDS

Sunday
December 7, 1941

THE NFL ON PEARL HARBOR DAY

Three NFL games were under way when Japan attacked Pearl Harbor on December 7, 1941. In New York's Polo Grounds, where fans were celebrating "Tuffy Leemans Day," the public address announcer interrupted his commentary to tell all servicemen to report to their units. The same was done at Chicago's Comiskey Park. At Washington's Griffith Stadium, the announcer paged high-ranking government and military personnel in attendance, and reporters were told to check with their offices.

EAGLES VS. REDSKINS GAME ACTION, DECEMBER 7, 1941

Even as the public address announcers were calling for military personnel to report to their stations, players like those in this December 7, 1941, game between the Philadelphia Eagles and Washington Redskins were unaware of Japan's attack on Pearl Harbor. More than 1,000 men interrupted or delayed their pro football careers to serve their country during World War II. Nineteen active or former players, an ex-coach, and a team executive lost their lives. Two players, Jack Lummus and Maurice Britt, and future American Football League commissioner Joe Foss each earned the country's highest military honor, the Congressional Medal of Honor.

> **"We didn't have enough players for someone to be taking a vacation in midseason…everyone who played back then showed up for every game. If you got hurt too bad to play, you retired."**
>
> **—Frank "Bruiser" Kinard**

By the time the crown was claimed in half-empty Cleveland Stadium when temperatures dipped as low as six degrees, Reeves had already determined that he would move his franchise rather than remain in Cleveland and compete in a shared market with the start-up Browns of the new AAFC. Although initially rebuffed by other NFL owners, he ultimately received a favorable vote after promising to pay visiting teams $5,000 above the normal share of gate receipts, to cover travel costs.

It was a crucial cross-country move that exemplified Reeves's nature as a visionary. The Rams were the first franchise in any professional sport to move to the West Coast. Still, the prospect of being prevented from using the potentially lucrative Coliseum, which seated over 100,000, threatened to undermine the deal.

There was no secret about which player the local writers envisioned with the Rams: Kenny Washington. A hometown hero who starred at UCLA, Washington was a high-profile victim of the color barrier that was never written into NFL bylaws but was practiced nonetheless.

"Kenny Washington was the greatest football player I have ever seen," college teammate Jackie Robinson declared years later in *Gridiron* magazine. "He had everything needed for greatness—size, speed and tremendous strength. Kenny was probably the greatest long passer ever."

NEW YORK GIANTS 1940 TRAINING CAMP PHOTO

From their Pearl River, New York, training camp, the New York Giants posed for this photo to demonstrate their war readiness and support for the U.S. armed forces.

THE NATIONAL FOOTBALL LEAGUE

BROOKLYN, N.Y.
CHICAGO (BEARS) ILL.
CHICAGO (CARDINALS)
CLEVELAND, OHIO
DETROIT, MICH.

GREEN BAY, WIS.
NEW YORK, N.Y.
PHILADELPHIA, PA.
PITTSBURGH, PA.
WASHINGTON, D.C.

310 SOUTH MICHIGAN AVENUE
CHICAGO, ILLINOIS

January 20, 1942

Mr. Ward L. Cuff
1919 N. 33rd Street
Milwaukee, Wisconsin

Dear Ward:

Your sacrifice of time and
the inconvenience you went to, to play in the
National Football League Champions-All Star
Game, is sincerely appreciated. The Naval
Relief benefitted from your fine efforts to
the amount of $26,529.83.

In addition to the fine feeling
you have for a job well done, I congratulate
you on the fine game, and I am extremely grateful to you for your cooperation.

Yours sincerely,

Elmer F. Layden
Commissioner

HTN

ELMER LAYDEN LETTER TO WARD CUFF, 1942

NFL Commissioner Elmer Layden sent this congratulatory letter to New York Giants back Ward Cuff, thanking him for participating in the 1941 NFL All-Star Game in New York. As Layden pointed out, the game's receipts went to the Naval Relief.

BRONKO NAGURSKI'S 1943 CHICAGO BEARS JERSEY

Chicago Bears fullback Bronko Nagurski was the incarnation of toughness and power, the standard against whom all runners of his era were judged. In addition to his powerful running, he had no peer as a blocker or tackler on defense. He was the complete player. When Nagurski couldn't get a $700 raise in 1938, he retired from football in favor of a professional wrestling career. But in 1943, when the demands of World War II left the Bears short of manpower, he rejoined the team for one final season, during which he played primarily at tackle. Nagurski ended his career by scoring a touchdown in the 1943 NFL Champion-ship Game against the Washington Redskins.

In 1939, Washington was the biggest college football star on the West Coast, leading the nation in total yards and sparking the Bruins to a top 10 ranking. Despite his achievements—and the ensuing uproar when the running back was not selected as a first-team All-America choice—he wasn't drafted by any NFL team. Instead, he played semi-pro football with the Hollywood Bears, heading a prominent list of African American players who might have starred in the NFL. The names of the bypassed, stars on the college level, were left to be remembered (barely, if at all) as mere footnotes. Among them: Ozzie Simmons; Willis Ward; Horace Bell; Wilmeth Sidat-Singh; Dwight Reed; Clarence Hinton; Ezzrett Anderson.

OFFICIAL **25c** PROGRAM

EAGLES-STEELERS vs GIANTS

OCTOBER 9, 1943

PHILADELPHIA, PA.

This Program Sponsored by Navy League Service

Opposite and right:

1943 PHIL-PITT AND 1944 CARD-PITT GAME PROGRAMS

The shortage of NFL players caused by the demands of World War II made it necessary for some teams to combine and play as merged squads. In 1943 the Philadelphia Eagles merged for one season with the Pittsburgh Steelers. The team was frequently referred to as Phil-Pitt or the "Steagles." The next season the Steelers merged with the Chicago Cardinals and were known as Card-Pitt. In 1945, the Boston Yanks merged with the Brooklyn Tigers and played as the "Yanks" with no reference to a city.

GRID REVIEW   Official Program   ✦   PRICE, TWENTY-FIVE CENTS

Steelers - Cardinals vs. Washington

FORBES FIELD
PITTSBURGH, PA.   MONDAY, SEPT. 18, 1944

SEGMENT OF GOALPOST FROM 1945 NFL CHAMPIONSHIP GAME

During the first quarter of the 1945 NFL Championship Game between the Washington Redskins and the Cleveland Rams, Redskins quarterback Sammy Baugh attempted a pass from his own end zone. Baugh's pass hit the goalpost and, according to the rules of the day, an incomplete pass thrown from behind one's own goal line resulted in a safety. The pass-turned-safety turned out to be the deciding points in the game as the Rams defeated the Redskins 15–14. Furious about the outcome, Redskins owner George Preston Marshall successfully had the rule changed in 1946.

ALL-AMERICA FOOTBALL CONFERENCE
(War-Time Player's Agreement)

THIS AGREEMENT made and entered into at _Glenview Ill_,
this _28th_ day of _March_, 194_5_, by and between the _Cleveland_
Franchise in
All American Conference, first party, hereinafter called the "Club", and
Otto Everett Graham Jr., of _Waukegun, Ill._,
second party, hereinafter called the "Player",

WITNESSETH:

WHEREAS, the Club is a member of the All-American Football
Conference, hereinafter called the "Conference", an unincorporated
association consisting of eight (8) professional football clubs; and

WHEREAS, it is a fundamental purpose of the Conference to
establish professional football, as played by the football clubs of
the members of the Conference, as a sport which will command the
respect and patronage of the American public, because of the high
standards of the Conference with respect to the integrity of members, players and officials and the skill of the players; and

WHEREAS, the Conference has engaged a "Commissioner", well
known to the world of sports and the American public as being of
unquestioned character and integrity, to act, independently of the
Conference, as final arbiter of all disputes between club and club,
and club and player, and generally to adopt, approve and promulgate
all proper rules and regulations to the end that the public may be
assured of wholesome entertainment; and

WHEREAS, the Club desires to engage the Player's skilled
services as a professional football player upon the terms and conditions hereinafter set forth, and the Player is agreeable to render
such services to the Club upon said terms and conditions;

NOW, THEREFORE, IT IS AGREED by the parties hereto, as
follows:

1. The Club hereby employs the Player to render skilled
service/as a professional football player in connection with
all football games of the Club, whether Conference or non-Con-
ference, during the/first football season following World War

Opposite and right:

OTTO GRAHAM'S
CONTRACT WITH AAFC
DURING THE WAR

Although they weren't scheduled
to play until 1946, All-America
Football Conference teams signed
players in 1945 who were still on
active duty during World War II.
The early signings were done to
get a jump on NFL teams who
would likely sign the returning
vets. Hall of Fame quarterback
Otto Graham agreed to a contract
with Cleveland's entry in the AAFC
that paid him $250 per month
while in the service and a
$1,000 bonus for signing.

"The game was played in
the middle of the field
when I broke in and the
center position had some
glamour to it. The centers
were called pivots. The
line play used to depend
a lot on the centers. Usually
the team that controlled
center-middle-guard position
was the team that won...
it was a lot of fun."
—Alex Wojciechowicz

(b) Dishonorable discharge from the Armed Services of the United States automatically cancells this agreement.

(c) This Agreement is also subject to the Constitution and By-Laws of the All-America Football Conference and the Rules and Regulations thereof.

14. As a further inducement to the Player to enter into this Agreement, the Player shall receive from the Club the sum of Two Hundred Fifty Dollars ($250 00) per month while in the Armed Forces of the United States during World War II, and continuing until incapacitated or his football ability handicapped to perform the services for which contracted herein or until the conclusion of the war and has honorable discharge shortly therefrom. And a bonus of $1000.00 for signing contract payable during the month of April, 1945.

15. (a) No verbal understandings between Club and Player not set forth herein shall be valid or binding upon the Club or the Player.

(b) This Agreement shall not be valid or effective unless and until approved by the President of the All-America Football Conference.

Executed in duplicated the day and year first above written.

Witness:

Cleveland Franchise of All-American League
(Club)
By Paul E. Brown
Otto Everett Graham Jr.
(Player)
1503 Jenkerson Ct.
(Home address of Player)
Waukegan, Ill.
Majestic 2221

DON HUTSON WITH HIS TROPHIES

Like most players of his era, Green Bay Packers super-end Don Hutson held down other jobs during the off-season. Hutson, seen here carefully arranging a few of his trophies, ran two successful businesses, Don Hutson Motors and a popular bowling alley, Don Hutson's Packers Playdium. Among the trophies Hutson is displaying at his bowling alley are the three NFL championship trophies the Packers won during his years with the team and his two Joe F. Carr NFL Most Valuable Player trophies.

DON HUTSON'S GREEN BAY PACKERS SIDELINE CAPE

Don Hutson was the NFL's first "super end." A two-way performer, Hutson was the NFL's leading receiver eight of his eleven seasons. His best year was 1942, when he caught 72 passes; the number two receiver that year caught just 27. Hutson, who wore this sideline cape, also placekicked and played safety. When he retired following the 1945 season he held eighteen major NFL records.

By the time Washington, at age twenty-eight, began his three-year stint with the Rams, beginning with the one-year contract signed on March 21, 1946, he was a shell of the electrifying player that he had been. He came to the NFL with damaged knees. Woody Strode, meanwhile, had also played with the Hollywood Bears and was Washington's handpicked choice to join him with the Rams in a move that was announced in May 1946.

Washington played three seasons with the Rams, logging just five career starts. His best season was in 1947, when he led the team with 444 rushing yards on 60 carries. Strode, a tall, sculpted end, barely registered an impact as a reserve in his single season with the Rams.

At the same time that Washington and Strode prepared to make history in the NFL, Bill Willis and Marion Motley pined for the chance to do likewise in the AAFC. The pivotal figure who determined their fate was coach Paul Brown.

Opposite:

DON HUTSON GAME ACTION

Don Hutson, "the Alabama Antelope," is still considered by many the greatest pass receiver who ever lived. Even though he retired in 1945, he is still a yardstick against whom any receiver is measured. Hutson caught a touchdown bomb on his very first play as a rookie and wound up with 99 career touchdown receptions, a record that stood for more than four decades. By the time he retired he had caught 488 passes; the second-place receiver at the time had just 190.

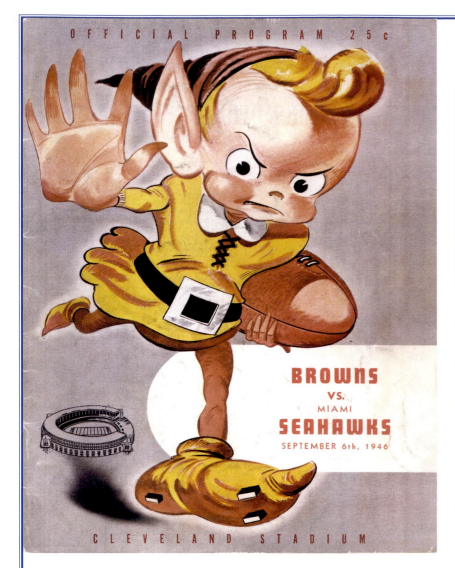

OFFICIAL PROGRAM 25c

BROWNS
VS.
MIAMI
SEAHAWKS
SEPTEMBER 6th, 1946

CLEVELAND STADIUM

1946 CLEVELAND BROWNS VS. MIAMI SEAHAWKS GAME PROGRAM AND GAME TICKET

The Cleveland Browns played their first game as members of the new All-America Football Conference on September 6, 1946, against the Miami Seahawks. The Browns, however, were without the services of two of their star players. Bill Willis and Marion Motley didn't travel with the team after "credible" threats were received stating that the two African American players would be shot from the stands if they played.

SID LUCKMAN AND GEORGE McAFEE LEAD THE BEARS

The Chicago Bears were a dominant team in the 1940s. Five times during the decade they played in the NFL Championship Game, winning four. Sid Luckman and halfback George McAfee, seen here planting a kiss on the cheek of his quarterback following the Bears' 24–14 win over the New York Giants in the 1946 Championship Game, were the team's main offensive weapons.

Motley, who had played for Brown in 1945 at Great Lakes Naval Station, was back in his hometown of Canton, Ohio, in the spring of 1946. According to his version of events, he was preparing to return to the University of Nevada–Reno when he wrote to Brown expressing an interest to join his new squad in Cleveland. Motley maintained that Brown replied to inform him that the Browns were set with their backfield personnel; Brown has said that he wanted Motley to join him in Cleveland all along.

Willis wrote to Brown, his former coach at Ohio State, and even visited him. After playing on a national championship team in 1942 under Brown and becoming the first African American player to earn All-America honors at Ohio State, Willis didn't see the NFL as an option because of the color barrier.

Instead, he pursued a coaching career. He landed at a historically black institution, Kentucky State, as head coach. But one season on the sideline was enough. He still wanted to play.

Although Brown told Willis that there was nothing in the bylaws of the new AAFC that prevented black players from playing, he didn't initially offer him an opportunity. So Willis decided to head north, agreeing to join the Montreal Alouettes of the Canadian Football League (CFL). He never got to Canada.

Paul Hornung, a sportswriter for the *Columbus Dispatch* (not the Hall of Fame football player of the same name) who happened to be close to Brown, convinced Willis to make a detour before heading north and visit the Browns' training camp in Bowling Green, Ohio. Hornung told Willis he believed Brown would give him a tryout.

Lou Haman, the Alouettes' general manager trying to lure Willis to Canada, didn't want to believe the sudden turn of events. He bet Willis a Stetson hat that Brown wouldn't offer him a tryout.

Willis got the hat. When he arrived at Bowling Green and chatted with Brown, the coach immediately told him to get fitted for a uniform. The next day, Willis was on the practice field lining up at middle guard and blazing past centers who included Mo Scarry and Frank Gatski, repeatedly reaching quarterback Otto Graham before plays could develop.

Brown was so impressed—or unconvinced—by Willis's quick acceleration that he positioned himself at the end of the scrimmage line on one knee to determine whether he was lining up offside. Willis quickly earned a roster spot.

A few days later, as he was working in a mill, Motley received a call from assistant coach Blanton Collier inviting him to camp. Collier, who had followed Brown to Cleveland after coaching on his staff at Great Lakes Naval, had lobbied the head coach to bring in the twenty-six-year-old Motley. (Nearly two decades later, Collier succeeded Brown as head coach.)

"I was the luckiest guy who ever played football. I came along at the right time, under a great coach with a great team. Our only thought was to win for each other, for the glory of the team. You never set records for yourself in football. It's not like baseball where you hit on your own. It's an overall thing; if one man fails, the team fails. I know that sounds like a pep talk, but it's a fact."

—Sid Luckman

"I remember clearly, on one of the first scrimmage plays, that a rookie halfback was knocked cold trying to bring down Bill Osmanski. That play served as a valuable lesson for me. Whenever I ran with the ball, I had a picture in my mind of that back there on the ground, cold as a stone. I would run as fast as I could if there was any daylight."

—George McAfee

Following spread:

HISTORIC CONTRACTS

In 1946, four African American pioneers reintegrated pro football, ending a thirteen-year "color barrier." Marion Motley and Bill Willis signed with the Cleveland Browns of the All-America Football Conference, and Woody Strode and Kenny Washington with the NFL's Los Angeles Rams.

All-America Football Conference

Uniform Player's Contract

BETWEEN

CLEVELAND BROWNS

herein called Club, and *Marion Motley* ,

of *Canton, Ohio* , herein called Player.

The Club is a member of the All-America Football Conference, herein called the Conference. The Constitution and Rules of the Conference define the relationship between Club and Player and vest in a Commissioner (herein called the Commissioner) powers of control and discipline and of decision in case of disputes.

In consideration of those facts and of the promises of each to the other, Club and Player agree as follows:

1. Club hereby employs Player to render skilled services as a football player during the Conference football season of 194*6*, including Club's training season, exhibition games, Conference games and post-season championship games.

2. For said services Club will pay Player a salary per season of $ *4,000* , of which 75% shall be payable in semi-monthly instalments commencing with the first and ending with the last regularly scheduled Conference game of Club and the balance of 25% shall be payable at the end of said last game.

In addition Player shall be entitled to all amounts allocated to him by the Commissioner or the Conference Rules for post-season play-offs and championship games.

3. Player agrees to perform his services hereunder diligently and faithfully and to conform to high standards of personal conduct, fair play and good sportsmanship and to Conference Rules and Club Regulations respecting player conduct.

4. Player agrees that until August 1 of the year following the last football season covered by this contract, he will not play football otherwise than for Club except with the approval in writing of the Commissioner and Club.

5. Player represents and agrees that he has exceptional and unique skill and ability as a football player, that his services to be rendered hereunder are of a special, unusual, extraordinary and intellectual character which gives them peculiar value which cannot be reasonably or adequately compensated for in damages at law, and that Player's breach of this contract will cause Club great and irreparable injury and damage. Player agrees that, in addition to other remedies, Club shall be entitled to injunctive and other equitable relief to prevent a breach of this contract by Player. Player represents that he has no physical or mental defects, known to him, which would prevent or impair performance of his services.

6. The Conference Constitution and Rules are hereby made a part of this contract and Club and Player agree to accept and comply with their provisions, all amendments thereof and all decisions of the Commissioner thereunder. Player also accepts as part of this contract the Regulations printed on the reverse hereof and such reasonable modifications of them and such other reasonable regulations as Club may announce from time to time.

7. Club may terminate this contract if Player should at any time (a) fail, refuse or neglect to render his services hereunder, (b) in any other manner breach this contract or the Conference Constitution or Rules or the Regulations incorporated herein, (c) fail, in the opinion of Club's coach, to exhibit sufficient skill to qualify as a member of Club's football squad, or (d) become disabled from performing his services hereunder; provided, however, that, subject to the notice required by the Regulations, Player's disability resulting directly from injury sustained in the performance of his services under this contract shall not affect Player's right to receive his full salary for the season in which the injury was sustained. If this contract is terminated by Club during its regular Conference schedule, Player shall receive as his full compensation such proportion of his salary as the number of days of his service during such Conference schedule bears to the total number of days in such Conference schedule. If this contract is terminated during the training season, payment by Club of Player's expenses and his transportation as provided in the Regulations, shall be full compensation for Player's services during the training season and Club shall not be obligated to pay any part of salary.

8. Player agrees that he may be fined or suspended by the Commissioner or the Club for violation of this contract, provided that any termination of this contract or fine or suspension by Club shall be appealable to the Commissioner in accordance with the Conference Rules.

9. On or before August 1 of the year next following the last football season covered by this contract, by written notice to Player, Club may renew this contract for the football season of that year on the same terms, including salary rate, as those stipulated herein, unless Player and Club agree upon a higher or lower salary. Such right of renewal and the promise of Player not to play otherwise than for Club have been taken into consideration in determining the salary specified herein and Club's undertaking to pay said salary is the consideration for said renewal right and promise and Player's services.

10. This contract may be assigned by Club, and Player shall report to the assignee promptly (as provided in the Regulations) upon notice of such assignment. Upon and after such assignment, all rights and obligations of the assignor hereunder shall become and be rights and obligations of the assignee and the assignee shall become liable to Player for his salary and the assignor shall not be liable therefor. All references in this contract to Club shall be deemed to mean and include any assignee of this contract.

11. Disputes between Player and Club may be referred to the Commissioner and his decision shall be accepted by all parties as final; provided that any such dispute or any claim by either party against the other shall be presented in writing to the Commissioner and to the party complained against within 10 days from the date it arose.

12. This contract sets forth the entire agreement between the parties. No verbal agreements or understandings between Club and Player shall be valid or binding.

A copy of this contract shall be filed with the Commissioner by Club within 10 days after its execution. This contract shall have no force or effect if disapproved by the Commissioner within 10 days after such filing.

SIGNED in triplicate this *10th* day of *August* , 194*6*.

CLEVELAND BROWNS

By *Paul Brown*
(Club)

WITNESSES:

Fred R Heisler

W. Robert Vogts

Marion Motley
(Player)

1205 Dondee ave SE Canton, Ohio
(Home address of Player)

All-America Football Conference

Uniform Player's Contract

BETWEEN

CLEVELAND BROWNS

herein called Club, and ___Wm Willis___

of ___Columbus, Ohio___, herein called Player.

The Club is a member of the All-America Football Conference, herein called the Conference. The Constitution and Rules of the Conference define the relationship between Club and Player and vest in a Commissioner (herein called the Commissioner) powers of control and discipline and of decision in case of disputes.

In consideration of those facts and of the promises of each to the other, Club and Player agree as follows:

1. Club hereby employs Player to render skilled services as a football player during the Conference football season of 194_6_____, including Club's training season, exhibition games, Conference games and post-season championship games.

2. For said services Club will pay Player a salary per season of $__4,000__, of which 75% shall be payable in semi-monthly instalments commencing with the first and ending with the last regularly scheduled Conference game of Club and the balance of 25% shall be payable at the end of said last game.

In addition Player shall be entitled to all amounts allocated to him by the Commissioner or the Conference Rules for post-season play-offs and championship games.

3. Player agrees to perform his services hereunder diligently and faithfully and to conform to high standards of personal conduct, fair play and good sportsmanship and to Conference Rules and Club Regulations respecting player conduct.

4. Player agrees that until August 1 of the year following the last football season covered by this contract, he will not play football otherwise than for Club except with the approval in writing of the Commissioner and Club.

5. Player represents and agrees that he has exceptional and unique skill and ability as a football player, that his services to be rendered hereunder are of a special, unusual, extraordinary and intellectual character which gives them peculiar value which cannot be reasonably or adequately compensated for in damages at law, and that Player's breach of this contract will cause Club great and irreparable injury and damage. Player agrees that, in addition to other remedies, Club shall be entitled to injunctive and other equitable relief to prevent a breach of this contract by Player. Player represents that he has no physical or mental defects, known to him, which would prevent or impair performance of his services.

6. The Conference Constitution and Rules are hereby made a part of this contract and Club and Player agree to accept and comply with their provisions, all amendments thereof and all decisions of the Commissioner thereunder. Player also accepts as part of this contract the Regulations printed on the reverse hereof and such reasonable modifications of them and such other reasonable regulations as Club may announce from time to time.

7. Club may terminate this contract if Player should at any time (a) fail, refuse or neglect to render his services hereunder, (b) in any other manner breach this contract or the Conference Constitution or Rules or the Regulations incorporated herein, (c) fail, in the opinion of Club's coach, to exhibit sufficient skill to qualify as a member of Club's football squad, or (d) become disabled from performing his services hereunder; provided, however, that, subject to the notice required by the Regulations, Player's disability resulting directly from injury sustained in the performance of his services under this contract shall not affect Player's right to receive his full salary for the season in which the injury was sustained. If this contract is terminated by Club during its regular Conference schedule, Player shall receive as his full compensation such proportion of his salary as the number of days of his service during such Conference schedule bears to the total number of days in such Conference schedule. If this contract is terminated during the training season, payment by Club of Player's expenses and his transportation as provided in the Regulations, shall be full compensation for Player's services during the training season and Club shall not be obligated to pay any part of salary.

8. Player agrees that he may be fined or suspended by the Commissioner or the Club for violation of this contract, provided that any termination of this contract or fine or suspension by Club shall be appealable to the Commissioner in accordance with the Conference Rules.

9. On or before August 1 of the year next following the last football season covered by this contract, by written notice to Player, Club may renew this contract for the football season of that year on the same terms, including salary rate, as those stipulated herein, unless Player and Club agree upon a higher or lower salary. Such right of renewal and the promise of Player not to play otherwise than for Club have been taken into consideration in determining the salary specified herein and Club's undertaking to pay said salary is the consideration for said renewal right and promise and Player's services.

10. This contract may be assigned by Club, and Player shall report to the assignee promptly (as provided in the Regulations) upon notice of such assignment. Upon and after such assignment, all rights and obligations of the assignor hereunder shall become and be rights and obligations of the assignee and the assignee shall become liable to Player for his salary and the assignor shall not be liable therefor. All references in this contract to Club shall be deemed to mean and include any assignee of this contract.

11. Disputes between Player and Club may be referred to the Commissioner and his decision shall be accepted by all parties as final; provided that any such dispute or any claim by either party against the other shall be presented in writing to the Commissioner and to the party complained against within 10 days from the date it arose.

12. This contract sets forth the entire agreement between the parties. No verbal agreements or understandings between Club and Player shall be valid or binding.

A copy of this contract shall be filed with the Commissioner by Club within 10 days after its execution. This contract shall have no force or effect if disapproved by the Commissioner within 10 days after such filing.

SIGNED in triplicate this __8th__ day of __Aug.__, 194_6_.

CLEVELAND BROWNS

By ___Paul E Brown___
(Club)

WITNESSES:

___W. Robert Voigts___

___N. F. Conkright___

___William Willis___
(Player)

___172 Talmadge St___
(Home address of Player)

(PLAYER'S COPY)

THE VERSATILE BILL DUDLEY'S MVP TROPHY

In 1946 Pittsburgh Steelers halfback Bill Dudley led the NFL in four statistical categories: rushing, interceptions, punt returns, and lateral passes attempted. An exceptionally versatile player, Dudley scored nine different ways during his career, including passing, receiving, rushing, punt and kick returns, interceptions, and a fumble recovery. He also kicked field goals and extra points.

❝I survived on thinking.❞

—Bill Dudley

Willis and Motley, launching careers that earned them immortality in the Pro Football Hall of Fame, had never met until the bruising fullback arrived in camp. Years later, Willis recalled Brown's quick no-nonsense introduction: "Meet your new roommate."

They quickly developed a bond that lasted for the rest of their lives.

Brown had a long-established reputation for fairness and coached black players on every level, including the years his Washington High School team in Massillon, Ohio, was the dominant prep team in the state. He never considered himself as an agent for social change, but that's precisely what he achieved. While maintaining that he merely wanted the best players, he eventually acknowledged that he decided to bring Willis and Motley aboard after training camp had begun in order to minimize the attention that might be generated because of their roles as pioneers.

Willis contended that he experienced no issues with teammates as he broke in with the Browns. Motley, though, recalled some tension.

After only one practice, Brown promoted Motley to the second string. Motley later contended that some teammates resented his quick rise on the depth chart. Brown may have sensed that too, as he quickly pushed Motley back to the fourth string and allowed for a gradual climb up the ladder. Over the long haul, there was no denying the vital role that Willis and Motley each played in the Browns' success: four AAFC championships and then, after the club joined the NFL in 1950, six consecutive conference titles.

Willis, whose middle guard role evolved into the middle linebacker position, earned all-league honors in each of his eight seasons with the Browns. Motley played nine pro seasons, the first eight with the Browns. He won an AAFC rushing crown in 1946, led the NFL in rushing in 1950, and for his career averaged 5.7 yards per carry (which would be highest in history for a running back if his AAFC statistics were included). His average rush of 17.09 yards during a 1950 game against Pittsburgh (11 carries, 188 yards) remains the highest single-game average for a running back in NFL annals.

Motley was the second African American inducted into the Hall of Fame (in 1968, a year after Emlen Tunnell), but a compelling case can be made to suggest that he merely scratched the surface of his potential as a gamebreaker. Listed at 6'1" and 238 pounds, Motley was bigger than many of the linemen of his era and in his prime faster than just about any other player. That combination of speed and power was tough to tackle, and was one of the reasons that Paul Zimmerman,

OTTO GRAHAM'S MVP TROPHIES
During his ten years with the Cleveland Browns, quarterback Otto Graham led his team to four consecutive All-America Football Conference titles, six NFL divisional crowns, and three NFL championships. He was named MVP in the AAFC in 1947 and co-MVP in 1948, and NFL MVP in 1951, 1953, and 1955.

the esteemed *Sports Illustrated* pro football writer, declared in his two versions of *The Thinking Man's Guide to Pro Football* that he believed Motley was the greatest player in pro football history.

Motley averaged just 8.3 carries per game during his career—an astonishingly low rate and about half that of the premier running back of the 1940s, Philadelphia's Steve Van Buren. In addition to his rushing prowess, he averaged 13 yards per catch during his career and was arguably the game's best blocker—helping to key Cleveland's passing attack as he protected Otto Graham. He was a complete player. Brown once said that Motley, who played both ways early in his career and later on defense in key situations, could have made the Hall of Fame as strictly a linebacker.

Long after they retired, Motley and Willis carried contrasting views of Brown. Willis grew closer to Brown after retirement; Motley grew disenchanted with his former coach, whom he felt didn't do

> "Who the hell likes to lose? Sure, I'm a tough loser. Who isn't? If you don't want to win all the time, you've got no business holding a job in sports. You should get a soft spot like selling ribbons behind a counter."
>
> —Earle "Greasy" Neale

SAMMY BAUGH DAY, 1947

One of quarterback Sammy Baugh's best single-game performances came on "Sammy Baugh Day" in 1947 when he passed for 355 yards and six touchdowns against that year's eventual champions, the Chicago Cardinals.

[Said in 1936]

❝I may be a nut on this subject, but my idea is that pro football will be a helluva thing in a few more years.... Our game is making definite strides forward, strides with each year.❞

—Charles W. Bidwill Sr.

enough to help him land a coaching job in the NFL. When the NFL absorbed four AAFC teams in 1950, ten of the eighteen black players in the league that season played for either the Browns or the Rams.

Still, the path to equality in pro football that had been staked out by the four pioneers who broke the color barrier was anything but smooth. Years after making history, Strode famously quipped to *Sports Illustrated*, "If I have to integrate heaven, I don't want to go."

That statement reflected some of the resistance and slights—verbal, physical, and psychological—that the pioneers met. After absorbing unnecessary punishment during a particularly grueling game in 1946, a series of flagrant blows ignored by game officials, Washington uttered softly to a white teammate, "It's hell to be a Negro."

Motley could relate. His fingers were left disfigured for the rest of his life because opponents made it a habit to stomp on his hands as he lay on the turf at the end of plays. This practice, in addition to other cheap shots that included elbows to the face at a time when helmets didn't include face masks, was routinely ignored by officials.

Finally, referee Tommy Hughitt threw a flag and declared, "Enough." Motley never forgot Hughitt, whose action to penalize offenders was ultimately followed by other officials.

"Of course, the opposing players called us 'nigger' and all kinds of names like that," Motley, after retiring, told sports columnist Myron Cope. "This went on for about two or three years, until they found out that Willis and I were ballplayers."

Motley and Willis, roommates for camp and road games, used to compare mental notes about which opponents were prone to cross the line. They often took retribution into their own hands by dishing out retaliatory punishment within the rules, but they typically had the support of teammates who were sensitive to their plight. Willis said that lineman Lou Rymkus, who had previously played for the all-white Redskins before joining the Browns and was among the team's biggest players, was the ultimate enforcer. Willis recalled that Rymkus told him, "Just show me who he is. I'll take care of it."

Obviously, during a period in America that preceded the civil rights era, the double standards and indignities were hardly limited to the playing field. When Washington and Strode, for example, took their first road trip with the Rams in 1946, to Chicago, they were barred from staying with the rest of the team at the Stevens Hotel. They wound up at the Persian Hotel, a lavish property that catered to blacks.

> **"In those days the more things a player did, the more pay he could demand. I could run, kick, pass, and catch, and that made me a valuable property."**
>
> **—Charley Trippi**

SAMMY BAUGH'S SCULPTED HAND

Many considered quarterback Sammy Baugh an artist on the football field. In 1947, Corinne Griffith Marshall, looking for an unusual gift to present her husband, Washington Redskins owner George Preston Marshall, commissioned an artist to sculpt Baugh's passing hand.

THE CARDINALS' "DREAM BACKFIELD" (CHARLEY TRIPPI ON THE BENCH)

The Chicago Cardinals recorded only one winning season between 1932 and 1945. But in 1947, after owner Charles Bidwill signed Georgia halfback Charley Trippi (62) to a $100,000 contract—the largest ever in the NFL up to that time—things began to change. Along with quarterback Paul Christman, fullback Pat Harder, and halfback Elmer Angsman, Trippi completed Bidwill's "Dream Backfield" that led the Cardinals to their first title since 1925. Sadly, Bidwill passed away in April and didn't witness his team's championship season.

BALTIMORE COLTS
GREEN-AND-SILVER JERSEY

The original 1947 Baltimore Colts were a replacement franchise for the failed Miami Seahawks of the All-America Football Conference (1946–49). When the AAFC was absorbed by the NFL following the 1949 season, the Colts were one of three franchises admitted into the senior circuit. After a disappointing 1–11 season in 1950, the Colts franchise was canceled. From 1947 through 1950 they wore green-and-silver uniforms. In 1953 the Dallas Texans franchise was transferred to Baltimore and assumed the Colts' name but kept the Texans' blue-and-white colors.

" I didn't mind leaving football because I played eleven years and had enough. I ran out of gas. At my age, I hurt just to think of having played. I don't miss playing the game. **"**

—Tony Canadeo

Bob Waterfield, the star quarterback, went to the Persian Hotel later to inform Washington and Strode that their accommodations had been arranged at the Stevens. They opted not to leave. Count Basie was playing in the club lounge. Waterfield stayed for hours. The trio drank to the tunes of Basie.

Later that year, Willis and Motley were dealt the discrimination card in an unabashedly more threatening fashion. Death threats were made against the two players before the Browns were to travel to Miami to face the Seahawks. With Florida's laws calling for segregation that even extended to the field, and the prospect of violence, Brown left Willis and Motley in Cleveland—and gave them each a $500 bonus.

Years later, Willis recalled how Brown explained the situation. "I don't want you to be subjected to any kind of foolishness," Brown told the players. "Next year, they will not be in the league." In 1947, the Miami Seahawks indeed vanished from the AAFC.

Willis, who died in 2007 at the age of eighty-six, was the last survivor of the four pioneers. Although the honors never stopped coming—in the final year of his life he was feted at halftime of an Ohio State game, recognized by the U.S. Congress at the annual Pro Football Hall of Fame Game, and recognized by the Ohio House of Representatives— he refused to consider himself in the same category as trailblazers from the civil rights era.

Still, in the NFL universe, there's no denying the significance of the path that the tandems of Willis and Motley and Strode and Washington took in 1946 for the growth of the game. It's no wonder that until his death, Willis watched the African American players and coaches of today's era with a sense of pride.

"I feel like kin to them," he said. "There's a connection. I feel a part of it in some way."

NEITHER RAIN NOR SLEET NOR SNOW

A blinding snowstorm created near-impossible playing conditions in the 1948 NFL Championship Game between the hometown Philadelphia Eagles and Chicago Cardinals. Snow fell so fast that the yard lines and sidelines were undetectable. Eagles halfback Steve Van Buren scored the game's only touchdown on a five-yard run in the fourth quarter, giving the Eagles a 7–0 win. Van Buren, assuming that the game would be canceled, almost missed the start of the game. Unable to get his car out of his driveway, he was forced to take a trolley to Philadelphia's 69th Street, and then the Market Street subway to City Hall, transfer to the Broad Street Line, ride the subway to Lehigh Avenue, and walk the last seven blocks to the stadium.

> " I made a lot of long runs. I ran from scrimmage and I ran back kicks and I played safety and ran back passes…. I'd just love to run against these four-man lines they have nowadays. "
> —Steve Van Buren

1948 NFL CHAMPIONSHIP GAME BALL

In blizzard-like conditions, the Philadelphia Eagles defeated the Chicago Cardinals 7–0 in the 1948 NFL Championship Game. Fullback George Muha was presented this game ball by his teammates for his strong play that included a critical five-yard first-down run that set up halfback Steve Van Buren's touchdown, the game's only score.

The 1950s
FOUR FOR THE AGES

STEVE SABOL

Opposite:

COACH PAUL BROWN

Coach Paul Brown built a pro football dynasty in Cleveland, posting a 167–53–8 record, four All-America Football Conference titles, three NFL crowns, and only one losing season in seventeen years. In the four seasons the Browns operated in the AAFC, they lost just four games. When the Browns joined the NFL in 1950, they continued their winning ways, playing in the next six championship games and winning the title in 1950, 1954, and 1955.

*H*ula hoops and rock 'n' roll. Elvis and Marilyn. Penny loafers, 3-D, and Howdy Doody. I grew up in the 1950s, and I thought those years were great. The football sure was. And that's what I remember most.

IN 1952 MY DAD took me to my first NFL game to see the Eagles and the Redskins at old Shibe Park. As the teams were warming up, my father pointed to a player and said, "There's Sammy Baugh." He didn't say anything else. He didn't need to. Everyone knew about Sammy Baugh. It was like pointing out the Washington Monument or Independence Hall. Nothing else needed to be said. Right before kickoff, my dad said something else. "Watch Number 60 on the Eagles. That's Chuck Bednarik. He's going to kick the ball, run downfield, and make the tackle himself." Sure enough Bednarik kicked off, beat everyone downfield, and made the tackle. Sometimes a dad just knows. At least mine did.

Football in the 1950s had fewer rules than today, which left plenty of room for characters, the kind of roustabouts and rogues who could capture a kid's imagination. Bob St. Clair, who ate raw meat. Leo Nomellini, who moonlighted as a pro wrestler under the name Leo the Lion. Were the players actually better back then, or did they just have better nicknames? Hard to say for sure, but I do know that I loved *Jaguar Jon* Arnett, *Crazy Legs* Hirsch, Dick *Night Train* Lane, and, of course, *Concrete Charlie* Bednarik.

By the time NFL Films really got rolling in the mid-1960s the world had changed. So had the NFL. The league was booming, becoming ever more popular, profitable, regulated, and respectable. It's safe to say a lot was gained in the '60s, but I thought there was a risk that something else would be lost; namely, the stories of the men who made the game.

> "The most pleasant way of life is to have a job you love, and I love football coaching. Money is relatively unimportant to me, once I've taken care of the comforts of my family."
>
> —Paul Brown

PAUL BROWN ARTIFACTS

Coach Paul Brown wore this sideline jacket during his stellar coaching career with the Cleveland Browns. These autographed footballs are from the 1954 and 1955 title games, both won by the Browns.

And I knew they were stories worth knowing. I'd seen some of them with my own eyes. But I also knew that nostalgia can be a seductive liar, and that memory is no substitute for film. So I set out to preserve the memories of the '50s the best way I knew how. Camera in hand and soundman in tow, I headed out across the country to interview the men I'd seen as a boy. It took a long time.

It was worth it. We interviewed hundreds of players and coaches. I heard comedies, tragedies, knee-slappers, and even a few head-scratchers. And really, what better way to understand an era than by listening to the men who were part of it.

The place to begin any story of the 1950s is listening to Paul Brown and his Cleveland Browns, who played in seven championship games in that memorable decade. If George Halas is the George Washington of pro football, then Paul Brown is its Thomas Jefferson. He created a framework that defined the profession and strategies that modernized the sport. Brown was the first coach to use notebooks and classroom techniques extensively. He invented the draw play, the passing pocket, and the single-bar face mask. It was his idea to put coaches in the press box with phones so they could talk to the coaches on the sideline. He was the Jefferson, the Einstein, and the Marconi of pro football. His team was the perfect expression of his vision of how the game should be played.

PAUL BROWN: In my opening lecture to the team I always said to them that I didn't care whether they were black, white, Catholic, Protestant, or Jewish. I was after the forty best football players. If you're a bum, a boozer, a chaser, that kind of person, I don't want you on our team.

DANTE LAVELLI; END, BROWNS: Paul Brown stood for what America stood for: hard work, dedication, and loyalty. He called them the Eternal Verities. Many of us were just home from World War II, so when he stressed discipline, we already understood. He expected us to pay attention, be presentable, we had to wear white shirts at dinner and be mannerly. He always said, "Don't slurp your soup."

ABE GIBRON; GUARD, BROWNS: Paul Brown wanted high-class players. We were in the middle of a team meeting and Paul was diagramming a play on the blackboard. Doug Atkins broke wind. Paul said, "How can you be so disgusting during a meeting of this nature?" Two days later he traded Atkins to the Bears.

LOU SABAN; LINEBACKER, BROWNS: The night before our first title game in the All-America Conference our captain, Jim Daniel, had a few drinks and got into a spat with some cops.

PAUL BROWN: I couldn't have that happen to not only one of my players but the captain. So when he came to the park I just simply said, "Jim, for the welfare of this team and the future of our organization, you are dismissed. You may go." That was all there was to it.

LOU SABAN: He fired our captain before the championship game! You just don't do that. But Daniel's backup was a good football player too, so Jim wasn't going to be missed. Paul saw the opportunity to get that team in the palm of his hand forever, and he took it. If Otto Graham had been arrested there's no way Paul would have cut him. That would have hurt the team. This didn't hurt our team at all. We beat the New York Yanks, 14–9.

OTTO GRAHAM; QUARTERBACK, BROWNS: Paul Brown revolutionized pro football. Within a few years, everybody was patterning themselves after the Browns. He started off each year by giving us these thick playbooks filled with blank sheets of paper. We had to write everything. For ten straight years, I had to do this. That's one of the reasons I quit. I got so sick and tired of doing this damn thing. Every week we had a test. We had several good quarterback prospects come in here and they didn't do very well on the test. The next day they were gone. If a guy wasn't going to work at it, he wasn't going to be here.

ABE GIBRON: The thing was, everyone cheated like crazy on those tests. They used crib sheets with all the answers. Hell, I remember

> **"If I wanted numbers, I'd not have quit when I did."**
> **—Jim Brown**

FOOTBALL DRYER

Not every idea is a good one. Coach Paul Brown experimented with this cast-iron contraption designed to dry footballs during rainy games. The wet football was inserted in the metal container and slowly rotated past two heating coils. Unfortunately, the electric heating unit not only dried the football, it baked the leather, turning the soft, pliable ball into a rock-hard projectile.

> **"Glory? No, there's not much glory in it. But there is self-satisfaction and we have to do with that. When the newspapers say somebody ran 50 yards to a touchdown and they don't tell who made the blocks, it hurts a little."**
> **—Roosevelt Brown**

THE 1950 CHAMPIONSHIP GAME

In their first year in the NFL after dominating the rival All-America Football Conference for four seasons (1946–49), the Cleveland Browns had a lot to prove. Were they as good as the best in the NFL? A 10–2 regular season suggested yes, but their exciting 30–28 win over the Los Angeles Rams in the NFL Championship Game confirmed it. In that game quarterback Otto Graham conducted two near-perfect fourth-quarter drives. The first, a 65-yard touchdown drive, pulled the Browns within a point of the Rams, 28–27. On the Browns' next possession, Graham fumbled, but the defense held and forced the Rams to punt. With 1:48 remaining Graham drove his offense 57 yards to the Rams 11, and with 28 seconds remaining, Lou Groza kicked the winning points.

seeing Chuck Noll do it, and Paul would brag about how smart Chuck Noll was. I think Paul believed that by making up those crib sheets, the players learned the formations of the plays. We had some real dumb guys and Paul figured that by their copying down the plays a couple of times…hey, after a while, even the dumb guys start to remember it.

CURLY MORRISON; FULLBACK, BROWNS: All coaching films were taken from up in the press box from the sideline. When I was traded to the Browns from the Bears we never looked at the sideline films. That was for TV. With the Browns we looked at films that were taken by an end zone camera. This is how you could really read the defenses and you could really see the techniques of certain players. And that was so important in those days. The difference in being able to see the coverage from the end zone was night and day. It just opened up things. We were way ahead in preparation those days. But we also had a great quarterback in Otto Graham.

Quarterback Otto Graham embodied the Paul Brown ideal. He was as handsome as Tyrone Power and an exemplary family man.

THE UMBRELLA DEFENSE

New York Giants Coach Steve Owen unveiled his famous "umbrella defense" in 1950. It was specifically designed to stop the high-powered passing attack of the Cleveland Browns. The Giants lined up in a traditional 6–4–1 defense with a six-man line, but when Cleveland's Otto Graham faded back to pass, the Giants defensive ends dropped back to help the four defensive backs form an "umbrella shield." Key to the success of Owen's umbrella was the play of defensive backs Emlen Tunnell (45) and Tom Landry (49), seen here defending Browns receiver Dante Lavelli.

> **"I could make tackles until I'm fifty. Your body may go, but your heart doesn't."**
>
> **—Emlen Tunnell**

> **"That was a big moment, going into the NFL** *[in 1950]*. **I'll bet 25,000 fans from Cleveland went to Philadelphia. We weren't apprehensive. We knew we had a good club, one that really could throw the football. We weren't as stunned as some of the NFL fans when the Browns won, 35–10."**
>
> **—Dante Lavelli**

A happily married father of three, he helped found the Fellowship of Christian Athletes. He won more consistently than any quarterback in history, leading his Browns to six straight NFL Championship Games (after winning four straight titles in the All-America Football Conference). Fifty-five years after he last took a snap, Graham still boasts the highest average in history at 8.62 yards per pass attempt (9.0 if you count in the AAFC years). Current experts insist the yards per pass attempt is the single most important stat when evaluating a passer. "Automatic Otto" also ran for 44 touchdowns (again counting the AAFC), the record for a quarterback.

> **"It took a tackle agile enough to be used like an end** *[in the Giants' umbrella defense]*.
> **You had to be able to rush inside and outside. I was lucky. I was blessed with speed. It covers a multitude of sins.... I could run 100 yards in 10.1. At the time, it was very unusual to have that kind of speed and play in the interior line."**
>
> **—Arnie Weinmeister**

> "No one seems to know what the guards are doing. They don't keep a record of your blocks."
>
> —Stan Jones

BUDDY YOUNG

Running back Buddy Young (76), pictured here with the 1951 New York Yanks, began his career in 1947 with the New York Yankees of the All-America Football Conference. He was among the first African Americans to play pro football after the "color barrier" was broken in 1946. The 5'4" Young sometimes joked that he found more prejudice against his height than his color. One of the fastest runners of his day, Young also played for the Dallas Texans (1952) and Baltimore Colts (1953–55).

PAUL BROWN: Otto was the greatest athlete I ever coached. In 1946 he played for us in the AAC and in the winter he was a forward for the Rochester Royals in the NBA. On a football field there was nothing he couldn't do. When he wasn't throwing the ball, he was running with it, or catching it, or punting it. The only thing he didn't do was call the plays. I did that. In our system, success depended on discipline, timing, and controlling the movements of the players on the field during a game. I decided that I would call the plays from the sidelines and relay them into the huddle by alternating my guards.

OTTO GRAHAM: When Paul began calling the plays from the bench, I disagreed, but the whole thing was exaggerated over the years. I didn't like it, but I didn't resent it. Calling a play is nothing more than a guess. You see those movies where the quarterback raises up from the huddle, looks at the defense, then ducks down and calls the play. Well, that's baloney. Paul could see as much or more from the sideline than I could from the huddle. Paul called the plays and the records show we won three NFL championships, so he called 'em

OTTO GRAHAM'S DOUBLE-NUMBERED JERSEY

In 1952 the NFL established a new numbering system for players by position. The rule had one exception: "nationally known players" who had been in the league for at least three years were allowed to keep their old numbers. Cleveland Browns quarterback Otto Graham, perhaps the best-known player in the league, chose to go along with the new rule rather than use his obvious status to bypass the change. Although the Browns may have appreciated Graham's willingness to conform, his selflessness wasn't exactly rewarded. Rather than provide the star quarterback with a new jersey, the Browns' equipment manager merely sewed the number 14 over the still visible outline of his famous Number 60.

pretty good. Paul was light-years ahead of everybody. But he was a cold piece of work; cold as a February icicle.

BOBBY MITCHELL; HALFBACK, BROWNS: Paul was a difficult man to please. After every game he'd say, "Quiet...we'll go over what we did wrong." He'd take out this piece of paper and it would drop all the way to the floor. We said, "Gee, we just beat these guys 38 to nothing!" He tried to bring out the best in us by telling us that our best wasn't good enough. He liked to needle me. He'd get right in my face and say, "Do you know what? You're killing our football team. Maybe you're not good enough, Bobby Mitchell."

OTTO GRAHAM: There were times when I hated his guts, I could have killed him. Other times I felt something close to love. All I know is, when I got into coaching I found myself doing and saying the same things that used to make me so mad at him. One night, I ran out of the pocket a couple times for what I considered a very valid reason. I didn't want to get my bones broken. He took me out, sent in George Ratterman, and walked over to one of his assistants, five, six feet away from me. Loud enough for me to hear him he said, "At least now we have someone in there with the guts to stay in the pocket." I wanted to get up and slug him. I couldn't do it but I wanted to. A short time later, I was in the game and I said, "I'm not leaving this pocket if they tear my damned head off." And, I have to admit, I played better.

66 **All players at times resent the things done by the head coach. I'd get upset with _[Paul]_ Brown and I didn't appreciate the planning and organization he brought to his job. Now that I'm older I realize that Brown was as good as any man who ever coached this game.** 99

—Otto Graham

66 **I was as big as the linemen I ran against, so I didn't worry about them. And once I ran over a back twice, I didn't have to run over him a third time. He had reservations by then.** 99

—Marion Motley

66 **I concentrated on the ball. The split second the ball moved, I charged and I always came at a different angle.... I could unleash a pretty good forearm block and a rather devastating tackle too.** 99

—Bill Willis

RATTERMAN'S RADIO RECEIVER HELMET

In 1956, Cleveland Browns coach Paul Brown had quarterback George Ratterman secretly equipped with a helmet fitted with a special radio receiver. The radio receiver helmet enabled Brown to send plays in to his quarterback from the sideline. Though the prototype, worn during the preseason and first three regular season games, was largely successful, NFL commissioner Bert Bell wasn't ready to accept the new technology as a part of the game. The commissioner sent a memo to each team informing them that any such equipment was strictly prohibited. So until 1994, when the coach-to-quarterback helmet was reintroduced, the only receiver a team could use during an NFL game was a wide receiver.

CRAZY LEGS AND FEARS

One of pro football's most explosive receiver tandems was the Los Angeles Rams' Elroy "Crazy Legs" Hirsch (40) and Tom Fears (80). Fears led the NFL in receiving in each of his first three years in the league, including an 84-catch season in 1950, a record that stood for a decade. His 18 catches in one game in 1950 stood as the high-water mark for fifty years. In 1951, Hirsch, nicknamed because of his odd running style, established a single-season reception record of 1,495 yards gained.

CURLY MORRISON: The 1955 championship in Los Angeles was Otto Graham's last game. We beat the Rams 38–14 and Otto went out in style, passing for two touchdowns and running for two more. Paul took Otto out with about two minutes to play and the entire stadium, 90,000 fans, stood up and cheered for Otto Graham. Rams fans, everybody. It was a great moment; I get chills talking about it. As Otto ran off the field he said, "Thanks, Coach," and Paul Brown looked at him and said, "Thank you, Otto," and that's all that was ever said. It was a special final moment between a great coach and his greatest player.

[Commenting on his nickname, "Crazy Legs"]

"Any name is better than Elroy."

—Elroy Hirsch

[Describing his philosophy as an assistant coach with the 1964 Packers]

"It's not a matter of staying at the same level—you have to get better. You have to come up with something new and some new finds. And at the same time, everybody else is getting hungrier—and stronger—every year, because they are drafting ahead of you, and consequently obtaining better talent."

—Tom Fears

Otto Graham and the Browns represented excellence in all phases of the game except the ability to control the roughneck Detroit Lions, led by their freewheeling, high-living quarterback Bobby Layne. Other quarterbacks had a more graceful delivery, threw longer or prettier passes, were bigger, faster, or stronger. But none prodded, drove, threatened, scolded, or inspired like Layne. The Lions were NFL champions in '52, '53, and '57.

BOBBY LAYNE; QUARTERBACK, LIONS: We cut up the Browns like a boardinghouse pie, and that's real small pieces. Me and Otto played against each other eight times. I could only win seven of them.

PAT SUMMERALL; END, LIONS, CARDINALS, GIANTS: Bobby was the most dynamic leader I ever met. He would party Saturday night, beat you on a Sunday afternoon, and party again Monday night. He loved being around his teammates and his parties were more like spiritual gatherings, except not much religion was discussed.

BOBBY LAYNE: When I was with the Lions, they'd fine me all the time for missing curfew—$100, $200, $500, whatever it might be. So one time, I slid a check under the coach's door as I was going out. After a while, he knew how late I was going to be by the size of the check.

DOAK WALKER; HALFBACK, LIONS: Bobby's helmet had no face mask. He wore no hip pads, no thigh pads, and no knee pads. He'd put one strip of tape on his ankle because there was a fine if you sprained your ankle and you weren't taped. You wouldn't let your twelve-year-old kid wear the shoulder pads he had.

BOBBY LAYNE: Playing quarterback isn't always about what you do with your arm, it's about being tough when your teammates need you the most. It's important to learn your playbook and master your technique…and then forget all that bullshit and just play.

JOHN HENRY JOHNSON; FULLBACK, LIONS, 49ERS, STEELERS: There was only one thing Bobby loved better than a tall beer, and that was winning football games. Bobby called his own plays and would kick out anybody the coach sent in with one. He liked to make up little trick plays. He saved a dilly for the Giants. He called it the "Wait-a-Minute Play." As Bobby bent over the center, halfback Tom Tracy suddenly shouted, "Wait a minute." Without moving from his crouch, Bobby looked around. "What's the matter?" he called. On the word "matter," the center snapped the ball through Bobby's legs directly to me and I raced for a touchdown. Unfortunately, an official, faked out by the play, called us offsides.

> **"You know, I've always had confidence in myself. I still think I could do more things better than any other back that ever lived."**
> **—Doak Walker**

THE VERSATILE DOAK WALKER

Halfback Doak Walker, who starred for the Detroit Lions from 1950 to 1955, was known for his versatility. He rushed, passed, caught passes, returned punts and kickoffs, and even filled in on defense when needed. The former Heisman Trophy winner also handled Detroit's placekicking duties. To help him switch from halfback to placekicker between plays, Walker added a zipper to his prelaced kicking shoe for a quick change.

> **"I never said a word in my life to a receiver who dropped the ball. I'll admit that I sure raised hell with the guy who blew an assignment, though. There's no excuse for that."**
> **—Bobby Layne**

Opposite:

DETROIT'S DECADE

Four times during the 1950s the Detroit Lions and the Cleveland Browns met in the NFL Championship Game; three times the Lions were victorious. In the 1952 Championship Game, quarterback Bobby Layne and halfback Doak Walker led Detroit to its first title in seventeen years. Walker rushed for 97 yards, including a third-quarter 67-yard run for a touchdown. In the 1953 Championship Game backup end Jim Doran caught a game-winning 33-yard touchdown pass from Layne with 2:08 left in the game. The Lions' third win over Cleveland was a 59–14 slaughter delivered by quarterback Tobin Rote, who replaced an injured Layne in midseason.

DOAK WALKER: In 1955 we won only three games and Bobby had a disappointing season, so he offered to take a $2,500 cut in his next year's contract [Layne was making $18,000 a year]. The Lions knew it was not a stunt and they agreed to cut his salary.

SAM HUFF; LINEBACKER, NEW YORK GIANTS: One time in New York, Bobby held the ball too long and I got in clean and I held him up in the air. I didn't body-slam him down on the turf. I would've hurt him. I held him and the whistle blew. He looked at me and he said, "Thanks, Sam." I said, "No problem." You didn't try to hurt that guy. There was a special respect that we always had for Bobby Layne.

> **"I'd much rather play defense than offense…you get more satisfaction from the job. You can really express yourself a helluva lot more defensively. I always enjoyed tackling. The contact is a persistent challenge to you. A good hard tackle gives you a lift, a thrill, and I don't mean to be sadistic."**
>
> —**Joe Schmidt**

JOE SCHMIDT'S HELMET

Joe Schmidt didn't invent the middle linebacker position as it evolved in the 1950s; he just played it better than it had ever been played before. An All-NFL choice ten times, Schmidt was also named to ten consecutive Pro Bowls during his thirteen-year career with the Detroit Lions.

> **"Television creates interest and this can benefit pro football. But it's only good as long as you can protect your home gate. You can't give fans a game for free on television and also expect them to pay to go to the ballpark to see the same game."**
>
> —**Bert Bell**

"There's far more to playing fullback than just running with the football. Everybody wants to run with the ball, that's the quickest way to get the headlines and lot of newspaper space. But how many times does a back peel off a long run by himself? I'll tell you—absolutely none."

—John Henry Johnson

JOHN HENRY JOHNSON

One of the most punishing runners of his era, John Henry Johnson joined the San Francisco 49ers in 1954 after spending a year in the Canadian Football League. Johnson completed the 49ers' "Million Dollar Backfield" that included Hugh McElhenny, Y. A. Tittle, and Joe "the Jet" Perry. At the time of his retirement in 1966, Johnson's 6,803 career yards rushing was the fourth highest in NFL history.

JOE PERRY'S SAN FRANCISCO 49ERS UNIFORM

Joe Perry played thirteen seasons with the San Francisco 49ers before being traded to the Baltimore Colts in 1961. After two seasons with the Colts he returned to San Francisco for one final season. A member of the 49ers' famous "Million Dollar Backfield," he was the first running back to record back-to-back 1,000-yard seasons.

"I was an oddity. I was the first big man in the league who could run. I was a track man....We put in a system of the tackles pulling out around the ends.... I was able to get around and get downfield without a back running over the top of me."

—Bob St. Clair

"The gratifying thing was when I'd gained the respect of not only my teammates but of everyone else throughout the league, including the officials. They accepted me as a man. Not as a black man or a white man, but as a man."

—Joe Perry

"I really like to play football. It's tough and it's hard and no pro football owners can pay a player enough for the punishment they take. You just have to like it—and I do."

—Leo Nomellini

"You play as hard and as tough as you can, but you play clean. We hit each other hard, sure. But this is a man's game and any guy who doesn't want to hit hard doesn't belong in it."

—Sam Huff

> "I was always scared. It was like when I was a little kid. I used to have to walk through a dark alley to get home at night. There was a light at the end of that alley and doorways, dark doorways, on both sides of the street. Well, I wouldn't walk on either side. I'd run down the middle of the street for the light. But I'd run with the anticipation that there was someone trying to get at me in each of those doorways. It was the same in football. I could just feel them coming for me. I could hear their footsteps."
>
> —Hugh McElhenny

HUGH "THE KING" McELHENNY

Halfback Hugh McElhenny was considered the greatest "thrill runner" of his era. As a rookie with the San Francisco 49ers, he recorded the season's longest punt return (94 yards), the longest run from scrimmage (89 yards), and the top rushing average (7.0 yards per carry). Known for his long stride and high knee action, McElhenny, with his breakaway speed and unique ability to change direction at will, left defenders dazed and confused. From 1954 to 1956 the 49ers backfield included McElhenny, quarterback Y. A. Tittle, and fullbacks Joe Perry and John Henry Johnson. It is the only full-house backfield to have every member enshrined in the Hall of Fame.

Y. A. TITTLE

QUESTION: How difficult was it having that much talent in the same backfield—Joe Perry, John Henry Johnson, and Hugh McElhenny? Was it difficult to decide who got the ball?

TITTLE: Well, I needed a calculator to figure out who got to carry the most times and I never wanted to hurt anybody's feelings, because any one of those three backs was capable of making short yardage or going the distance. McElhenny was a broken-field runner—skillful and classy. John Henry Johnson was a hard-nosed, give-and-take, sock-'em-in-the-eye runner. Joe Perry had greased-lightning speed so all I had to do was try to keep track of how many times each got the ball. I didn't want any of them mad at me, and I think they got their fair share. Some of it just came naturally. Joe Perry was just a workhorse. He could carry the ball thirty times a game. McElhenny was sort of a…he was fancy-dancy runner and really not a classic every-down style runner. So he didn't carry the ball as many times as Joe Perry or John Henry. So I didn't really have any problems. McElhenny got to carry the ball at certain times but Joe Perry was really the workhorse.

"I was a strict, straight-arrow quarterback when I came to the 49ers. I learned to become free….I had always tried to please every coach I ever played for, I guess to the point I became their mirror image. I was conservative always…I learned to do the unusual things…I learned to run the bootleg…I was a good thrower."

—Y. A. Tittle

[Responding to critics in 1953 that he was one-dimensional and that all he could do was pass]

"Now, you take a goalie in big-league hockey. He's not supposed to rush out of his cage and throw body-checks all over the rink. Or a pitcher who wins twenty games is a bum if he doesn't hit .300. And Joe Louis wasn't a great fighter—all he could do was punch. If that's ridiculous, so are these so-called theorists. I'm not paid to do anything but throw and call plays….A lot of smart men have tried to figure out ways to score, and none of them ever invented a quicker way than to pass and keep on passing."

—Norm Van Brocklin

"We hit with these *[as he holds out his forearms]*. That's where you get your power, not from your legs or your shoulders or anything else. There will be times out there…when you forget all the things you ever learned, but remember this: with the snap of the ball, move. Move and be rough."

—Ernie Stautner

JOHNNY U

No two pieces of equipment are more associated with one player than quarterback Johnny Unitas's famous Number 19 jersey and his classic high-top shoes. Amazingly, Unitas, who wrote the book on quarterback play, got off to a slow start as a pro. A ninth-round draft choice of the 1955 Pittsburgh Steelers, he was cut before he even threw one pass in a game. Signed by the Baltimore Colts after a season of semipro football, he watched as his first pass was intercepted for a touchdown. Making matters worse, he fumbled on his next two possessions. But his shaky debut was soon forgotten. During his legendary career Unitas amassed 40,239 passing yards and 290 touchdowns, and his record of at least one touchdown pass in forty-seven consecutive games still stands at this writing.

While Layne was respected, and Graham was admired, Johnny Unitas was feared. With the possible exception of Jonas Salk, John Foster Dulles, and Annette Funicello, no one public figure so personified the '50s for me as did Johnny U. He was a classic, in the sense that he belonged to a class of which he was the only and definitive member.

RAYMOND BERRY; WIDE RECEIVER, COLTS: John was a field general. He had this rare ability to make the game conform to his will. He controlled the tempo, decided the tactics. He was a chess master who played the game several moves ahead of everyone else.

JOHN UNITAS; QUARTERBACK, COLTS: Our coach [Weeb Ewbank] never called the plays. He turned the game plan over to me. The guys up in the press box, they would ask me, "What do you want to know?" I said, "If you can find any kind of a tendency on them as far as their rushing linebackers, let me know. Otherwise, just sit there and enjoy the game." Once in a while Weeb would send things in to me like, "Tell John to make the first down," or "Tell John we gotta score a touchdown here," but that was fine with me. The decision was mine.

"Quickness was the best thing I had going for me. That, and concentration. I'd always line up so I could see three offensive linemen at the same time…the tackle in front of me, plus the guard and center. The moment any of those three guys moved a muscle, I was gone. The key to that was concentration. The guy in front of me better be just as quick, because if I got that split-second jump and got my hands on his shoulders, he was finished."

—Gino Marchetti

"We didn't make much money, but we had a lot of fun…nothing but fun. Whoever thought that kids who enjoyed the game on all those sandlots would get to play the game on the pro level? That's pretty special."

—Art Donovan

THE 1958 NFL CHAMPIONSHIP GAME

The 1958 NFL Championship Game is often cited as the "Greatest Game Ever Played." It definitely reached epic proportions late in the game as Baltimore Colts quarterback Johnny Unitas began one of the great drives in pro football history. Starting from his own 14-yard line, he connected with halfback Lenny Moore for an 11-yard gain, followed by three consecutive completions to Raymond Berry. Then with seven seconds remaining, Steve Myhra booted a 20-yard field goal, sending the game into overtime. It marked the first time a championship game would be decided in sudden death. The Giants won the coin toss but were forced to punt. Seizing the opportunity, Unitas drove 80 yards in 13 plays. Finally, after 8 minutes and 15 seconds, fullback Alan Ameche scored from a yard out to give the Colts a 23–17 victory.

1958 CHAMPIONSHIP GAME— GIFFORD CARRIES THE BALL

Leading the Colts 17–14 in the final minutes of the fourth quarter of the 1958 NFL Championship Game, it appeared all the Giants had to do was run out the clock. Using four running plays and a completed pass, they moved from the 19 to their 40. Then on third-and-four, halfback Frank Gifford carried for what he thought was a first down. "I made the first down," Gifford insists. "But [Gino] Marchetti broke his leg....There was a lot of confusion. A lot of time passed by while they carried Marchetti off the field. When they finally spotted the ball, it was placed short of the first-down marker." The Giants were forced to punt. The Colts responded with a field goal that sent the game into overtime, after which the Colts scored again to win 23–17.

"To me, Vince *[Lombardi]* was the difference between my becoming a good pro player and just another halfback. He turned my life around. Anything I accomplished in this game, I owe to him."

—Frank Gifford

"Luck is something which happens when preparation meets opportunity. One play may make the difference in winning or losing a game. I must be prepared to make my own luck."

—Raymond Berry

"There's no thrill in football like popping the ball to a receiver who has a step on his man in the open."

—Bob Waterfield

"You've got to know when to rush. Overanxiety can hurt you. Knowing when comes with experience and nothing else."

—Andy Robustelli

"When I joined the team we started winning, shutting out two teams to win the championship. When you win, everything is great."

—Pete Pihos

"My object is to stop the guy before he gains another inch. I'm usually dealing with ends who are trying to catch passes, and if I hit them in the legs they may fall forward for a first down. There is nothing I hate worse than a first down. It means I have to stay out there three more plays. I grab them around the neck so I can get back to the bench and sit me down."

—Dick "Night Train" Lane

"Money is important without a doubt, but everything is relative. I happened to like the era in which I played. I liked the close-knit family atmosphere of the Detroit Lions. There were only thirty-three players then and we felt like a family, from the front office down. That aspect of the game has changed and I'm not sure I like it."

—Yale Lary

"There are only two things necessary. First, you get the best players. Then you get a coach who can get the best out of them."

—Dan Reeves

"What I planned to do through professional football was play one or two years, save some money, go into coaching, be able to buy my house, and pay for it outright. Thirteen years later, they almost had to tear the uniform off me, I love the game so much."

—Mike McCormack

"Sure, I play rough. But that's what the Rams pay me for, and that's what the fans pay to see. We've got a few dirty players in the league, let's be honest about it. But everyone knows who they are, and they don't get away with much. There's a big distinction between playing hard and playing dirty."

—Les Richter

LEO NOMELLINI; TACKLE, 49ERS: Unitas was fearless. Out of the corner of his eye, when he could see you coming, I swear he'd hold that ball a split second longer than he really needed to—just to let you know he wasn't afraid of any man. Then he threw it on the button.

JOHN UNITAS: The Bears had a bounty on me for $500. I never found that out until after the year was over. One of the players told me. They said, "Anybody that knocks him out of the ball game gets an extra $500." I never worried about that. A quarterback who's looking at the rush instead of his receivers shouldn't be playing in the NFL.

JOHNNY SAMPLE; DEFENSIVE BACK, COLTS, REDSKINS, JETS: John wasn't graceful or nifty, he was actually kind of awkward, but he had a helluva arm, strong. He could knock the nuts off a low-flying duck. He was a daring passer and he used surprise as a weapon. If we thought he'd call the obvious play, he'd do the unexpected. If we anticipated the unexpected, he'd try the obvious.

WEEB EWBANK; COACH, COLTS, JETS: Unitas was excellent at reading defenses, but he was also the first to master the art of "looking off"—looking at one side of the field or even faking a throw to make the defense flinch and then suddenly throwing the ball elsewhere. The great quarterbacks always complete the "one-on-ones." When a guy was wide open John never missed him, he always hit him.

1958 NFL CHAMPIONSHIP GAME

Among the Hall of Fame's artifacts from the championship game is this football; coach Weeb Ewbank's offensive game plan; the shoe worn by Steve Myhra when he kicked the field goal that sent the game into sudden death; and a segment of the goalpost. Twelve future Hall of Famers played in this historic game.

[Explaining why he hit receivers so hard whether they held onto the ball or not.]

"The best pass defense is the respect of the receivers. If they figure they're going to get hit as soon as they touch the ball, they're not so relaxed about catching it."
—Jack Butler

Before the decade ended, Unitas led the Colts to two world championships. The first, in 1958, has been called the "Greatest Game Ever Played." But with eight fumbles and eight quarterback sacks it was hardly that. It was really fifty-eight minutes of prelude setting the stage for an unforgettable sudden-death overtime finish. In 1959 Johnny U and his Colts defeated the New York Giants for the second time, winning easily 31–16 in Baltimore. The game was played in Memorial Stadium, which has since been demolished. I filmed many games there and I remember that on the façade there was a memorial dedicated to those who lost their lives in World Wars I and II. The last line on the façade read, "Time will not dim the glory of their deeds."

While football is certainly not as important as wars, that line seems appropriate in the context of Johnny Unitas, and also of Bobby Layne, Otto Graham, and Paul Brown—names that ring down through history with good reason. They were the most memorable men in a decade that proved pro football was no fad. It was a good game going on great. It's safe to say that it has outlasted hula hoops, McCarthyism, bomb shelters, and the bunny hop, and has held its own with rock 'n' roll.

A WINNING COMBINATION

During his nine years with the Baltimore Colts, Weeb Ewbank coached six future Hall of Famers: Johnny Unitas, Raymond Berry, Lenny Moore, Art Donovan, Jim Parker, and Gino Marchetti. Depicted here with their coach are Berry, Moore, and Unitas.

Opposite:

TELEGRAM ANNOUNCING OLLIE MATSON'S TRADE

This is the telegram sent by the Los Angeles Rams to the NFL office on February 28, 1959, announcing the trade of nine players to the Chicago Cardinals in exchange for halfback Ollie Matson. The deal was orchestrated by then–Rams general manager and future NFL commissioner Pete Rozelle. Matson played fourteen seasons in the NFL, gaining 12,884 combined yards via rushing, receiving, and returns. A gifted athlete, he also won silver and bronze medals in the 1952 Summer Olympics.

"**The things I cherish most are the Olympic medals and the Hall of Fame. In the Olympics you're competing against the best there are. It isn't the Iowa State Fair. It's the world championship. The Hall of Fame is the same. Think of the hundreds of thousands who have played football. Think of the thousands who have played pro football. And you're one of seventy-four** *[as of 1972]* **who made it.**"

—Ollie Matson

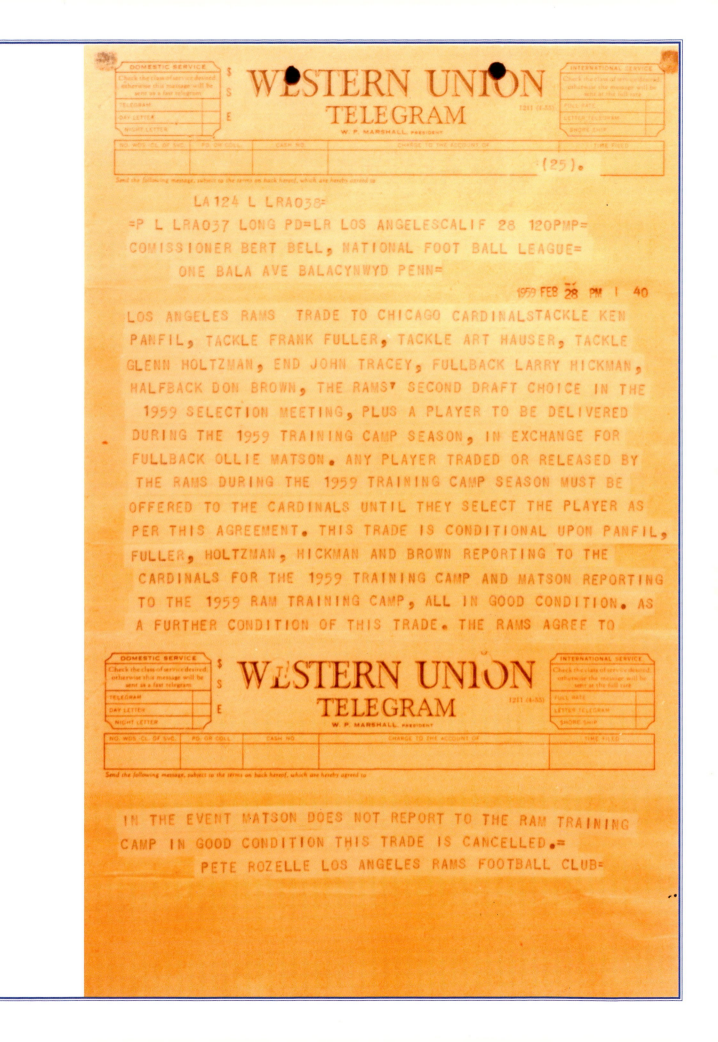

LA124 L LRA038=

=P L LRA037 LONG PD=LR LOS ANGELESCALIF 28 120PMP=

COMISSIONER BERT BELL, NATIONAL FOOT BALL LEAGUE=

ONE BALA AVE BALACYNWYD PENN=

1959 FEB 28 PM 1 40

LOS ANGELES RAMS TRADE TO CHICAGO CARDINALSTACKLE KEN
PANFIL, TACKLE FRANK FULLER, TACKLE ART HAUSER, TACKLE
GLENN HOLTZMAN, END JOHN TRACEY, FULLBACK LARRY HICKMAN,
HALFBACK DON BROWN, THE RAMS' SECOND DRAFT CHOICE IN THE
1959 SELECTION MEETING, PLUS A PLAYER TO BE DELIVERED
DURING THE 1959 TRAINING CAMP SEASON, IN EXCHANGE FOR
FULLBACK OLLIE MATSON. ANY PLAYER TRADED OR RELEASED BY
THE RAMS DURING THE 1959 TRAINING CAMP SEASON MUST BE
OFFERED TO THE CARDINALS UNTIL THEY SELECT THE PLAYER AS
PER THIS AGREEMENT. THIS TRADE IS CONDITIONAL UPON PANFIL,
FULLER, HOLTZMAN, HICKMAN AND BROWN REPORTING TO THE
CARDINALS FOR THE 1959 TRAINING CAMP AND MATSON REPORTING
TO THE 1959 RAM TRAINING CAMP, ALL IN GOOD CONDITION. AS
A FURTHER CONDITION OF THIS TRADE. THE RAMS AGREE TO

IN THE EVENT MATSON DOES NOT REPORT TO THE RAM TRAINING
CAMP IN GOOD CONDITION THIS TRADE IS CANCELLED.=
PETE ROZELLE LOS ANGELES RAMS FOOTBALL CLUB=

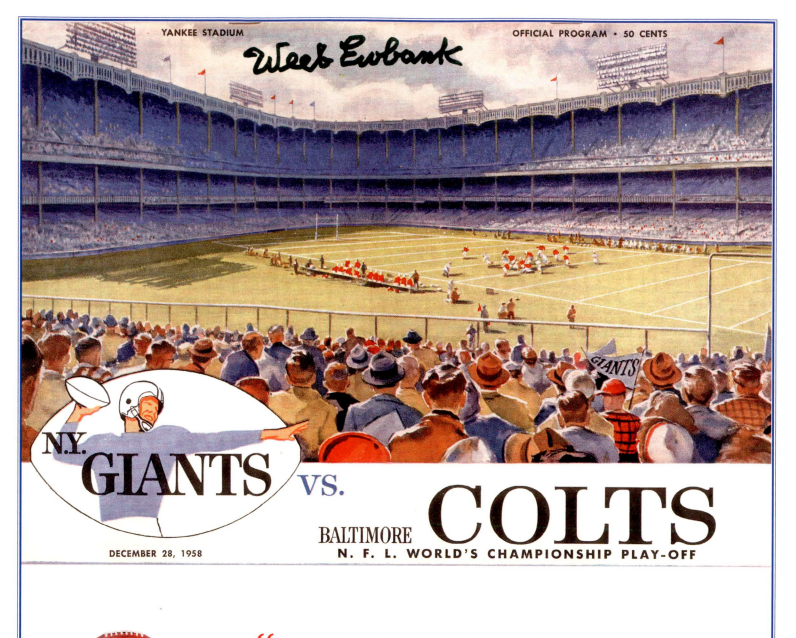

YANKEE STADIUM

Weeb Ewbank

OFFICIAL PROGRAM · 50 CENTS

N.Y. GIANTS VS. **BALTIMORE COLTS**

DECEMBER 28, 1958

N. F. L. WORLD'S CHAMPIONSHIP PLAY-OFF

"The big play comes from the pass. God bless those runners because they get you the first down, give you ball control, and keep your defense off the field. But if you want to ring the cash register, you have to pass."

—Sid Gillman

"It would be foolish for me to say I expected to play football until I am incapable of doing an adequate job. Football has been good for me, for my body and my mind, and I'm anxious to put some of the things I've learned from it into business. Ever since I started playing football back in high school in Washington, D.C., I have been associated with men who have been very helpful for me. My friends are amused by some of the things I tell them, but believe me, I'm better for having played the game."

—Len Ford

"Kicking was something I did because I had the talent. I always considered myself a tackle."

—Lou Groza

"Just being there. Just winning all those games. That's what it was all about for me."

—Frank Gatski

"All that stuff about trickery we read about.... Mighty few games have been won with tricks. They're won first by preparation and second by desire."

—Bill George

"People remember me as suddenly quite angry when an opponent held or tripped me. The reputation that I would become a one-man wrecking gang when someone did me wrong followed me everywhere. I guess it's true that that sort of stuff would stir me up. In fact, sometimes it would take something like that to get me going in a game. But I took exception to that kind of treatment from an opponent when I was playing hurt, which I did a lot. When I was hobbling around with a sore leg and some guy kicked me, I let him know I didn't like that."

—Doug Atkins

"I'd really never thought much about pro ball. I never even remember talking to a pro scout or filling out a questionnaire when I was in college. In those days, a lot of NFL clubs did much of their scouting from football magazines."

—Jack Christiansen

"We were a lot of rabble-rousers. We lived high on the hog but on Sunday we were dedicated."

—Lou Creekmur

"If you try to follow the ball, any slick quarterback can fool you. But if you concentrate on watching a few key offensive players, they'll lead you right to the play."

—George Connor

The 1960s

THE MAN WHO MADE THE DECADE

DAVE ANDERSON

Opposite, above:

PAUL HORNUNG SIGNS
WITH THE PACK

Using a bonus selection, the Green Bay Packers made Notre Dame Heisman Trophy winner Paul Hornung the first choice in the 1957 NFL draft. However, after two undistinguished seasons under two head coaches, it appeared Hornung's career was in jeopardy. That changed in 1959, when Vince Lombardi was named the Packers' head coach. Lombardi made Hornung his starting halfback and paired him with second-year fullback Jim Taylor to create one of the most productive running back tandems in NFL history.

Opposite, below:

LOMBARDI'S PACKER SWEEP

Paul Hornung and Jim Taylor perfected Vince Lombardi's seemingly unstoppable "Packer Sweep." Hornung led the league in scoring three consecutive years (1959–61), while Taylor rushed for more than 1,000 yards in five consecutive seasons (1960–64). Lombardi called the sweep his number one play "because it requires eleven men to play as one for it to succeed, and that's what team means."

With the final desperate seconds flashing on the Franklin Field scoreboard, Green Bay Packers quarterback Bart Starr took the snap at the Philadelphia Eagles' 22-yard line, glanced left, and threw a pass to fullback Jim Taylor, who barreled toward the end zone. Defensive back Bobby Jackson cut down Taylor at the eight-yard line and Chuck Bednarik, the two-way linebacker and center known as Concrete Charlie, sat on him to make sure, as time expired, that he stayed down.

"YOU CAN GET UP now," Bednarik finally told him. "This *!&#* game is over." The Eagles had won the 1960 NFL Championship Game, 17–13, but in the Packers' locker room Coach Vince Lombardi's words established their future domination of the '60s. He told his players that perhaps they had not realized before the game that they could have won, but he knew now that there was no doubt in their minds.

"That's why we'll win it all next year," he promised. "This will never happen again. You will never lose another championship game."

Vince Lombardi's Packers never did. They won the title in 1961 and 1962 and again in 1965, as well as Super Bowl I in 1966 and Super Bowl II in 1967—the only franchise to win three consecutive championships (twice—in 1929–31 and in 1965–67!), the only franchise to win five in seven years, the only franchise with a total of eleven NFL championships (it added a twelfth in 1996 with Mike Holmgren as coach and Brett Favre at quarterback, and a record thirteenth in 2011 with Mike McCarthy as coach and Aaron Rodgers at quarterback). All those titles gilded the glory of one of the NFL's oldest franchises, organized on August 11, 1919, in the editorial room of the *Green Bay Press-*

> **"I'm Coach Lombardi's representative on the field. I'm doing what he would be doing if he were the quarterback. If he's happy with the way I do my job, I don't care how anybody else reacts."**
>
> **—Bart Starr**

MERLIN OLSEN JERSEY

Merlin Olsen was the stabilizing leader of the Los Angeles Rams' "Fearsome Foursome" that also included Deacon Jones, Rosey Grier, and Lamar Lundy. Merlin was selected to play in the Pro Bowl in every one of his fourteen years in the league.

> **"Football is a great deal like life in that it teaches that work, sacrifice, perseverance, competitive drive, self-lessness, and respect for authority is the price that each and every one of us must pay to achieve any goal that is worthwhile."**
>
> **—Vince Lombardi**

Gazette by Curly Lambeau, its hometown star tailback and coach for thirty-one seasons, and financed by the Indian Packing Company's purchase of the original blue-and-gold jerseys. But between their 1944 title and Lombardi's arrival in 1959, the Packers were an embarrassment to the little town in northern Wisconsin on the often icy shores of Lake Michigan. During the 1958 season, their 1–10–1 record was the league's and the franchise's worst, but the new coach, in a booming voice that could melt snow, had his pride and his plan.

"I have never been on a losing team, gentlemen," he barked when the players gathered at training camp. "I do not intend to start now."

Lombardi, a block-of-granite guard at Fordham, had been a head coach only at St. Cecilia's High School in Englewood, New Jersey, where he won state titles (and taught chemistry, physics, algebra, and Latin) before moving to Army, then a national power, as an assistant coach under Earl "Red" Blaik, and then to the New York Giants as what would now be considered their offensive coordinator. Those Giants, with Frank Gifford, Charlie Conerly, Andy Robustelli, and Sam Huff, won the 1956 title and took the Baltimore Colts into sudden-death overtime in the 1958 Championship Game. Lombardi had been promised the Giants' head job when Jim Lee Howell retired, but when the Packers called, he decided to depart to Green Bay.

"I want it understood," he told the committee that oversaw the publicly owned Packers, "that I am in complete command here."

What nobody realized was that those 1–10–1 Packers in 1958 had seven future Hall of Famers just waiting to be prodded and polished: Starr, Taylor, running back Paul Hornung, center Jim Ringo, tackle Forrest Gregg, linebacker Ray Nitschke, and defensive tackle Henry Jordan. In their 1959 opener, they upset the Chicago Bears,

> **"I've accomplished all of my goals...I've played in the Pro Bowl, been named best center in the league, been a member of a championship team, and now I've established a record that will last for some years after I'm through."**
>
> **—Jim Ringo**

> **"They say you don't get much recognition on the offensive line, but there is a lot of satisfaction if you know you're doing your job and the coaches know it. Our backs always knew they didn't make those long runs by themselves."**
>
> **—Forrest Gregg**

❝You can take the best team and the worst team and line them up and you would find very little physical difference. You would find an emotional difference. The winning team has a dedication. It will have at its core a group of veteran players who set the standard. They will not accept defeat.❞ —Merlin Olsen

9–6, en route to a 7–5 season in the new green-and-gold uniforms that Lombardi ordered. The "G" on the helmet would be added by Dad Braisher, the Packers' longtime equipment manager, in 1961 when, fortified by three future Hall of Famers (defensive end Willie Davis, safety Willie Wood, and cornerback Herb Adderley), they were 11–3 and routed the Giants 37–0 for the championship. Hornung, on leave from Army service at Fort Riley, Kansas (arranged by Lombardi's phone call to President John F. Kennedy), ran for a six-yard touchdown, kicked field goals of 17, 22, and 19 yards, and added four extra points for a record 19 points.

THE RAMS' FEARSOME FOURSOME

Although several teams—including the San Diego Chargers, New York Giants, and Detroit Lions—featured defensive lines known as the "Fearsome Foursome," the best known and arguably the best group of players was the Los Angeles Rams' 1960s version consisting of defensive tackles Merlin Olsen and Rosey Grier and defensive ends Deacon Jones and Lamar Lundy. Chicago Bears linebacker Dick Butkus called the Rams foursome "the most dominant line in football."

PETE ROZELLE NAMED NFL COMMISSIONER

Thirty-three-year-old Pete Rozelle was a surprise choice to replace Bert Bell as NFL commissioner in 1960. He went on to become the premier commissioner of all professional sports. Rozelle created and maintained the NFL's image of stability and integrity; negotiated the first league-wide television contract; skillfully managed the AFL-NFL "war," merger, and the league restructuring that followed; and developed the Super Bowl into the world's most successful single-day sporting event. Pictured with Rozelle at his hiring announcement are (left to right) NFL owners George Halas (Chicago Bears), Frank McNamee (Philadelphia Eagles), and George Preston Marshall (Washington Redskins), as well as Eagles executive Joe Donohue.

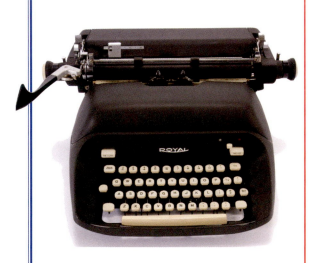

NFL COMMISSIONER PETE ROZELLE'S TYPEWRITER

Although a true visionary, Rozelle did resist innovation in at least one area—his office equipment. Rozelle proudly used this beat-up old typewriter throughout his entire thirty-year reign as NFL commissioner.

Lombardi's Packers were new and different, and so was the NFL. Pete Rozelle, the young commissioner, had moved the league offices from Philadelphia to the media market of midtown New York, eased the expansion to Dallas and Minnesota, and ushered through Congress the television policy that split millions equally among the fourteen teams and has kept the Packers prosperous in small-market Green Bay. The 1960 population there was only 62,888; in Brown County it was only 125,082.

In 1962 the Packers were even better despite Hornung's knee injury that limited him to 219 rushing yards and six field goals. They were 10–0 before a 26–14 loss in Detroit on Thanksgiving Day when the Lions defense, led by 6'5", 300-pound tackle Roger Brown, sacked Starr 11 times. They quickly regrouped, finished 13–1, and froze the Giants, 16–7, on Jerry Kramer's three field goals at Yankee Stadium in near-zero weather with swirling 25- to 40-mph winds that blew Y. A. Tittle's passes every which way. Jim Taylor, spitting blood from a badly cut tongue, rushed for 85 yards, including a seven-yard touchdown, after leading the league with 1,474 yards and 19 touchdowns. Middle linebacker Ray Nitschke, forcing two fumbles and tipping a pass into an interception, was voted the most valuable player.

"I think that I was proud of…my staff played obviously a major part…popularizing the sport, with the early promotional activities of NFL Properties, merchandising, NFL Films, all the work that we put on the Super Bowl to make that a top attraction. All those things, I feel very good about—I think they played a big part in popularizing the league."

—Pete Rozelle

"THE DUTCHMAN," QUARTERBACK NORM VAN BROCKLIN

In the final game of his twelve-year career, quarterback Norm Van Brocklin led the Philadelphia Eagles to a 17–13 victory over the Green Bay Packers in the 1960 NFL Championship Game. Thus "The Dutchman" was the only man to defeat a Lombardi-coached Green Bay team in championship game play. "Old Van completed them when the Eagles needed them," commented Lombardi on Van Brocklin's performance. This is the jersey he wore that day and his 1960 league MVP trophy.

> **"I wrapped my arms around him. I wrapped my arms around him and squeezed. I knocked him down and I lay on him. Then I watched the clock. I watched those seconds tick off and I watched that clock hit zero. Then I let loose, 'Okay Taylor,' I said, 'You can get up now. This game is over.'"**
>
> *[On stopping Jim Taylor from scoring the game-winning TD on the last play of the 1960 NFL Championship Game.]*
> **—Chuck Bednarik**

HALL OF FAMER CHUCK BEDNARIK'S 1960 CHAMPIONSHIP BLAZER

Chuck Bednarik played both center and linebacker for the Philadelphia Eagles. The NFL's last true "iron man," in the 1960 NFL title game Bednarik played 58 of a possible 60 minutes and made a game-saving tackle. With the Eagles leading 17–13 late in the second half, quarterback Bart Starr threw a short pass to Jim Taylor, who headed toward the end zone for the go-ahead touchdown. Bednarik, the oldest player on the field at thirty-five, tackled Taylor short of the goal line and held him down as the clock ran out. This is Bednarik's 1960 championship blazer.

"This game is more mental than physical. Every club is loaded with guys who have something physically or they wouldn't be here. It's the guys who are right mentally who come out on top. It's the guys who don't make the big mistakes who win. Maybe that's why I do well in big games. When the pressure's on, guys get tight. By my very nature, I'm a loose character. I'm not great physically. So I've had to learn to use what I have intelligently, to avoid mistakes."

—Paul Hornung

As Lombardi left the Packers' locker room, patches of white adhesive tape were everywhere. Dirty towels were crumpled in the lockers. Newspapers littered the floor. Lombardi glared at two men on the stadium staff who were relaxing in the trainers' room. "You," the coach said sharply, "can clean up this mess, you know."

Any other NFL coach probably never would have noticed the debris. Or if he had, he would have ignored it, especially if his team had just won the title. But not Lombardi, who lived by a severe code of discipline. And little did he know in those hours after winning the 1962 Championship Game that he soon would be required to clean up the mess of Hornung's suspension for gambling on NFL games, a mess all the more hurtful to Lombardi because Hornung, for all his playboy reputation, was the coach's favorite player. After hearing rumors of Hornung's betting, Rozelle had assembled more than a dozen former FBI agents to investigate. In early April 1963 he showed Hornung's signed confession to Lombardi.

"You've got to do," Lombardi told the commissioner, "what you've got to do."

Hornung, along with defensive tackle Alex Karras of the Lions, was suspended indefinitely. Five other Lions each were fined $2,000 for betting on one game they did not participate in; the Lions franchise was fined $2,000 on each of two counts for ignoring reports of gambling by players. But the headlines and highlights mostly blared Hornung's name.

LANCE ALWORTH'S JERSEY

San Diego Chargers flanker Lance Alworth, a seven-time American Football League All-Star, was the first player from the AFL to be enshrined in the Pro Football Hall of Fame. Known for his smooth and spectacular moves, Alworth caught passes in a then-record 96 consecutive games and led the AFL in receptions three times.

LANCE ALWORTH

QUESTION: What was the key to the success of the Chargers' offense in the 1960s AFL?

ALWORTH: There were an awful lot of fine players on the Charger football team, a lot of talented guys, back when the NFL and AFL were fighting for talent. We were lucky enough to be able to gather a few of those guys in, and at the same time we had the master of offense, what I think was the early West Coast offense, that Sid Gillman defined and put into play. The biggest reason why that offense worked and was good, particularly for me, was John Hadl at quarterback. John was a great quarterback. I don't think anything happened in a game that surprised him or that he couldn't change himself during the ball game. If anything developed in the game he'd take care of it and adjust to it. It really helps the receiver knowing that the quarterback knows exactly what's going to happen and when it's going to happen and he can adjust if necessary and still get the ball to you. And that is what John did. He didn't throw the most beautiful pass in the world, but I'll tell you what, you check his stats, he was fabulous. With him guiding Sid's game plan, we did put up a few stats that I think they may break 'em sometime…but if I recall correctly, a lot of them still stand and it's been a long, long time.

"I made a terrible mistake," he acknowledged. "I realize that now. I am truly sorry. What else is there to say?"

Lombardi knew what else to say. Hornung had grown up and lived in the off-season in Louisville, Kentucky, where the Kentucky Derby and racetrack gambling was a way of life. Lombardi told him, "No racetrack, no Derby. Keep your nose clean and I'll do my best to get you back." Without Hornung, the Packers were good (11–2–1), but not good enough in a season stained by President Kennedy's assassination in Dallas. The Chicago Bears won the West by one-half game, then edged the Giants, 14–10, for owner George Halas's sixth title in his thirty-sixth season as coach. And just as Lombardi hoped, on March 16, 1964, Hornung, along with Karras, was reinstated.

When Hornung told Lombardi, "I'll be there in early May to start working out," the coach snapped that mid-April would be better. As Hornung said later, "We compromised on mid-April."

The Packers won their opener with the Bears, 23–12, then lost to the Baltimore Colts, 21–20, when Hornung missed an extra point—an ominous sign for an 8–5–1 season, tied with the upstart Minnesota Vikings for second in the West before the Cleveland Browns surprised the Colts, 27–0, in the championship game. Taylor rushed for 1,169 yards and scored 15 touchdowns, but Hornung had only 415 rushing yards, caught only nine passes, and made only 12 of 38 field goals.

Y. A. TITTLE'S WELL-WORN SHOULDER PADS

Quarterback Y. A. Tittle passed for 33,070 yards and 242 touchdowns during his stellar seventeen-year career (1948–64), most notably with the San Francisco 49ers and New York Giants. The superstitious Tittle wore the same shoulder pads throughout his entire career. These tattered pads are now prominently displayed at the Hall of Fame.

"If a man can catch the ball, he can catch it, and that's all there is to it. Coaching may make him a little better, but not much. It's born to a person. It's innate."

—Lance Alworth

"There's always a place for people who can play. I'll tolerate how you look and what you do if you can play football and help us win."

—Weeb Ewbank

WEEB EWBANK FLANKED BY HIS HALL OF FAME PASS-CATCH DUO

Weeb Ewbank was the only coach to win championships in both the American Football League and National Football League. Ewbank won NFL titles with the Baltimore Colts in 1958 and 1959 and Super Bowl III as head coach of the AFL's New York Jets. Both of Ewbank's championship teams featured Hall of Fame quarterback-receiver combinations. The Colts' passing game starred Johnny Unitas and Raymond Berry, while his Jets offense was led by Joe Namath and Don Maynard.

"I don't really look at it like I'm the greatest receiver. After you play a while anybody can break certain records. Longevity is the key. The record I'm proudest of is being the first guy to get 10,000 yards in receptions. Others may do it, but I'm the first and only one guy that can be the first."

—Don Maynard

"Coach Lombardi is very fair. He treats us all the same way...like dogs."

—Henry Jordan

"Catching a game-winning touchdown is more of a thrill than winning gold medals. You play football for your team, not for yourself."

—Bob Hayes

When the Packers gathered for training camp in 1965, Lombardi had a new kicker-punter: Don Chandler. Hornung struggled until the next-to-last game, when he scored five touchdowns at Baltimore in a 42–27 victory that preserved a Western Conference playoff with the Colts at Lambeau Field.

Injuries had benched Unitas and his backup, Gary Cuozzo, so Tom Matte, usually a halfback, was the Colts' quarterback, with the plays written on his taped forearm. The Colts had a 10–0 halftime lead and Starr was out with battered ribs, but quarterback Zeke Bratkowski guided Hornung's one-yard touchdown and Chandler booted

TOM MATTE'S FAMOUS WRISTBAND

In 1965, after injuries sidelined Baltimore Colts quarterbacks Johnny Unitas and Gary Cuozzo, halfback Tom Matte was pressed into duty as the team's signal caller for the season finale against the Los Angeles Rams. Uncertain about his play-calling ability, Matte had his wife, "who could write real small," create a miniature "cheat sheet" that he attached to his wristband. In a stunning upset, Matte and the Colts defeated the Rams 21–17. The following week, in a playoff game for first place in the Western Conference, the Colts again played tough but were upended 13–10 in overtime by the Green Bay Packers.

a tying 27-yard field goal that the Colts argued was wide right. In overtime, Colts kicker Lou Michaels missed from 47 yards, and the Packers won, 13–10, on Chandler's 25-yarder after 13 minutes, 39 seconds. In the snow-softened championship game a week later, the Packers dominated the Browns, 23–12. Hornung rushed for 105 yards, including a 13-yard touchdown sweep. The defense held Jim Brown to 50 yards in his final game after nine stellar seasons.

The Packers' third NFL title under Lombardi occurred at a historical crossroads in pro football. The American Football League had been around since 1960, but its six championships had been won by teams with quarterbacks the NFL had discarded—the Houston Oilers twice with George Blanda, the Dallas Texans with Len Dawson, the San Diego Chargers with Tobin Rote, the Buffalo Bills twice with Jack Kemp. Early in 1965 the New York Jets' showbiz owner, David "Sonny" Werblin, put together a $427,000 offer over three years that Joe Namath, a whip-armed quarterback out of Alabama, couldn't refuse. For all the millions that the AFL owners had lost in overpaying college stars to build "the other league," Namath's then-stupendous contract, along with the five-year ABC network television deal that Werblin had pursued with NBC, showed that the AFL was here to stay.

> "The idea just hit me while I was flying home from my last attempt to buy the Cardinals. I knew that other cities were interested in getting pro football teams and I decided the answer had to be a new league."
> —Lamar Hunt

RAY NITSCHKE

Linebacker Ray Nitschke, according to Hall of Fame quarterback and teammate Bart Starr, was a "classic example of Dr. Jekyll and Mr. Hyde." Off the field he was a thoughtful, caring person. On the field, he was a ferocious middle linebacker who at times seemed truly to enjoy hitting people. A fierce competitor, Ray was the heart of the great Packers defense of the 1960s.

"It's the only way I can play. After all, I'm not the biggest guy or the strongest guy either. I have to make up for lack of size with aggressiveness. I've always learned that the best way to play the game is to hit your opponent a little harder than he hits you. It's self-preservation."

—Ray Nitschke

Opposite:

SCRAMBLIN' FRAN TARKENTON

Quarterback Fran Tarkenton attracted widespread attention as an exciting scrambler who took plays from sideline to sideline. Add his 3,674 yards rushing to his stunning passing totals and you have 50,677 yards—almost 29 miles—of offensive progression. On this play Tarkenton had good reason to scramble out of the pocket, as two of the game's most ferocious hitters, linebacker Dick Butkus and end Doug Atkins, were in hot pursuit.

"I scramble because I'm good at it, because I can twist and dodge those big pass rushers better than most guys and we get a lot of touchdowns that way....A quarterback has to maintain his cool while a 300-pound pass rusher is firing at him like a Sidewinder missile, and at the last second, before his feet get knocked out from under him, he has to stick that ball right on some receiver's left ear."

—Fran Tarkenton

"I just don't like to get tackled. When that defensive man tackles me, it means he's beaten me. I'm just not going to give up. I'm not going to give him that satisfaction. It's the challenge of the moment. It doesn't matter who the tackler is—or the team. It's me against him. I won't give in; I hate to get beat."

—Jackie Smith

American FOOTBALL LEAGUE

609 FIFTH AVENUE
NEW YORK 17, N.Y.
HA 1-2424

JOE FOSS • COMMISSIONER

December 6, 1963

Mr. Pete Rozelle, Commissioner
The National Football League
1 Rockefeller Plaza
New York, New York

Dear Pete:

Much talking has been done of late by the public and press as
to when the American and National Football Leagues will meet in
a championship game. I feel strongly that the time has arrived
for the inauguration of such an annual game.

Therefore on behalf of the AFL, I re-issue an official challenge
to the NFL for the first game to be played at the conclusion of
the 1964 season with the winners of the respective league divisional
playoffs opposing one another.

The '64 season, as you're well aware, Pete, will be our fifth
year of operation, certainly a sufficient period for our teams
to have achieved a high talent and maturity level.

It was in the exact same year of their existence that the Cleveland
Browns moved from the defunct All-America Conference into the NFL.
The Browns, as you'll recall, quickly proved a representative of
the so-called "neophite league" of that era was more than capable
of holding its own. They won the league title that very first year.

Nevertheless, any argument as to which team would win the initial
AFL-NFL game is of secondary importance. The overriding fact is
the establishment of a World Series of professional football is
necessary to the continued progress of our game if we're to be
true sportsmen and not merely businessmen in sports.

Pro football has now attained the status where many regard it as
our national sport. What could be more fitting then than for us
to match baseball in having an annual classic between the leagues?

BOSTON PATRIOTS • BUFFALO BILLS • KANSAS CITY CHIEFS • DENVER BRONCOS
HOUSTON OILERS • NEW YORK JETS • OAKLAND RAIDERS • SAN DIEGO CHARGERS

Pete Rozelle
National Football League   December 6, 1963
New York, New York

I think now is the time for action rather than talk, Pete, and if
you concur I'll be available to commence arrangements for the game
at your earliest convenience.

Sincerely,

Joe

JOE FOSS
Commissioner

JF:mi

Opposite and left:

A "SUPER" CHALLENGE—
JOE FOSS'S LETTER TO PETE ROZELLE

American Football League Commissioner Joe Foss
sent this letter to NFL Commissioner Pete Rozelle
on December 6, 1963, to "re-issue" the AFL's challenge to
the senior circuit to play an annual championship game
starting at the end of the 1964 season. Foss wrote that
"the time has arrived for the inauguration of such an
annual game." As unlikely as Foss's proposal must
have seemed, he was in fact just three years premature,
as the AFL and NFL met in the first Super Bowl
following the 1966 season.

"Yes, football is a sport, but it is a business too.
A man has to have something to sell not only in
football, but in any profession. The only commodity
I have is my body. I want to make it the best at its
task. I want to be sure the people who come out to
see me get their money's worth. But I do not
become giddy from that roar-of-the-crowd stuff.
I do a lot of work for my self-satisfaction.**"**

—Bob "Boomer" Brown

– 2 –

"It shouldn't take much calculating to decide whether to pay $5 or $50,000 for a seat at a football game. I had just
such a choice a few years back and, contrary to what you might expect of a sane man, I chose the higher-priced seat.
It wasn't that I was interested in the view, but the $50,000 entitled me to any seat in the house; I had finally become
what I had long wanted to be—the sole owner of a pro football team.**"**

—Ralph Wilson Jr.

Opposite:

LINEBACKER SAM HUFF

Because his early NFL tenure was spent with a winning team in high-profile New York, Sam Huff became one of the most publicized players of his day. At the age of twenty-four, he appeared on a *Time* magazine cover. He was the subject of a television special, *The Violent World of Sam Huff*. Almost overnight, he became the symbol of the new glamour era for defensive football. Known for hard-hitting duels with some of the game's greatest running backs, Huff played in six NFL title games and five Pro Bowls and was named to the All-Decade Team of the 1950s.

A MAN'S GAME

Sam Huff excelled as a middle linebacker for thirteen seasons with the New York Giants (1956–63) and the Washington Redskins (1964–67, 1969). He once said, "This is a man's game and any guy who docsn't want to hit hard doesn't belong in it." These are the jersey and shoes Huff wore in his final season with the Giants.

> "Most offensive linemen get themselves in trouble by being too aggressive. They get hit a couple of times and they forget their prime assignment and want to hit back. Then, bang, the defensive man goes by them. An offensive lineman has got to stay in there. Take a beating without committing himself. That's the only way."
>
> —Jim Parker

"I had a style all my own. The way I ran, lurchy, herky-jerky, I kept people off guard so if I didn't have that much power when I hit a man, hell, he was off balance and I could knock him down. If you drew a line straight down the field…I might deviate ten yards on each side of the line. I used more movements to elude tacklers…I used the whole field.**"**

—**Gale Sayers**

GALE SAYERS'S SIX TDS

Chicago Bears halfback Gale Sayers scored a then–NFL record 22 touchdowns in 1965, his rookie season. And in the next-to-last game, playing on a muddy field that would have stalled most runners, Sayers scored an NFL record-tying six touchdowns against the San Francisco 49ers. Included in his sensational spree were an 80-yard pass-run play, a 50-yard rush, and a 65-yard punt return. Sayers's six-touchdown performance tied Chicago Cardinals fullback Ernie Nevers's 1929 touchdown record that still stands today.

The AFL's impact was reflected in a Louis Harris survey in October 1965 when sports fans chose pro football (41 percent) as their favorite sport, jumping over baseball (38 percent) for the first time. Tired of paying more and more expensive rookie contracts, the NFL and AFL realized that it was time to stop cutting each other's financial throats.

After a series of secret meetings between representatives of both leagues, the merger agreement was announced on June 8, 1966: while the leagues would maintain separate schedules through 1969, the first AFL-NFL Championship Game (soon known as the Super Bowl) would be played in January 1967; the first combined draft would be held in 1967; regular-season games involving at least twenty-six teams would begin in 1970, when the two leagues would officially merge

to form an expanded NFL with two conferences, American and National. Rozelle was named commissioner. Al Davis, briefly the AFL commissioner, who had been the coach and general manager of the Oakland Raiders, rejoined the Raiders.

In Green Bay, Lombardi had a new challenge. If his Packers were to be champions again, they not only had to win the NFL title, they also had to win the Super Bowl against whichever team came out of the AFL. They roared through the season with a 12–2 record. Starr threw 14 touchdown passes, and only three interceptions.

WELCOME TO THE NFL

On September 2, 1966, Miami Dolphins running back Joe Auer returned the opening kickoff of the Dolphins' inaugural game 95 yards for a touchdown against the Oakland Raiders. The following year New Orleans Saints wide receiver John Gilliam took the opening kickoff in his team's inaugural game 94 yards for a touchdown against the Los Angeles Rams.

"Football as a team game demands sacrifice and discipline. You've got to think of the guy playing next to you and try to help him. To do that you have to sacrifice. You have to give yourself to your teammates. You have to discipline yourself in order to sacrifice."

—Jim Otto

PETE GOGOLAK HELPS BRING PEACE

In 1964 Cornell kicker Pete Gogolak became the first soccer-style kicker in pro football when he signed to play for the American Football League's Buffalo Bills. Following the 1965 season, he again made news when he signed a contract with the New York Giants of the rival NFL. The Giants' signing of Gogolak caused an escalation of attempts by both leagues to "steal" each other's star players. The practice proved costly for both leagues and eventually contributed to the decision to seek peace through a merger. This is the nameplate that was removed from Gogolak's Bills jersey after he signed with the Giants.

JIM BROWN

When Cleveland Browns fullback Jim Brown retired in 1965 he was at the top of his game. After just nine seasons, he held every major rushing record. More than just a one-dimensional running back, Brown caught passes, returned kickoffs, and even threw three touchdown passes. His then–career record of 12,312 rushing yards and 15,459 combined net yards put him in a class by himself. Brown, the NFL's Rookie of the Year in 1957 and MVP in 1957, 1958, and 1965, is still regarded by many as the game's greatest running back.

> "I'm the best defensive end around. I'd hate to have to play against me!"
> —David "Deacon" Jones

PEN USED BY LYNDON JOHNSON TO SIGN LEGISLATION THAT ALLOWED MERGER OF AFL AND NFL

President Lyndon B. Johnson used this pen on November 8, 1966, at the signing ceremony for Public Law 89-800, the Suspension of Credit Act, which carried a rider approving the merger of the American and National football leagues.

Public Law 89–800

THE SUSPENSION OF CREDIT ACT WHICH CARRIED A RIDER APPROVING
THE MERGER OF THE NATIONAL FOOTBALL LEAGUE AND
THE AMERICAN FOOTBALL LEAGUE

This pen, used by the President of the United States at the formal signing of the above-mentioned public law on November 8, 1966, was presented to Pete Rozelle, Commissioner of the National Football League, by Congressmen Bates, Boland, and O'Neill of Massachusetts

"When you're on the field, you have to concentrate 100 percent....This tough reputation I'm supposed to have represents a different part of football. You have to have enough pride to want to be the best. When no one completes any passes on your side or runs your hole, that gives you a better feeling than what someone says about you in a book."

—Dave Wilcox

"I don't think age makes any difference when you're a quarterback....Heck, if a quarterback is with the right team, he could play at sixty. The secret to quarterbacking is not throwing passes but play selection, reading defense, and motivating the team. There are plenty of guys around who can really throw the ball but don't make it because they don't have those other qualities."

—George Blanda

COIL RECOIL

The yellow coil is a segment of the special heating system installed under the Lambeau Field turf, designed to prevent the ground from freezing. However, the system couldn't withstand Green Bay's minus-13-degree temperature and failed.

LOMBARDI'S LAST GAME AT LAMBEAU FIELD

This bench was used by Green Bay Packers coach Vince Lombardi during the December 31, 1967, NFL Championship Game, the last game Lombardi coached at Lambeau Field. In what has become known as the "Ice Bowl," the Packers defeated the Dallas Cowboys 21–17 on a last-minute one-yard quarterback sneak by Bart Starr.

Player bench from last game Vince Lombardi coached at Lambeau Field. Green Bay, Dec. 31, 1967

RAYMOND BERRY'S BALTIMORE COLTS UNIFORM

Baltimore Colts end Raymond Berry and quarterback Johnny Unitas formed one of pro football's most productive pass-catch duos. Together they led the Colts to four playoff appearances and two NFL championships between 1958 and 1965. Berry, known for running precise routes, caught a then-record 631 passes for 9,275 yards and 68 touchdowns during his thirteen-year career.

❝I came into the league without any fuss. I'd just as soon leave it that way. There's no difference I can see in retiring from pro football or quitting a job at the Pennsy Railroad. I did something I wanted to do and went as far as I could go.❞

—Johnny Unitas

❝If you don't get hurt, you haven't played. As long as I can remember you always paid for what you got in football. It never has changed and it never will.❞

—Larry Wilson

❝You have to recognize that you are going to get beaten once in a while. You just can't dwell on it. You just have to concentrate on not letting the same man beat you again.❞

—Herb Adderley

HERB ADDERLEY

QUESTION: When you were told by Lombardi that he planned to switch you from a running back to defensive back, as a first-round pick were you surprised, and what do you think motivated him to make the move?

ADDERLEY: My first year, I was asked to play the left corner in the second half in Detroit against the Lions because it was an emergency situation....My second year, I received a call from Coach Lombardi informing me that the left corner was my position. Yes, I was surprised, and happy about the move, because I wanted to play....Lombardi was motivated to make the switch for two reasons: he told me that I was too good of an athlete to be sitting on the bench, and number two, Jim Taylor and Paul Hornung were future Hall of Fame running backs.... That fact gave me little or no chance to replace either one...the move to defense was a great move for me, and for the Green Bay Packers.

Elijah Pitts, often inserted for Hornung, scored 10 touchdowns. They retained the NFL title, 34–27, in Dallas when safety Tom Brown intercepted Cowboys quarterback Don Meredith's frantic fourth-down pass in the end zone. But in Super Bowl I at the Los Angeles Memorial Coliseum, they now had to oppose the Kansas City Chiefs, 31–7 winners in Buffalo on Dawson's two touchdown passes and a 72-yard interception return by safety Johnny Robinson.

To uphold the honor of the much older NFL, Lombardi and the Packers knew they had to win. At halftime, the Chiefs were down by only 14–10, but after a tongue-lashing by Lombardi, the Packers took charge. Willie Wood intercepted Dawson's tipped pass and hurried 50 yards to set up the first of Pitts's two touchdowns. Wide receiver Max McGee, out all night in defiance of Lombardi's curfew because he had caught only four passes all season and didn't expect to play, snatched Starr's 37-yard touchdown pass as the injured Boyd Dowler's replacement in the first half and later snared a 13-yard touchdown. He was a star, if not the MVP of the 35–10 triumph. Starr took the MVP.

For Lombardi, most of the postgame questions concerned the two leagues' relative strength. "Their defensive backs are weak," he said, "weaker than I thought they'd be. That's where we beat them. They also didn't have enough depth." After a pause, he added, "I don't think Kansas City compares with the top teams in the NFL. Dallas is a better team. There, you made me say it. Now I've said it."

SUPER BOWL I

The Green Bay Packers earned the right to represent the NFL in the first AFL-NFL World Championship Game. The AFL's representative was the Kansas City Chiefs. In a one-sided affair, Lombardi's veteran team proved to be too much for Kansas City, crushing the Chiefs 35–10. Proving it wasn't a fluke, the Packers repeated as world champions the next year, defeating the Oakland Raiders 33–14.

"You've got to do your best against the man opposite you on every play. You're less than a man if you let this guy win a battle when he shouldn't."

—Willie Davis

"SUPER BOWL": THE NAME

Kansas City Chiefs owner Lamar Hunt didn't create the Super Bowl but he did give the game its name. Hunt offered the name "Super Bowl" after a toy he'd seen his children play with called a Super Ball. Although the name was not immediately adopted—the first two games were officially referred to as the AFL-NFL World Championship Game—this photo shows how the name was already gaining acceptance, as it was spelled out on the sidelines during the halftime show of the first AFL-NFL Championship Game.

"You got to enjoy punishment, because you are going to deliver so much of it, and you are going to get so much of it. That's why you have to pay your dues on the practice field. If you are prepared you don't really feel the punishment during the game."

—Jim Taylor

SUPER BOWL MVP BART STARR

During his sixteen-season career, Green Bay Packers quarterback Bart Starr led his team to six division and five NFL titles, and two Super Bowl victories. The poised precision passer earned game MVP honors in both Super Bowl I and Super Bowl II. Starr wore this jersey in Super Bowl I, in which he completed 16 of 23 passes for 250 yards and two touchdowns.

JIM TAYLOR SCORED FIRST RUSHING TD IN SUPER BOWL HISTORY

Fullback Jim Taylor, who gained more than 1,000 yards in five straight seasons (1960–64), wore this jersey during the 1966 season, his last with the Green Bay Packers. In Super Bowl I—his final game with the team—Taylor ran for 56 yards and scored the first rushing touchdown in Super Bowl history.

> **"**Determination probably was my trademark. I was talented, but so were a lot of people. I'd like people to tell you I was the toughest guy they ever played against.**"**
>
> —**Willie Wood**

BOB DEE'S BOSTON PATRIOTS HELMET

Defensive end Bob Dee retired from pro football after just two seasons with the Washington Redskins. Then he heard about the new American Football League and decided to return to the game. In 1960 he signed with the AFL's Boston Patriots. Dee scored the AFL's first touchdown when he recovered a fumble in the end zone in a preseason game against the Buffalo Bills on July 30, 1960. Dee wore this helmet for 107 consecutive games before giving it up just before his final retirement in 1967.

As the 1967 season approached, Lombardi had another opportunity to accomplish what had only been accomplished once before—by this same franchise—win three consecutive NFL championships. Aging and retooled, the Packers hurried to a 9–2–1 start before losses to the Rams and the Steelers created a Western Conference playoff with the Rams in Milwaukee, their three-game home in that era. They prevailed, 28–7, as linebacker Dave Robinson blocked a 24-yard field goal try, Travis Williams scored two touchdowns, and Starr, who completed 17 of 23 passes, found Carroll Dale for a 17-yard touchdown.

For the second straight year, the Packers' opponent in the NFL title game would be the Cowboys, who in the Eastern playoff had routed the Browns, 52–14. This time the site was Green Bay, where the temperature at kickoff was 13 degrees *below* zero, the wind chill

"Every football game is mental. Winning or losing often depends upon the mental approach of the team.... I try and get myself 100 percent right mentally for *every* game. That way I don't have to 'psych up' for any particular game.**"**

—Billy Shaw

"I always wanted to take an organization and make it the best in sports. I admired the New York Yankees of George Weiss for their power, intimidation, fear, and big people. I admired the Brooklyn Dodgers under Branch Rickey for their speed and player development. I felt there was no reason the two approaches couldn't be combined into one powerful organization.**"**

—Al Davis

DICK BUTKUS'S HELMET, 1969
Nicknamed "the Maestro of Mayhem," middle
linebacker Dick Butkus wreaked havoc on
opposing offenses. A hard-hitting instinctive
player, Butkus racked up a then-record 25
fumble recoveries and 22 interceptions during
a nine-year career with the Chicago Bears
that was cut short by a serious knee injury.

was 46 degrees below, and the game would be frozen forever in history as the Ice Bowl.

Lombardi had installed an $80,000 blanket of electric heating
coils under Lambeau Field to keep the grass relatively soft, but the
system failed. The grass was slick, if not icy in spots. Lombardi told
his players, "No gloves if you handle the ball," and two without gloves,
Starr and Dowler, combined for eight-yard and 46-yard touchdowns
before George Andrie's seven-yard fumble return and Danny Villa-
nueva's 21-yard field goal narrowed the Packers' halftime lead to
14–10. In the fourth quarter Dan Reeves's option pass to Lance Rentzel
for a 50-yard touchdown put the Cowboys ahead 17–14, but with 4
minutes, 50 seconds remaining, Starr and the Packer offense trotted
out to their 32-yard line.

"I've got to be a jump ahead. I like to do things on reaction. I don't like
to wait and think. If you do that you're always late."

—Bobby Bell

"I don't look at myself as an innovator. I look at myself as a coach who is
striving desperately to win....Every head coach has to be a dictator...
my only concern is doing it my way and winning."

—Hank Stram

"There's only one thing I've ever
wanted to do. Play pro football.
Everyone seems to be made for
something, and I've always felt that
playing football was the thing I was
supposed to do. I love the game
and I don't want to get out of it.
If anything happened where I
couldn't play pro ball, I don't know
what I'd do. I'd support my wife
doing something, but I sure
wouldn't be happy."

—Dick Butkus

"All I ask my blockers is four seconds. I try to stay on my feet and try not to be forced out. Any time they make me do something I'm second best at, they're defeating me. I beat people by throwing, not running. And I won't let them intimidate me."

—Sonny Jurgensen

"The defenseman, he's at a disadvantage. If he tries to cover me man-to-man, that is unheard of. I'm not bragging about my ability. All I'm saying is, there's a lot of field out there for him to cover. I'm not a cocky individual. I'm confident, but you have to go out there confident. If you come hesitating, that defenseman, he has you in his back pocket. You got to aim at him with authority, make him worry about you, and not you worry about him. You can't do anything in your life if you don't go at it with confidence."

—Bobby Mitchell

"I'm like a guy packing a lunch and going to work. A ditch-digger breaks up clods of dirt, but he doesn't do it because he hates dirt. He's just got a job to do. I generally approach football the same way. But I have discovered that if I can play the game in an angry mood, I play better."

—Ron Mix

WILLIE LANIER'S UNUSUAL HELMET

Kansas City Chiefs linebacker Willie Lanier, nicknamed "Contact" for his hard-hitting style, wore this unusual helmet that includes extra padding on the outside shell designed to help absorb the impact of his hits on opponents. Lanier, a perennial all-league performer, was the defensive star in the Chiefs' upset win over the Minnesota Vikings in Super Bowl IV.

DALLAS'S "DOOMSDAY DEFENSE"

Defensive tackle Bob Lilly was the first-ever draft choice of the Dallas Cowboys and the foundation for the team's great defensive unit that became known as the "Doomsday Defense." During his fourteen seasons with the Cowboys (1961–74), Lilly played in five NFL/NFC title games and two Super Bowls.

"I continually remind myself that the one thing I must be careful not to do is try too hard. When I relax, stay cool, and think of what I have to do on every play I find things work out a whole lot better than getting sentimental or inspirational."

—Lenny Moore

"I don't try to think about replacing Jim Brown. When I was sitting on the bench two years, I used to compare myself to the backs that were starting around the league and I knew I was as good as most of them. I just want to be one of the best backs in the league, not a superman like Jim Brown was."

—Leroy Kelly

" Let me stress that I've never intentionally made a dirty play in my life, because this is the way I like to live. But if you come near me and you're not in the pattern and I have a chance to hit you—I'm gonna hit you. I think it's half of survival on the corner. You've got to make them conscious of you. Because if he can run his route unimpeded, go down there and set you up—he's gonna kill you. "

—Dick LeBeau

" I'm convinced I'm better than anybody else. I've been convinced of that for quite a while. I haven't seen anything out there that I couldn't do and do well....I get annoyed with myself for doing something wrong....I tell myself, 'You're the best, damn it, do it right.' "

—Joe Namath

JOE NAMATH

Plagued by knee injuries throughout much of his career, quarterback Joe Namath wore this custom-made knee brace during the New York Jets' storybook 1969 season that concluded with a 16–7 victory over the Baltimore Colts in Super Bowl III. Although the Colts were favored by as many as 20 points, Namath brashly guaranteed a Jets victory. The Jets' win is remembered as one of the biggest upsets in all sports.

"This is it," Starr said. "We're going in."

Starr threw to halfback Donny Anderson for six yards, fullback Chuck Mercein, who had rushed for only 56 yards after his midseason signing, ran for seven, and Starr hit Dowler for 13. After Anderson slipped for a nine-yard loss, Starr found him for 12 and nine, then hit Mercein for 19. Mercein ran for eight to the three-yard line. Anderson plunged to the one for a first down. Anderson again, no gain. Time out, 20 seconds left. Anderson again, inside the one. Time out, 16 seconds. Starr hurried to the sideline to confer with Lombardi, but a tying field goal was not considered.

"Run it," Lombardi ordered, "and let's get the hell out of here."

In the huddle, Starr called, "Thirty-one wedge and I'll carry the ball," between right guard Jerry Kramer and center Ken Bowman. At the snap, Starr moved behind Kramer's block on Cowboy tackle Jethro Pugh and crawled into the end zone. Touchdown. Don Chandler added the extra point. Packers, 21–17.

On to Super Bowl II against the Oakland Raiders and several future Hall of Famers that Al Davis had assembled: center Jim Otto, tackle Art Shell, guard Gene Upshaw, wide receiver Fred Biletnikoff, cornerback Willie Brown, and kicker George Blanda. But that week

Jets Give AFL First Super Bowl Win, 16-7

Joe Guaranteed It

TOTAL FIRST DOWNS	Jets	Colts
First downs rushing	21	18
First downs passing	13	7
First downs by penalty	10	9
TOTAL YARDS	1	2
No. offense plays	337	324
Avg. gain per play	74	64
NET RUSHING YARDS	4.5	5.1
Total rushing plays	142	143
NET PASSING YARDS	43	23
Gross yds gained passing	195	181
Yards lost attempt. pass	206	181
PASSES	0-11	0-0
Avg. gain per pass	20-17-0	41-17-J
PUNTS	6.4	4.4
	4-38.8	3-44.3
FUMBLES	1	1
PENALTIES	5-28	3-23
TOTAL RETURN YARDS	24	139
No. & Yds. punt ret.	1-0	4-34
No. & Yds kickoff ret.	1-25	4-103
No. & Yds interrept. ret.	4-9	0-0
No. & Yds. misc. ret.	0	0

By LUTHER EVANS
Herald Sports Writer

The world will listen the next time Broadway Joe Namath guarantees the New York Jets will win a football game.

The sideburned superswinger became a super prophet Sunday by quarterbacking the New York Jets to a 16-7 victory over Baltimore in the third annual Super Bowl.

Just Thursday night at the Miami Touchdown Club, the cocky 25-year-old had stood on a podium, a double shot of Scotch on the rocks in his right hand, and pledged: "The Jets will win Sunday . . . I guarantee it."

The world laughed.

An astounded Orange Bowl

crowd of 75,377, — including moon-flight astronauts Frank Borman, Jim Lovell and Bill Anders — saw the Jets ascend the pinnacle of pro football on Namath's arm, Jim Turner's toe, Matt Snell's legs and four interceptions.

Namath's precision passes set up a four-yard touchdown run by Snell in the second quarter and three subsequent field goals by Turner, world champion kicker.

Turner booted a 32-yard field goal in the third quarter, connected on a 30-yarder later in the period, and was

true with nine-yard effort early in the fourth quarter.

That was sufficient to earn the Jets $15,000 each while forcing the Colts to settle for $7,500 each.

Long before Jerry Hill cracked the final yard off left tackle for the Colt TD, even

Sore-armed Johnny Unitas had to come off the bench as Earl Morrall's replacement to lead the National Football League champions on a shutout-averting 80-yard touchdown drive with just 3:19 remaining.

Namath may have been wrong when he boldly said there were four or five quarterbacks in the American Football League better than Earl Morrall. He proved Sunday there is at least one such in the AFL — Joe Namath.

such avid Colt fans as Vice-President-elect Spiro T. Agnew and Bob Hope faced up to one fact:

On put-up or shut-up day, the magnificent lip — provided fantastic protection by the Jets' line — completed 17 of 28 passes for 206 yards and did not suffer a single interception.

In the "inferior" AFL, the defensive secondaries are supposed to be the most inferior of all phases. Hah!

The Jets intercepted three Morrall passes and picked off one of Unitas' heaves, All

three thefts against Morrall came with the Colts threatening — by Randy Beverly in the end zone, Johnny Sample at the Jets' two-yard line and Jim Hudson at the Jets' 11.

No wonder when the startling game ended, a stunned NFL writer held his head in his hands and mumbled, "I wonder how a whole week of stories (all wrong) will taste."

Fullback Snell, the first man which Baltimore's game plan said must be stopped, was seldom contained by the

Turn to Page 6D, Col. 1

the Packers' Pro Bowl guard, Jerry Kramer, who would collaborate with writer Dick Schaap on their classic book *Instant Replay*, had a hunch that Lombardi was about to retire.

With the Packers holding a 16–7 halftime lead, Kramer told his teammates, "Let's win this for the old man." They did, 33–14, for a record-tying third consecutive NFL championship that more than justified Green Bay's nickname of "Titletown."

Weakened by an arthritic hip and digestive problems, Vince Lombardi soon announced that he would no longer coach the Packers but would remain as general manager. Under Phil Bengtson, who had been Lombardi's defensive coordinator, the Packers slipped to 7–5–2 as the Colts rolled to a 13–1 record, eliminated the Vikings, 24–14, and the Browns, 34–0, in the playoffs, and rolled into Super Bowl III as a 17-point favorite over the AFL champion Jets. Longtime NFL loyalists smirked at Joe Namath, the shaggy-haired quarterback who guaranteed an upset, but before that 1968 season Lombardi had unusually positive words for him.

"His arm, his release of the ball are just perfect," Lombardi said. "Namath is as good a passer as I've ever seen. My judgment has to be limited because I haven't had any personal contact with him, and with a quarterback, personal contact is the most important thing, but from what I've seen on the films, he's a perfect passer."

"JOE GUARANTEED IT": SUPER BOWL III

At a Thursday night banquet just three days before Super Bowl III, Joe Namath stepped to the speaker's podium and announced, "The Jets will win Sunday… I guarantee it." When Namath and the Jets delivered a 16–7 win over the Baltimore Colts, the stature and credibility of the rival AFL reached the same level as the established NFL. The Super Bowl, a mismatch the first two years, suddenly had new meaning.

> **" I've always wanted to be a super ballplayer, always wanted to be a star. I want to be the best in this league and that's what I work on. "**
> **—Carl Eller**

Opposite:

LOMBARDI'S PACKER SWEEP

"At that time I was the first player from a small black school drafted in the first round. It said a lot for the Gramblings, the Prairie Views, and all the other black colleges. It was important for me to be picked in that round, at the very beginning."

—Buck Buchanan

"My job was not catching passes. My job was to stop the receiver from catching it. If I could have played fifteen or twenty years without an interception, that would have been fine. Anything beyond stopping a receiver, that's gravy."

—Willie Brown

Perfect was not a word Lombardi often used about anybody or anything, but Joe Namath was as perfect as a quarterback could be: 17 completions in 28 passes for 206 yards and no interceptions in Coach Weeb Ewbank's ball-control offense that smothered the Colts, 16–7, and justified the AFL's maturity. The Kansas City Chiefs, with seven future Hall of Famers (coach Hank Stram, Dawson, defensive tackle Buck Buchanan, linebackers Willie Lanier and Bobby Bell, cornerback Emmitt Thomas, and kicker Jan Stenerud), stunned the Vikings, 23–7, in Super Bowl IV after Lombardi, who admitted having "missed the fire on Sunday," returned in 1969 as the Washington Redskins' executive vice president, general manager, and coach.

The Redskins improved to 7–5–2 with rookie running back Larry Brown, whom Lombardi discovered had a hearing problem when signals were called. "Get this young man a hearing aid," he ordered. Brown thrived, leading the NFL with 1,125 rushing yards in 1970, a season that Lombardi never saw. Ravaged by cancer, he died on September 3, 1970. He was fifty-seven. Including the postseason, he had a career 105–35–6 record as the Packers' head coach. The Super Bowl trophy would be named the Lombardi Trophy and his influence would endure for decades. When Larry Brown was on his way in 1972 to leading the NFL in rushing again, he was asked how George Allen, then the Redskins' coach, had helped him. "Lombardi made me," Brown snapped.

Just as Lombardi made the '60s.

"I thought I knew a lot of football by that time *[entering the pros]*. But once I got in the NFL, I found out I really didn't know very much at all. There are things you learn in the NFL, such as what defenses do, how an individual player reacts, where every man should be at a given time, that you don't even think about in college."

—Mike Ditka

"I think catching passes is judgment, mostly. I've got good vision; good peripheral vision. I think sometimes I can see things the defensive back doesn't see. I watch for him to make his move—you've got to study the guys in this league—and if he's a fraction late compensating for mine, then I've got him beat. When you've got the jump, size doesn't matter."

—Tommy McDonald

"A man has to figure out what has to be done and how to do it. You have to be able to spin out of a block, recognize a play immediately, and then react accordingly. I figure I'm as strong as anyone else; so getting the job done becomes a matter of pride and determination."

—Bob Lilly

❝I don't look at someone and think that he can't beat me. If you play long enough, you're going to get beat. The question and the key to your effectiveness is how often.❞

—Jimmy Johnson

❝I want the respect of my teammates. Would you believe that we *[linemen]* sit and grade each other? And I don't think there are too many of us underpaid.❞

—Gene Hickerson

❝Why do I play pro football? I guess the main reason is I always wanted to do it. I enjoy doing it. I enjoy the competitiveness of it. I enjoy the money we make.❞

—Len Dawson

The 1970s
DEFENSE WINS CHAMPIONSHIPS

RICK GOSSELIN

J oe Greene was in the stands for the first Super Bowl of the 1970 decade. He was on the field for the last one. In between, he witnessed the defensive metamorphosis of professional football.

THE 1960s WAS THE golden era of quarterbacking in the NFL. There are twenty-three modern-era passers in the Pro Football Hall of Fame, and more than half of them took snaps in the 1960s. NFL MVPs Johnny Unitas, Bart Starr, Norm Van Brocklin, and Y. A. Tittle were among the dozen Hall of Fame quarterbacks who performed during that decade. Fellow MVPs and Hall of Fame runners Jim Brown, Jim Taylor, and Paul Hornung joined them on NFL fields.

The AFL also arrived on football's landscape in the 1960s and carved out its own offensive niche with a swashbuckling, bombs-away style. The league produced its own stable of Hall of Fame quarterbacks in George Blanda, Len Dawson, Bob Griese, and Joe Namath. Not surprisingly, the first four Super Bowl MVPs in the 1960s were all quarterbacks.

So the decade was all about offense. It was about the power sweep of Vince Lombardi, the two-minute drill of Johnny Unitas, and the vertical stretch of Al Davis. But this was all about to change, quickly and dramatically, in that very first game of the 1970 decade—Super Bowl IV on January 11, 1970.

Greene attended the game that day as another face in the crowd of 80,000. He had just finished his rookie NFL season. This was before he ever played in a Pro Bowl. Before his celebrated Coca-Cola commercial. Before he truly became "Mean" Joe Greene. On this day he was simply Joe Greene, fan of football.

The NFL champion Minnesota Vikings wheeled into Tulane Stadium on Super Sunday with the highest-scoring offense in all of

Opposite:

STEEL CURTAIN

The Pittsburgh Steelers' "Steel Curtain" defense lived up to its name in Super Bowl IX. "Mean Joe" Greene and company held the Minnesota Vikings' running game to just 17 yards and the offense to just 119 total yards. Vikings quarterback Fran Tarkenton, who was under constant pressure from Greene, Ernie Holmes, Dwight White, and L. C. Greenwood, was sacked for a safety and completed just 11 passes for an average of less than four yards per completion as the Steelers won 16–6.

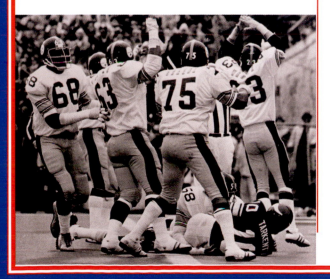

"There's no imagination….Every game is a carbon copy of the next…the creativity has gone out of football because too many coaches are lazy. What I'm talking about is research. I'm talking about getting into the fiber of the game….I'm the curious sort… discovery, that's something that really excites me. People always ask me why I look at football films so long. It's because every time I look at them I see a new thing. You look at the same film twenty times and then, bang, something jumps out at you."

—Chuck Noll

football—even higher than the pass-crazy juggernauts of the AFL. Pro Bowl quarterback Joe Kapp orchestrated a Minnesota attack that averaged 27.1 points per game—offensive might that established the Vikings as a two-touchdown favorite over the AFL champion Kansas City Chiefs.

But the Chiefs brought their own muscle, one that no Super Bowl has seen before or since. *Defensive muscle.* The Chiefs remain the only Super Bowl team in history to lead a league across the board in defense—running, passing, scoring, and total defense. They lined up future Hall of Famers at all three levels: tackle Buck Buchanan, linebackers Bobby Bell and Willie Lanier, and cornerback Emmitt Thomas.

Kansas City's four-man line of Buchanan, Curley Culp, Aaron Brown, and Jerry Mays averaged 6'4", 267 pounds across. Minnesota's offensive line averaged 6'2", 249. The Chiefs brutalized the smaller Vikings up front and harassed Kapp all afternoon, sacking him three times, forcing him to scramble on two other occasions, causing a fumble, and finally knocking him from the game in the fourth quarter with a shoulder injury. The Kansas City defense forced four turnovers and the Chiefs steamrolled the Vikings, 23–7.

The adage, "Offense sells tickets, defense wins championships," did not originate with that Super Bowl. But the Chiefs provided an exclamation point with their performance against the Vikings.

Greene heard that adage from Steelers coach Chuck Noll during his rookie season. That was a key reason Pittsburgh spent a first-round draft pick on Greene. Noll wanted a defense—a defense like the Chiefs'. He wanted to win championships.

VINCE LOMBARDI'S FUNERAL

Solemnity and sadness marked the faces of Paul Hornung, Bart Starr, and Willie Davis as they stood together outside the church following the funeral mass of their friend and coach Vince Lombardi, who died on September 3, 1970, at the age of fifty-seven.

KICKING THEIR WAY INTO HISTORY

On November 8, 1970, Tom Dempsey, who was born without toes on his right (kicking) foot, kicked his way into the NFL record book when he connected on a 63-yard field goal attempt to give his New Orleans Saints a last-second victory over the Detroit Lions. On October 25, 1998, Denver Broncos kicker Jason Elam matched Dempsey's long-standing mark with a 63-yarder against the Jacksonville Jaguars. Oakland's Sebastian Janikowski also kicked a 63-yarder in 2011.

ALAN PAGE'S MINNESOTA VIKINGS JERSEY

Minnesota Vikings defensive tackle Alan Page was named the NFL's MVP in 1971 and the NFL Defensive Player of the Year in 1971 and 1973. A nine-time first- or second-team All-NFL choice, Page was also elected to nine consecutive Pro Bowls. Page was not only a student of the game, but attended law school while playing and now serves on the Minnesota Supreme Court.

"I play for myself. The team is second. But if every individual does the best he can do, within the confines of what the team wants done, that's got to go a long way toward making the team better."

—Alan Page

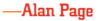

"All I'm interested in is knocking people off their feet and making them respect me. When those number 20s and 30s show up in front of me, I sorta feel good. I know they're defensive backs and probably 50 or 60 pounds smaller than me. If I hit them hard enough, the next time they might give ground and it'll make the job easier."

—Larry Little

"In my case, I'd say speed is my strong point. Some are faster, but I can run as fast sideways as I can straight ahead, which few can. I can accelerate fast and shift speeds smoothly. I'm small, but that helps me to hide. I mean it. I'm hard to spot behind big linemen. Also, it's hard to get down to my legs, which is the only place to bring me down. I'm strong, I have good balance, and I make good use of my arms, which I swing to break tackles. I run skittery, like a mouse eluding a cat. I can't explain my moves. I don't think any good runner can. I can't copy anyone. I don't know what I'm doing until I do it, then I can never repeat it. It's some kind of instinct."

—Floyd Little

"Those who evaluated me never thought I was as good as I thought I was. You see, I came into pro football with a heckuva purpose. I looked upon it as a helluva challenge to prove something. Being the first black middle linebacker placed me in an unusual position."

—Willie Lanier

"I thought Kansas City would win that ball game because of their defense," Greene said. "That was the first great defense. We tried to emulate the Chiefs."

The Chiefs ushered in a new era of football—defensive football. Nicknames were spawned and dynasties launched.

Doomsday arrived in Dallas. Miami thrived with a bunch of No Names. Pittsburgh erected a Steel Curtain. Purple People Eaters took the Vikings to three more Super Bowls in the 1970s, and an Orange Crush made the Denver Broncos the toast of the AFC.

The best way to defend against the great quarterbacks of the 1960s was to slow them at the play's start—rush them, harass them, tackle them. Deacon Jones helped the Los Angeles Rams become an elite NFL team and a championship contender by the end of the prior decade with his head-slap on blockers and self-proclaimed "sack" of quarterbacks.

WILLIE LANIER

QUESTION: Being the first black middle linebacker, did you feel an added pressure to succeed?

LANIER: Every moment of my entire career in the NFL I felt the weight of responsibility, being the first black middle linebacker to play the game. The ability to have, what I would say, a pragmatic approach to the game was important, one that was not based on emotion, but having to be based on excellence, the way you performed, a very cool confidence of strategy along with physical play. That's what I thought had to be noted by those who had not allowed a man of my color to play, to recognize that in the management of the position, I was equal to anyone. The physical skills obviously could be there, but the management skills would have to be seen, more than just the physical outcome. The only reason I can see for a head coach getting credit for something good is that he gets so much blame when something is bad. The whole secret, I think, is to not react to either the good or the bad.

MONDAY NIGHT FOOTBALL
Monday Night Football made its debut in 1970. The three-man broadcast team featured commentary by Howard Cosell and Don Meredith and the play-by-play call of Keith Jackson. Jackson was replaced by Frank Gifford the next year.

"It's entertainment. It's no more important, or less important, than any other form of entertainment. It's a business, too, like other forms of entertainment. Some people are getting rich on it, but there's nothing wrong with that."

—Dan Fouts

"The hardest thing will be no more locker rooms. No more Sundays. No more airplanes and training camps. You see each other torn down, angry, happy, injured. You shower with these guys, eat with these guys, sleep with these guys. You don't spend that much time with your wife. You see them hurt. You see them give up everything for you. You really get to love these guys. I know I'll miss that."

—Ken Houston

The notion that defenses could become offensive by chasing quarterbacks gained momentum. Defensive linemen were becoming as valuable a commodity as offensive skill players. The Atlanta Falcons selected defensive end Claude Humphrey from tiny Tennessee State with the third overall selection of the 1968 draft, and the Steelers claimed Greene from even tinier North Texas State with the fourth overall choice of the 1969 draft.

"I don't think of myself as a great all-around athlete who can make contributions in many facets of the game. My role is to make the power running game work. A lot of plays I run are momentum plays. They are not designed for long gains. If you make four or five yards, everyone is happy. It's not a spectacular strategy but I've lived and breathed it and I know it works."

—Larry Csonka

A PERFECT PAIR
IN A PERFECT SEASON

In 1972 the Miami Dolphins became the first NFL team to go undefeated in both the regular season and postseason. Key contributors were fullback Larry Csonka and halfback Mercury Morris. Csonka rushed for 1,117 yards while Morris rushed for 1,000 yards. It was the first time in NFL history that two backs on the same team rushed for 1,000 yards in the same season.

LARRY CSONKA

QUESTION: How did having a receiver like Paul Warfield on the line help the Dolphins' running game?

CSONKA: Well, I think the most positive thing about having a guy like Warfield on the team was that fact he posed such a threat that he was not a guy that the defense could just take lightly and just do a one-on-one or a man coverage on him. He drew fire. In other words, in a third-and-very-short situation the safeties could not risk cheating up and getting on the line in order to help stop a power running game which I was part of. In fact they had to back off, because if Griese, the quarterback, faked to me on the power dive, pulled the ball out, and turned and had a one-on-one situation with Paul, because the defense had safeties up to stop me on the short dive and to help the linebackers stop me, then of course Warfield would be in the one-on-one position to the outside. Several times that worked for us. After teams saw other teams on the films get burnt with that situation, it made the power running game work a little better because there weren't as many men in the box lining up at the line of scrimmage.

RUNNING BACKS IN THE 1970S

In an attempt to encourage more passing, the NFL in 1972 decided to move the hash marks in from 20 yards to 23.5 yards. The result was more running. In fact, that year ten running backs—twice as many as the year before and the most in NFL history to that point—gained more than 1,000 yards. Great runners during the decade included Walter Payton, O. J. Simpson, Franco Harris, Floyd Little, John Riggins, Larry Csonka and, later in the decade, Earl Campbell and Tony Dorsett.

"Our offense is geared to get me into the secondary. Much of my success when I get past the line of scrimmage is based on two factors. One: I'm usually faster than the secondary. Two: I'm usually bigger than they are....I have very good peripheral vision...and I know where everyone is supposed to be."

—O. J. Simpson

O. J. SIMPSON'S RECORD-BREAKING SEASON

O. J. Simpson wore this jersey in the 1973 season finale against the New York Jets. Going into the game, he needed just 60 yards to establish a new NFL single-season rushing record. His 200-yard performance not only gave him the record but also a season total of 2,003.

THE IMMACULATE RECEPTION

Players from both teams and Raiders coach John Madden surround the officials working the 1972 AFC Divisional Playoff Game as they debate whether Franco Harris's catch of a deflected Terry Bradshaw pass was legal and a touchdown. The officials needed to ascertain whether Harris caught the ball before it touched the ground and whether or not the ball had been simultaneously touched by both the intended receiver and the defender, making Harris's catch legal. After a long delay and a phone call from the game referee to the NFL's supervisor of officials seated in the press box, the play stood as initially called—catch and touchdown.

"A player should not be measured by statistics alone. He should be measured by something more special, such as the sharing of team-mates and fans. Both the city of Pittsburgh and the Steeler team were building at the same time. It was a good feeling to be a part of it."

—Franco Harris

"Coaching isn't work. It's more than a job. It's a way of life…no one should go into coaching unless he couldn't live without it….Football is what I am. I didn't go into it to make a living or because I enjoyed it. There is much more to it than just enjoying it. I am totally consumed by football, totally involved. I'm not into gardening…or any other hobbies. I don't fish or hunt. I'm in football."

—John Madden

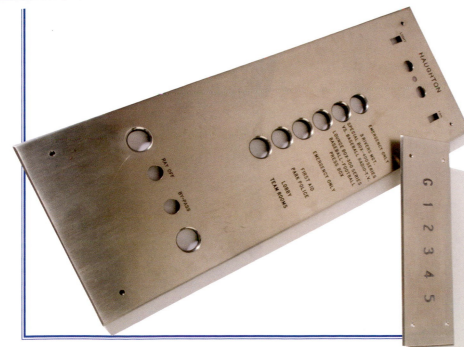

THE IMMACULATE RECEPTION REMEMBERED, THE TURF

This piece of turf was removed from Three Rivers Stadium by Franco Harris from the exact spot where he made his famous "Immaculate Reception" during the closing seconds of the 1972 AFC Divisional Playoff Game. After learning that the turf was scheduled to be re-placed, Harris decided he wanted a keepsake. "I saw in the paper that they were gonna change the turf at Three Rivers Stadium," he recalled. "So I said, 'Hmmm, I should go and get that area where I caught the ball.'" Fortunately, the demo crew had stopped for a break just before reaching the historic spot. "If I had been a few hours later, it would have been totally shredded. So they cut out the area for me," Harris remembered.

ELEVATOR PANEL FROM THREE RIVERS STADIUM

With 22 seconds left in the 1972 AFC Divisional Playoff Game and his team trailing the Oakland Raiders 7–6, Pittsburgh Steelers owner Art Rooney boarded the elevator that would take him to the Steelers' locker room. Expecting to console his team after their close loss, Rooney was stunned to learn, when the elevator doors opened, that his Steelers had somehow won. The Steelers' popular founder/owner missed the most famous play in his team's history, Franco Harris's "Immaculate Reception." This panel was taken from that elevator.

MEAN JOE GREENE

The Pittsburgh Steelers' number one draft pick in 1969, Joe Greene became the cornerstone of the franchise that dominated the NFL in the 1970s. A ten-time Pro Bowl selection, Greene was the NFL Defensive Player of the Year in 1972 and 1974 and a key part of the Steelers' first four Super Bowl championships.

> "I just want people to remember me as being a good player and not really mean. I want to be remembered for playing thirteen years and contributing to four championship teams. I would like to be remembered for maybe setting a standard for others to achieve."
>
> —Joe Greene

> "When I got the confidence from that man *[Coach Chuck Noll]*, that was when I became a pro quarterback. Prior to that, I wasn't making any progress. I knew that when I made mistakes, I was going to be benched. But when he said, 'Go make your mistakes, we're going to win with you,' that's when I became a quarterback."
>
> —Terry Bradshaw

TERRY BRADSHAW UNIFORM

Even though he was the first player selected in the 1970 NFL draft, success in the pro game did not come quickly for Pittsburgh Steelers quarterback Terry Bradshaw. But starting in 1972 he began a reign in which he led his team to four Super Bowl titles. A big-game performer, he was named MVP in Super Bowls XIII and XIV. This is his uniform from his final season, 1983.

In the 1950s, there was only one defensive player taken with the first overall pick of an NFL draft—defensive back Gary Glick by Pittsburgh in 1956. In the 1960s, there were two—linebacker Tommy Nobis by Atlanta in 1966 and defensive tackle Bubba Smith by Baltimore in 1967.

But in the 1970s, five defensive players were selected with the first overall selections of drafts, including three consecutive ends from 1972 to 1974: Walt Patulski in 1972, John Matuszak in 1973, and Ed "Too Tall" Jones in 1974. The Cowboys drafted Jones, then selected tackle Randy White with the second overall choice of the 1975 draft. Tampa Bay followed that up with the selection of end Lee Roy Selmon with the first pick in franchise history and number one overall in the 1976 draft.

Nine Super Bowl champions of the 1970s finished in the NFL's top ten in defense and eight finished in the top five. The 1972 Dolphins, 1974 Steelers, and 1977 Cowboys all won with top-ranked defenses. In addition, the 1973 Dolphins and 1978 Steelers led the NFL in scoring defense on the way to Super Bowl championships. A dominating defense became as vital to the Super Bowl championship equation as a franchise quarterback. And that domination on defense began up front.

The Dallas Doomsday Defense was anchored by Hall of Fame tackle Bob Lilly. The Purple People Eaters were moored by Hall of Famers Carl Eller at end and Alan Page at tackle. And Greene was the keystone of one of the greatest front sevens, defenses, and teams of all time—the 1970s Steelers.

> "I don't see any sense of trying to disprove the image. It doesn't bother me. I feel I play aggressive, but I don't play dirty. I'm not going to pick up opposing players or pat them on the back just to prove I'm a nice guy."
>
> —Jack Lambert

> "I like working hard and I liked doing the little things that would make you good. I loved football. I loved playing it."
>
> —Joe DeLamielleure

JOE DeLAMIELLEURE

JOE DeLAMIELLEURE: My rookie year in Buffalo they brought Paul Seymour and me to Buffalo in March and they were going to give us our physical and time us and all this even though they had already drafted us. Coach Ringo, who was the line coach, said, "I want you guys out in the parking lot," and we were literally in a parking lot at the motel where we trained in Blasdell, New York, and he said, "I'm going to mark off 40 yards and time you guys." So anyhow, I'm looking out in the parking lot watching our equipment man, Tony Marchetti, who's a Danny DeVito look-alike, marking off 40 yards. I didn't think much of it at the time. So we get out there, we're in sweats, heavy sweats—it's cold in March and everything. We're in Converse high-tops. So Ringo is at the other end of the 40 yards with his gym whistle and a cigarette hanging out of his mouth. He says, "Okay, when I blow the whistle you guys take off, we're going to time you." So anyhow he does, and Paul and I both take off and we're running as fast as we can and we think, "Hey, it's going pretty good," so Ringo instead of saying what the times are, he just shouts, "Jesus Christ, look at this." So we look and we're running 4.2 or 4.3 or something like that and Coach, all excited, says, "This is unbelievable." He's all happy and everything, maybe it was a 4.5, I don't remember exactly. But he goes, "You guys are really quick for your size." Then it hit me; I said, "Coach, look at the guy behind us who marked off the field here, Tony Marchetti. He probably had like a 27-inch inseam...so short he probably jumped off couches and chairs. Well, rather than measure the 40 yards, he just paced it off. Anyhow, Ringo measured it and it was 35½ yards. Frustrated and probably a little embarrassed, Ringo said, "Screw it, we already drafted you guys anyway."

SUPER BOWL VII

Even though the Miami Dolphins were 16–0 in the regular season and the playoff games to that point, they were still slight underdogs to the Washington Redskins in Super Bowl VII. Late in the game, with Miami leading 14–0, the Redskins scored on a flubbed pass attempt by kicker Garo Yepremian. Suddenly, with 1:14 remaining, the Dolphins' lead was in jeopardy. Their "No-Name" defense responded with a fourth-down sack of Redskins quarterback Billy Kilmer, preserving the club's perfect season.

All four members of the Pittsburgh defensive line became Pro Bowlers: tackles Greene and Ernie Holmes and ends L. C. Greenwood and Dwight White. Linebackers Jack Ham, Jack Lambert, and Andy Russell joined those linemen at Pro Bowls, and Ham and Lambert would later join Greene in the Pro Football Hall of Fame. So would cornerback Mel Blount.

The Steelers won a record four Super Bowls in the decade, winning back-to-back in 1974–75 and 1978–79. Pittsburgh ranked first in the NFL in defense in 1974, second in 1979, third in 1978, and fourth in 1975. But the Steel Curtain fashioned one of the greatest seasons in NFL annals in 1976, incredibly, in a non–Super Bowl season.

"The important thing is not what Don Shula knows or what any of my assistant coaches know. The important thing is what we can transmit to the people we're responsible for. That's what coaching is—the ability to transmit information."

—Don Shula

"I'm merely a representative of a great defense that doesn't get the recognition it deserves. I take great pride in that. I take great pride in having played for the greatest coach in the history of the game, Don Shula. I take great pride that I'm wearing the only ring in the history of the NFL that signifies we had an undefeated season."

—Nick Buoniconti

The Steelers lost their Hall of Fame quarterback Terry Bradshaw for four games during the season with neck and wrist injuries and could not afford to partake in any offensive shootouts with a backup taking the snaps. If Pittsburgh coveted a Super Bowl three-peat, Bud Carson's defense needed to slam the door shut on opposing offenses—and the Steel Curtain did just that.

The Steelers posted five shutouts in 1976, including three in a row at midseason, and held two other teams to a mere field goal. In all, the 1976 Steelers limited nine of their fourteen opponents to six points or less. Pittsburgh allowed only 138 points—38 fewer than any other team that season.

"It was heartbreaking when teams scored a touchdown on us," Greene said. "Our goal every week was to shut the opponent out. We didn't always accomplish that—but that was our goal. If it was fourth-and-one on the goal line, we'd rather have them go for a touchdown than kick a field goal. It was easier for us to stop a one-yard gain than to prevent a field goal. That was our mentality—we didn't want them to score."

"I think the biggest difference between defensive ends of today and when I played is they have more schemes today. Most of the linemen are specialists, whatever the hell that means. They seem to just want to put more pressure on the quarterback, but the total player or defensive end, I think he has to be tough on both the run and pass. That's the way it was back in my time. You had to play tough in both phases of the game."

—Elvin Bethea

GENE UPSHAW

Gene Upshaw was the first lineman who played guard exclusively to be elected to the Pro Football Hall of Fame. A key component of the Oakland Raiders' dominant decade of the 1970s, Upshaw played in ten AFL/AFC title games, three Super Bowls, and seven Pro Bowls.

"A wide receiver wants to catch a long touchdown pass. A defensive lineman wants to break in to sack a quarterback. I get my satisfaction pulling to lead those sweeps. That's a play where it comes down to just me and the defensive back. If I get him clean, we're going to make a long gain. If I miss him we don't gain a yard. I'm coming right at that defensive back weighing 260. He's 210 at the most and 185 some of the time. And he hasn't got a chance. I've got it in my head that whatever he does has to be wrong. If he goes to the outside, I'm going to put him out of bounds. If he goes inside, I'll knock him in, and if he stands there, man, I'm going right over him."

—Gene Upshaw

"I don't thrive on work. But I know what I have to do on Sunday, and I know what I have to do during the week to be able to do it on Sunday."

—John Riggins

That defensive excellence delivered the Steelers an AFC Central championship. But the Super Bowl express would run aground when the Steelers lost both starting running backs, Franco Harris and Rocky Bleier, with injuries in their playoff opener. Pittsburgh survived Baltimore that day but fell to Oakland, 24–7, in the AFC championship— and the Raiders went on to win the Super Bowl. Eight Steelers from that 1976 defense were selected to the Pro Bowl.

Two decades later, the game-by-game scores of Pittsburgh's 1976 season were pinned to a corkboard in the Valley Ranch office of Cowboys defensive coordinator Dave Wannstedt. That 1976 season served as an inspiration for the Pittsburgh native.

"**The thing about cornerback is you make one mistake and it can be a touchdown. It takes a certain kind of person to play the position. First and foremost, you have to be mentally strong.**"

—**Mel Blount**

"That's how you play defense," Wannstedt said. "That's what a championship defense looks like."

In 1992, Wannstedt coordinated the NFL's number-one-ranked defense and the Cowboys won their first Super Bowl in fifteen years.

But Wannstedt had another role model—a defense that walked those very same corridors at Valley Ranch.

The Dallas Doomsday defense opened the 1970 decade with Hall of Famers Lilly, safety Mel Renfro, and cornerback Herb Adderley in the starting lineup, and finished it with Hall of Fame defensive tackle Randy White and NFL All-Decade selections Harvey Martin and Cliff Harris on the field.

White and Martin shared Super Bowl MVP honors in 1978. Only seven times in Super Bowl history have defensive players taken home game MVP honors, but three of them came in the 1970s. Dallas linebacker Chuck Howley of Doomsday I was named the MVP of the 1971 Super Bowl—the only player from a losing team ever to capture the honor—and Miami safety Jake Scott was named MVP of the 1973 Super Bowl.

"**After having the best seven years in Redskin history, I really couldn't have given more of myself than I gave. I loved the team. I loved the city. I loved the team song.**"

—**George Allen**

GEORGE ALLEN

George Allen never had a losing season as head coach of the Los Angeles Rams and Washington Redskins. Allen's "Future Is Now" philosophy saw him make 131 trades during his career. His fiery enthusiasm for the game and preference for a veteran team endeared him to his players.

GEORGE BLANDA'S 2,000 POINTS

When quarterback/kicker George Blanda retired in 1975 after a twenty-six-year career with four different teams, he was just one month shy of his forty-ninth birthday. At the time of his retirement, his twenty-six seasons and 340 games played were NFL records, as were his 2,002 career points scored. This is the jersey the ageless wonder wore on December 21, 1975, and the ball he kicked that day to become the first player to score 2,000 career points.

> "I don't like the position the defensive lineman is in. I can beat the hell out of him all day long, then once—just once—he slips through and gets the quarterback. There he is, lying on the quarterback, and I'm embarrassed in front of 25 million people. I don't like his having that kind of advantage. The way you combat that is with aggression. I look at the first couple of plays as being of extra importance. In those first few plays, I try to remove any thought my opponent might have had that that was gonna be his day."
>
> **—Dan Dierdorf**

> "As you get older, you look back on your career and realize that you went through your life a lot quicker than a lot of people. You have a lot of failure and success in a matter of minutes on the football field. You've just got to handle it quicker."
>
> **—Fred Biletnikoff**

"SCRAMBLIN' FRAN" TARKENTON

Fran Tarkenton was an elusive scrambling quarterback who picked apart defenses for eighteen seasons with the Minnesota Vikings and New York Giants. At the time of his retirement, Fran owned every significant passing record—3,686 pass completions, 47,003 passing yards, and 342 touchdowns. Tarkenton wore this jersey on December 20, 1975, when he recorded his then-record 291st touchdown pass. The football is the one he threw in a 1976 game against the Chicago Bears to eclipse the all-time passing yardage mark.

The Cowboys had Hall of Fame quarterback Roger Staubach at the start of the decade, plus Hall of Fame running back Tony Dorsett at the finish. But the decade-long constant was the defensive brilliance of the Doomsday.

Six times from 1970 to 1978 the Cowboys held the opposition to 225 points or fewer, including a decade-low 194 in 1976. Even when the NFL went to a sixteen-game schedule in 1978, the Cowboys shined as a shutdown unit, allowing only 208 points on the way to their NFL-record fifth and final Super Bowl of the decade. Eleven different Dallas defenders went to Pro Bowls during the 1970s.

Like the 1977 Cowboys, Miami's No-Name defense allowed the fewest yards in their 1972 championship season. But the Dolphins were dubbed No-Names because the offense seemed to receive all the credit for those three consecutive Super Bowl seasons (1971–73).

Quarterback Bob Griese, fullback Larry Csonka, wide receiver Paul Warfield, and guard Larry Little all would go on to become Pro Football Hall of Famers. Only linebacker Nick Buoniconti gained enshrinement in Canton off that 1972 defense.

The Dolphins pitched six shutouts in those three Super Bowl seasons and a seventh in the 1971 AFC title game. The 1972 Dolphins also became one of only five defenses in history not to allow an offensive touchdown in a Super Bowl. The 1971 Doomsday and 1974 Steel Curtain were two of the others. Yet safety Dick Anderson was the only member of the No-Names selected to the 1970s NFL All-Decade team.

Minnesota's Purple People Eaters established their own tradition of defensive excellence in 1969 when they allowed only 133 points—the low-water point for the NFL in the 1960s. The Vikings also

"I like making All-Pro at cornerback. But I really hate to play it. It's the loneliest job they have."
—Mel Renfro

"When I'm on the sidelines I have to know what eleven men on offense do on every play, what eleven men on defense do on every play, and I've got to be able to tell them what's happening in a game if they're getting beat. I must be completely absorbed in the game. I must be thinking two or three plays ahead all the time as to what's coming. Therefore, I'm not even conscious of crowd response or great plays being made by either team. You can't do that and really concentrate. That's our system, and my system has really made me appear very cold on the sidelines."
—Tom Landry

TOM LANDRY

Noted for his impassive sideline demeanor, coach Tom Landry perfected the flex defense and multiple offense and revived the shotgun formation during his highly successful twenty-nine years at the helm of the Dallas Cowboys.
PHOTO: PAUL MOSELEY/FT. WORTH STAR-TELEGRAM

Opposite:

ROGER STAUBACH GAME ACTION
VS. VIKINGS
With just 24 seconds remaining and trailing 14–10 in the 1975 NFC divisional playoff game against the Minnesota Vikings, Roger Staubach threw what became the most celebrated pass of his career. From midfield, Staubach, aching with sore ribs, unleashed a wobbly pass downfield to wide receiver Drew Pearson, who caught it for the winning score. "It was just a Hail Mary… a very lucky play," Staubach offered in his postgame interview.

Right:

ROGER STAUBACH'S HELMET
FROM HIS FINAL SEASON
Nicknamed "Captain Comeback," Roger Staubach had a knack for snatching his team back from the brink of defeat. During his eleven seasons with the Dallas Cowboys, he orchestrated fourteen victories in the last two minutes or in overtime.

allowed fewer than 200 points in their next three Super Bowl seasons in the 1970s. But Minnesota never returned home with a Lombardi Trophy and that official stamp of greatness for its Purple People Eaters.

Alan Page became the first defensive player in NFL history to capture league MVP honors for the Vikings in 1971. Only one defensive player since then has won the award—linebacker Lawrence Taylor of the New York Giants in 1986. Page was elected to the Hall of Fame in his second year of eligibility.

But the absence of Super Bowl rings worked against the rest of the Minnesota defense. Safety Paul Krause set the NFL record with 81 career interceptions but had to wait fourteen years for that call from Canton. Defensive end Carl Eller, who played in four Pro Bowls in the 1970s and six in his career, waited twenty years for his enshrinement.

"I never thought much about pressure. My preparation gave me confidence. I believe if you work hard good things will happen to you….I believe in myself. Even in Little League, I wanted the ball hit to me for the last out. If you don't have that feeling *[as a quarterback]*, you can't expect the players around you to have it in the tight spots."
—Roger Staubach

"I'm not a believer in the long ball per se. The percentages are not good for the pass receiver or the passer in completing the long pass. If you're going to be successful at the passing game, you're going to have to make your living at the medium-distance to short passes. So many factors come into play with the long ball. You've got to have the arm, the judgment, the protection. Even if the receiver is an Olympic sprinter, it takes nearly four seconds to run 40 yards downfield from a crouch start. No offensive line can protect for that long today."
—Paul Warfield

QUARTERBACK BOB GRIESE

Miami Dolphins quarterback Bob Griese began wearing glasses in 1977 after revealing that he was legally blind in his right eye. On Thanksgiving Day that year, Griese threw six touchdown passes and might have added a record seventh but instead yielded to backup Don Strock to give him needed playing time. "The most unselfish player I've ever been around," Coach Don Shula said of his bespectacled quarterback.

"There is no great mystery to quarterbacking. You move personnel around in various formations, looking for the defense's particular patsy, and then you eat him alive."

—Bob Griese

"It came out in the paper once that I wasn't going to gamble as much as I had previously. It said I would just stick to basic defense. But I don't think I ever changed my style, and I don't think I will either. You have to have one style and stick to that and try to improve on what you're doing."

—Lem Barney

LEM BARNEY

QUESTION: Can you reflect briefly on your transition from college football to the pros? I know you got off to a quick start, but were you surprised and think it was easier than you expected?

BARNEY: Jackson State University was really my training ground for the pros. We had some guys that I played against while at Jackson State that were just phenomenal ballplayers and some of them are HOFers—and I think that Otis Taylor, who played at Prairie View, should be a Hall of Famer. Kenny Houston also played there. Kenny Burrows, a wide receiver, quick as lightning, and at Texas there was also Warren Wells, who played with the K.C. Chiefs. I had the occasion every year while at Jackson State to play against these guys as well as guys from Grambling State University under the tutelage of the great late Eddie Robinson…just some phenomenal athletes there as well. Richard Stebbins, I covered Richard; he ran the third leg on the 4-by-400, 440 relay over in Tokyo with Bob Hayes….Arkansas A&M, they had some phenomenal athletes, as well as Alcorn State University. To sum it up, playing at Jackson State University during practice was just like playing a game. I had guys like Harold Jackson to cover every day and Gloster Richardson. Harold went on to play with the L.A. Rams. Richardson played with the Chiefs. There was Speedy Duncan, who played with the San Diego Chargers, and I had to cover all of these guys along with John Outlaw. And when I got to school in '63 the slowest guy on our team in the 100-yard dash ran 10.5. Most guys were running 9.3 to 9.5 to 9.7 and so I could easily say that playing professionally was the easiest part of my four segments from middle school, high school, college, and the league.

The pros were more intellectual, bringing different plays to the table to work against your gifts and your skills and your talent. I enjoyed it, and I did get off to a quick start, but I truly always felt that I could make it in the pros. I ended up with fifty-six interceptions in the eleven-year career, so I guess I did okay.

[Said in 1981]

"This is a tremendously exciting profession, especially when you win. I've been very fortunate. I've played in two Rose Bowls and four Super Bowls in the last nine years. People say I perform well in the 'big' games. Maybe that's because I have more fun in those games. There is a sameness to the regular season…but when there is no next week, when six months of work is riding on every play and you come through, that's the ultimate. That's the rush we're all in this for."

—**Lynn Swann**

LYNN SWANN BALL

There may never be a more appropriate name for a wide receiver than Lynn Swann. His graceful moves and tremendous leaping ability seemed to defy the laws of physics and defined the skill set desired by future generations of pass catchers. Swann also used his breathtaking talent on the game's biggest stages, as evidenced by his MVP performance in Super Bowl X. The Pittsburgh Steeler had what may have been his best season in 1978 when he pulled in career highs in receptions (61), receiving yards (880), and TDs (11). During that season Swann was awarded this game ball after one of the best performances of his career, in a Monday night game on November 27 against the San Francisco 49ers.

EARL CAMPBELL RECORD FOOTBALL

Houston Oilers running back Earl Campbell joined Jim Brown as only the second player to lead the NFL in rushing in each of his first three seasons. A punishing runner, Campbell carried this football during the 1979 season finale against the Philadelphia Eagles when he notched his second consecutive rushing title and a handful of other single-season records, including most consecutive 100-yard games (seven) and most 100-yard games in a season (11).

"My definition of pressure is struggling to be yourself, and I knew who I was. I worked so hard throughout the week, Sunday was just another day at the office. I couldn't wait to be out there. I just hoped everyone else would show up, too. And when it was over, I quit football. Football didn't quit me."

—**Earl Campbell**

"I know Paul Brown knows how to win. I know that Hank Stram knows how to win. I know Bud Grant knows how to win, and certainly Vince Lombardi knew how to win. They don't necessarily use the same tactics. As a matter of fact, they're probably very different in many ways, but they all have that little something that sets them apart from the other coaches. But to define it would be impossible for me. It's a combination of things. It's their personality, their philosophy as far as life is concerned, the courage of their convictions, and certainly their intelligence in approaching the games. It's a combination of things, and they have it."

—Jim Finks

"Defense is seventy to eighty percent reaction. You can sense when things take place. But you cannot assume. You see something, a tip, and put it to use as an expectation. There's no guarantee this expectation will occur. But it gives you an edge and sometimes that makes a great difference in whether or not you are able to stop a play. To me, defense is perpetual motion; you've got one primary objective: get to the football."

—Chris Hanburger

"I always felt the best way to be able to do my best was to just get going and keep going for as long as I could."

—Mike Webster

"I never take a chance, I've got to get that man down any way I can. If I take a diving shot at him and miss the tackle, he's got a touchdown. I go for the interception only when I'm convinced that I can get it; if there's any doubt in my mind, I make the tackle. I don't have speed, but experience and quickness are more important."

—Paul Krause

THE NFL'S ALL-TIME INTERCEPTION LEADER

On December 2, 1979, in a game against the Los Angeles Rams, Minnesota Vikings safety Paul Krause broke Emlen Tunnell's record of 79 career interceptions. Krause wore this jersey that day and intercepted this football for his record 80th career pick. He added an 81st interception later in that same game.

❝A player once said that he and his mate had watched me from a distance during a close game. He said that as they looked at me, I didn't seem upset. So they figured that they didn't need to be upset either. That stuck with me. If my remaining calm could influence players, then it had value.❞

—Bud Grant

❝In my own case, I've always thought that one of the best things I've had going for me is my speed. I'm not as big and strong as some guards...but I think one of the things I can do best is block on a sweep.❞

—Tom Mack

❝It's not hard to catch footballs. Anybody can be a receiver. To be a complete receiver takes more than that, though. It's the ability to run patterns, honest-to-goodness, decent patterns. It's blocking...when you're not catching the ball, you've gotta do something else. And my thing is, I like to block. To be a total football player, you've got to play every play, and I like to play every play.❞

—Charley Taylor

❝I get a lot of respect out there. I guess all I want now *[1981]* is to be remembered as a nice guy, because all that counts now is that I know I can play. That's all I need now.❞

—Ted Hendricks

❝I'm not very emotional, but I'm as happy as anyone in the stadium when you're successful in situations like that....Just because I don't do cartwheels when I make a game-winning field goal doesn't mean I'm not extremely pleased.❞

—Jan Stenerud

❝To be great, you have to forget about pain. If it's not going to hurt you permanently, it's cheating your teammates if you don't play.❞

—John Hannah

❝Near the end of your career it's the next thing a player thinks about— how to stay in the game you've loved so long and played so long. This has been my life.❞

—Charlie Joiner

❝My main concern is not the records, but contributing as much as possible....My goal when I came to the NFL was to gain the respect of my peers and a certain amount of self-respect. I was never really interested in publicity or notoriety.❞

—John Stallworth

❝I got to prove to people I'm as good as they are saying. Sure, I got dollar marks for eyes, but I also have pride in my job. I don't care if I don't get a pass just as long as I can take two men with me on my pattern.❞

—John Mackey

"From the first time I was introduced to it, the game appealed to me. I'm competitive, which means I like to beat the other man."

—Jack Youngblood

[About playing for a team that lost all fourteen games in its first season and the first twelve of season number two]

"For the first time in my life, I was embarrassed to be recognized as a football player. I didn't even want to go to the grocery store. Everybody had a solution. Even the clerk would tell us what defense we should be using. Everyone had an answer... everyone but us."

—Lee Roy Selmon

Opposite:

JACK YOUNGBLOOD

Los Angeles Rams defensive end Jack Youngblood was as tough as they come. The five-time All-Pro choice played in seven consecutive Pro Bowls and a then–team record 201 consecutive games. Although Youngblood downplays it, the fact remains that after suffering a fractured left tibia in the first round of the 1979 playoffs, he still played every defensive down in the conference title game and Super Bowl XIV.

"In one sense the coverage makes me feel good, then in a sense it makes me mad. Why don't they leave me alone like any other tight end? Last year I would flex out and I could look up and know I had a touchdown. This year I look up and see the linebacker over me and the strong safety behind him and the weak safety hanging around nearby. I just wish they'd leave me alone."

—Charlie Sanders

JACK YOUNGBLOOD

QUESTION: As a defensive end, what was it like being drafted by a team that featured perhaps the best defensive end in the business at the time?

YOUNGBLOOD: When I was selected by the Los Angeles Rams and began to think about who my teammates might be, and then realized one of them was Deacon Jones, I automatically thought that was going to be a short trip to Los Angeles. They were going to give me a two-way ticket; it wasn't going to be a one-way ticket. On the other hand, when I got there I realized how truly blessed and fortunate I was that Deacon and Merlin Olsen both, for whatever reason, because of the goodness of their heart, I assume, saw something in that skinny kid out of the University of Florida and they embraced me and taught me how to play the game. They became my mentors.

QUESTION: Did you feel at that time that there was a sense—from either Deacon or even Merlin—that this is a threat, you being drafted by the Rams, or did you feel like this was a situation where they recognized you were there to help, not to threaten anyone?

YOUNGBLOOD: In that situation, there is always a sense of a threat with the new kids coming into camp. I sensed that during my career. There is always a sense of that. But when you have confidence in your own ability to play, you're always looking for good teammates, good players for your football team. I think that's how Deacon and Merlin approached it. I think that's what their perspective was: "Yeah, he's a threat to my job, but at the same time he's going to be a pretty good player."

QUESTION: How would Jack Youngblood do in today's NFL? What's the big difference today playing defensive end?

YOUNGBLOOD: Specialization has taken over the game. When we played, if it was sixty plays, you played sixty plays on defense, you played the run and the pass, and you had to be good at both. You had to be able to stop the run, get them to throw the football, and then rush the passer. So that's the change today, they specialize: they got guys, three big fat guys, who come in and play the run, and then they go and bring two stealth guys in who can come off the edge and rush the quarterback.

> "I happen to be a very emotional person. Whatever I get into, I get in over my head....I'm the type of guy who has confidence in what I believe in, which is key to the whole thing. If you have confidence in what you believe, then you're willing to see that it happens. Some people construe that as being tough, but it isn't being tough; it's being willing to do anything necessary to see that what you believe prevails."

—**Tex Schramm**

> "I look back now and I can see that the only advantage to being drafted high is financially. I think a player that comes up the way I did gets a lot more out of the game. If my career ended today or tomorrow I don't think I could say I got a bad deal. I have nothing bad to say about the game. I think it's because of the fact that I came up the way I did. I feel I earned my job and that I'm justified where I am."

—**Jim Langer**

[Said in 1980]

> "I don't think anybody knows as much about football as my people. We see more than anyone in the world. A coach or a player may see one game a week, but we see fourteen professional games every week."

—**Ed Sabol**

The Orange Crush was another superb defense that did not win a championship, coming up a game short against the Cowboys in the 1978 Super Bowl. But that Denver defense stood tall next to the other great defenses of the decade.

The Orange Crush allowed only 148 points that season, forced 40 turnovers, collected 35 sacks, and held seven opponents to single digits in scoring. End Lyle Alzado, linebackers Randy Gradishar and Tom Jackson, cornerback Louis Wright, and safety Billy Thompson were selected to the Pro Bowl in 1977, but only Wright was named to the 1970 All-Decade team. Not a one is in the Hall of Fame.

The 3–4 defense also surfaced in the NFL in 1975 when Bum Phillips slid Curley Culp from defensive tackle to nose tackle and added a fourth linebacker to his front seven—rookie Robert Brazile. The 1976 Raiders became the first 3–4 defense to reach a Super Bowl and the 1977 Broncos the second. The 1976 Raiders also became the first of a dozen 3–4 defenses to win a Lombardi Trophy.

Culp, a former NCAA heavyweight wrestling champion, became the first great nose tackle of the modern era and remains the prototype for the position. Brazile became a 1970s All-Decade selection, and Ted Hendricks, the prototype weakside backer in the Oakland 3–4, now has a bust in Canton. So does Elvin Bethea, who played end in Houston's 3–4 scheme.

Which brings us back to those 1969 Chiefs. In addition to the four Hall of Famers, end Jerry Mays and safety Johnny Robinson were named to the all-time All-AFL team. Culp, linebacker Jim Lynch, and cornerback Jim Marsalis joined them as AFL All-Stars.

That 1970 Super Bowl was a direct result of an offensive lesson the Chiefs learned in the 1960s—that 35–10 spanking from the Green Bay Packers in the first Super Bowl.

"After that, the Chiefs worked toward building a defense," Lanier said. "They realized they needed a stronger defense to give them a chance against the big, strong inside running games. So in 1967 they started building with myself and Jim Lynch coming in. Then they got the bump-and-run cornerbacks (Marsalis and Thomas) and traded for Curley Culp. That defense was built with the idea of being able to handle the power running games of the NFL and the passing games of the AFL."

Joe Greene was watching. So was the NFL. And the game would steam along on a defensive track in the 1970s.

"They teach us here to try to blow guys off the line of scrimmage and create holes. It's just a matter of either you do the job or you don't. Gladiators are what we are. Every week I feel it's like we're down there and it's do or die. Whoever wins in the pits, that's who controls the ball game."

—Art Shell

"I prefer to play consistent, error-free football. If you're doing your job well and defending your area, you might not get tested that often, or get a chance to make big plays. If I had been with another team, I might not have been thought of in the same light. We have a unique type of defense and it is honed around the kind of talent we have."

—Jack Ham

"A good lick ruins his *[the receiver's]* timing. If you can delay or reroute a receiver, you'll goof up a passer's timing and force him to look for a secondary receiver....I've been knocked around, but no one has run me over."

—Roger Wehrli

"I had a good career...I knew I had the stats....We didn't win enough championships when I was there *[Kansas City]*, but as far as a corner that could get the ball—I could get the football. I had great ball skills and speed."

—Emmitt Thomas

"With the Raiders we don't have to put up with any Mickey Mouse stuff. We don't have rules about keeping our chinstraps buckled on the sidelines. We don't have coaches encouraging a lot of false chatter on the practice field. The phony stuff is for losers. We're treated like intelligent human beings. We don't live by a lot of degrading rules. Our coaches don't harass us because they know we're winners."

—Dave Casper

"I feel I'm one of the top tackles...I love blocking, love the contact. There's a lot of satisfaction in knowing that you're moving your man out of there. Biggest of all is to put my man on the ground—I'm on top of him and the ball carrier is 10–15 yards downfield. That's satisfaction."

—Rayfield Wright

"Being an offensive lineman is about the most boring job in football. It's just a headbutting contest...the only satisfaction comes from knocking someone on his rear end. And if it helps score a touchdown, it is all the more satisfying."

—Ron Yary

The 1980s
THE NFL'S GREATEST DECADE?

IRA MILLER

NFL history is filled with milestone dates that many football fans can recite from memory. As if it were an onion, peel back the layers (or the years) and discover the game's history: 1920, the league's founding; or 1958, the so-called Greatest Game Ever Played; or 1960, the election of Pete Rozelle as commissioner; or 1966, the merger with the AFL and the ensuing first Super Bowl; or 1970, the start of Monday Night Football.

NO QUESTION, ALL OF them were important in the growth of professional football as modern America's game. Yet they all were little more than the appetizer to the decade that is the NFL's real main course: the 1980s. That is when the NFL we know now really began, when a series of events took place both on and off the field that set the stage for the game so many millions revere today.

Those events touched not only the players but the coaches, the front offices, and the structure of the league. That's why it's easy (for this writer, anyway) to make the argument that the '80s were the most significant ten years in NFL history.

For starters, the decade certainly produced plenty of all-time greats, being the heyday of coaches like Bill Walsh, Joe Gibbs, and Bill Parcells and players like Joe Montana, Lawrence Taylor, and Walter Payton. For another, it produced the roots of the free agency and salary cap system that created a more level playing field among franchises and remarkable competitive balance.

But there was more: the 1980s laid the foundation, in the two decades that followed, for the league's biggest expansion since the merger with the AFL. There is irony in that, because the trigger for expansion was the franchise movement that most of the league's owners opposed.

Opposite:

LESTER HAYES

Raiders cornerback Lester Hayes played linebacker in college before being switched to safety and then to cornerback in the pros. The cat-quick Hayes, however, never abandoned his linebacker's stance. A big-play defender, he mastered the intimidating bump-and-run technique and was one of the game's leading interceptors. In 1980 he recorded 13 interceptions, the second highest single-season total in NFL history.

PHOTO: JOHN W. McDONOUGH

ART SHELL'S SUPER BOWL XV HELMET

Oakland Raiders tackle Art Shell wore this helmet during the 1980 regular season and postseason, including Super Bowl XV. In a tribute to the Americans who were held hostage in Iran for 444 days and released from captivity just five days before the Super Bowl, a large yellow bow was attached to the outside of the Superdome. Miniature yellow ribbons were given to fans and a small yellow stripe was placed on the back of every player's helmet as a part of the tribute.

> **"I'm just tired of talking about the streak** *[consecutive games with a reception]*, **I'm just glad I did it, glad for the attention, but it's not that big a thing. I mean, I'm not bragging, but just going Sunday to Sunday, it will be a real rare game when I don't catch a pass."**
>
> **—Steve Largent**

> **"When I'm at my absolute best, I feel very relaxed. I'm laughing, having a good time. I feel smooth, loose, and confident. It doesn't matter who is defending me. If it's one guy, he's at a disadvantage. If it's two, they're at a disadvantage. When I'm on, it's a long day for the defense."**
>
> **—Kellen Winslow**

And still more, much more. Most significantly, during the '80s, the way the game was played changed, perhaps forever, the offensive emphasis shifting from running the ball to passing it.

Never again are we likely to see a team win a championship as the Miami Dolphins did in 1973, throwing only 11 passes in the Super Bowl. In the Super Bowl following the 1989 season, Montana threw 12 passes in the first period.

Of course, the '80s did not occur in a vacuum. The stage for change actually was set in the prior decade when the league liberalized its blocking rules, allowing offensive linemen to extend their arms and use their hands, making it easier for them to protect the quarterback. When the San Francisco 49ers hired Walsh as their coach and he drafted Montana to be his quarterback, the so-called West Coast offense came into vogue.

Prior to the change, linemen essentially had to keep their arms and hands close to their own body and block mostly with shoulders, forearms, and upper body. The new rule permitted blockers on passing plays to ward off opponents with their arms and hands, enabling them more easily to push the pass rushers away. This placed more of a premium on tall, lanky offensive tackles.

In the 1970s, many of the top coaches had been defensive specialists, such as Pittsburgh's Chuck Noll, Miami's Don Shula, and Dallas's Tom Landry. With the rules changes favoring the offense, the '80s produced offensive-minded coaches, disciples of gurus like Sid Gillman and Don Coryell. This group was headed by the 49ers' Walsh and the Washington Redskins' Gibbs, both of whom are in the Pro Football Hall of Fame.

In an eleven-year period beginning in 1981, San Francisco and Washington won seven Super Bowls.

And clearly, it was the competition between them—and between them and a few other contenders—that helped to elevate the 49ers to their status as team of the decade. Why? Quite simply because every champion needs a formidable rival. Where Ali had Frazier and Palmer had Nicklaus, the 49ers and Walsh had the Redskins and Gibbs—and also had the Giants and Bill Parcells and the Bears and Mike Ditka. Championships in the NFC did not come easily during this time, an era in which the 49ers and Bears posted 15–1 records and the Redskins and Giants topped out at 14–2.

The competition on the field also led to some memorable off-field sniping, modest by today's standards of trash talk but perhaps a bit out of character in those pre-Internet days. After the 49ers won their first Super Bowl and Walsh was anointed in the media as a "genius," he happened to mention that other coaches were calling him for offensive advice. He named some, including Gibbs. Famously, Gibbs read that quote, called a Washington columnist, and pointedly told him he had met Walsh only once in his life and they did not talk about football.

SAN DIEGO CHARGERS 1981 PLAYOFF GAME PLAYBOOK

The San Diego Chargers' 41–38 victory over the Miami Dolphins in the 1981 AFC Divisional Playoff Game is a classic. The overtime game produced playoff records for points scored by both teams (79), total yards by both teams (1,036), and passing yards by both teams (809). Although Chargers quarterback Dan Fouts completed 33 of 53 attempts for a franchise record of 433 yards and three touchdowns, it was tight end Kellen Winslow who stole the show. In addition to blocking a Dolphins field goal attempt on the last play in regulation, Winslow recorded a playoff record 13 receptions for 166 yards and a touchdown, despite suffering from a pinched nerve in his shoulder, dehydration, severe cramps, and a gash in his lower lip that required three stitches. This is the Chargers' playbook from that historic game.

TONY DORSETT

Superlative play from Dallas Cowboys running back Tony Dorsett was so routine that it was easy to not fully appreciate his career accomplishments. Eight times during his first nine seasons, Dorsett rushed for more than 1,000 yards. The only year he missed was the nine-game strike-shortened 1982 season, in which he still led the NFC in rushing.

PHOTO: AL MESSERSCHMIDT

"My career? It's one that I can live with. To be a running back in this league at 183 pounds, sometimes I wonder how I played this long. I'm the second-leading rusher and I played twelve seasons when at one point I thought I would only play five. When I leaf through the pages of my scrapbook someday, I can smile about what I have done."

—Tony Dorsett

DORSETT'S RECORD-BREAKING SHOES

Dallas Cowboys running back Tony Dorsett established an NFL record that will never be surpassed. In a Monday night game against the Minnesota Vikings on January 3, 1983, Dorsett pierced the Vikings defense for a 99-yard touchdown run. Remarkably, the record run came on a broken play. Ron Springs, the intended ball carrier, had mistakenly left the playing field, leaving the Cowboys offense with just ten men. As the ball was snapped, Dorsett realized the situation and improvised. He took the handoff from his startled quarterback and raced into the record book.

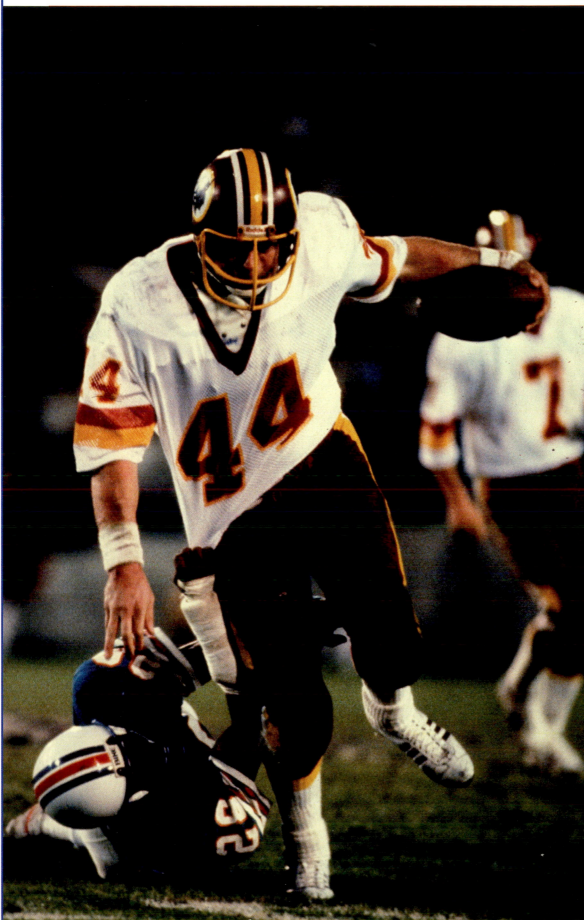

JOHN RIGGINS

John Riggins was a workhorse running back for the New York Jets and Washington Redskins for fourteen seasons. A first-round draft pick in 1971, Riggins gained 11,352 yards rushing for 104 touchdowns along with 2,090 receiving yards and 12 touchdowns. In Super Bowl XVII he earned MVP honors after gaining 166 yards rushing, including this 43-yard game-winning touchdown run.

PHOTO: AL GAMBOA

ERIC DICKERSON

JERSEY WORN BY
ERIC DICKERSON WHEN HE SET
THE ALL-TIME RUSHING RECORD

In 1983, Los Angeles Rams running back Eric Dickerson established rookie records, including most rushing yards (1,808). Prior to the start of his second season Dickerson was asked if he had a new yardage goal. "I've got figures in my head for this season," he replied, dodging the question. Whatever those figures were, by Week 15 against the Houston Oilers, it was apparent that he had a realistic shot at becoming the second back in NFL history to rush for more than 2,000 yards in a season. With three and a half minutes remaining and needing just six yards, Dickerson gained nine yards and a permanent place in pro football history. The carry gave him 215 yards for the game and 2,007 for the season, breaking O. J. Simpson's 2,003-yard single-season record. He gained an additional 98 yards in the season finale to finish with 2,105 rushing yards.

QUESTION: How tough was the adjustment from college to the NFL?

DICKERSON: I think I acclimated pretty quickly and I think the reason was my size and my speed. I am a big believer that in the NFL, if you are fast and you have the heart—that's what it comes down to, the heart to play the game—you can be very effective. I was big and I was fast. I remember one time we played, I think it was my rookie year, we played against the Detroit Lions and they were chasing me, and I'm running down the field and I turned around and I had the whole defense chasing me and even the defensive backs couldn't catch me and I was like, "I am passing all these guys, they can't catch me," it seemed so funny to me. I didn't think that it was easy, I just know that my speed and my size made a difference.

QUESTION: Were you aware of the record or were you just playing each game as it came along?

DICKERSON: Oh I was very, very cognizant of it because we had talked about it. We thought we could get it my rookie year, I was on pace, actually ahead of the pace. My rookie year though, it just kind of fell off. You know, a rookie is only used to playing ten or eleven college games in a season, counting your bowl games. Your first year in the NFL you're playing sixteen regular-season games and four pre-season games and then you get to the playoffs, so you're playing a total of twenty games. And it was probably around Week 10, I was just like, "*Wow*, I am beat down." I mean, I was just tired. When the season ended—I think it was Week 16, we didn't go to the playoffs—I went from 225 to like 207 or 206. I just dropped weight. I just wasn't used to that long season. And then the next year I said, "I'm going to be ready for this, I'm going to be ready for this long season." And we were going to try to get that record, because that was all our offensive linemen talked about: "We want that record of O.J. We want to be part of that."

The funny thing was, in some of the games the offensive linemen would come in at halftime and say, "How many yards does he have, how many yards does he have?" That's what made it real good. Jackie Slater got hurt that year and he was like our statistician. "You need to pick it up, you got over 100 yards, you need to try to get to 150 or 180 today. You fell off the pace last week." So that was the part that made it all fun.

QUESTION: What about O.J.? Do you remember how he handled it?

DICKERSON: You know, what I always say is this—O.J. did it in fourteen games and I did it in only fifteen games with one game left. What O.J. did was a great accomplishment. It's really hard to get that record. It really is.

A couple of years later, after the Giants held the 49ers without a touchdown in a playoff game, Parcells, a defensive specialist, sneered, "What do you think of that West Coast offense now?" And during the Bears' heyday, Ditka, taking a swipe at the reputations of both Walsh and his own estranged defensive coordinator, Buddy Ryan, said, "There's no sign on my door that says, 'Genius at work.'"

Walsh, a master psychologist, often referred to the East Coast "media establishment" not respecting his team. He made road games, particularly to New York, a crusade, and the 49ers responded; his teams actually won more games on the road than they did at home, and near the end of his career they began what became a league record eighteen-game road winning streak.

DICKERSON RUSHING RECORD WITH COACH ROBINSON

In 1984 Eric Dickerson, in just his second NFL season, rushed for 2,105 yards and broke the single-season rushing record of 2,003 yards set by O. J. Simpson in 1973. A clearly proud coach John Robinson holds the record football as he congratulates Dickerson on his milestone achievement.

"For me, it's a record, and all records are meant to be broken. I do cherish that record, but I think the one I look at most and means the most to me is my rookie rushing record. You get one shot at that. You don't get several. You get one."

—Eric Dickerson

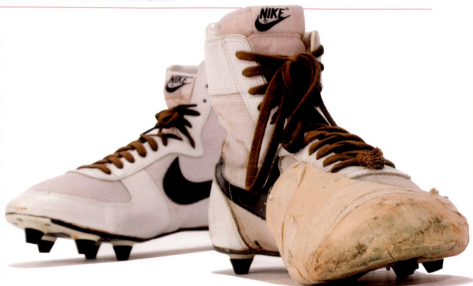

JACK LAMBERT'S SHOES

Pittsburgh Steelers linebacker Jack Lambert, known for his vicious tackling, superior pass defense, and overall toughness, suffered a severe toe injury in 1984 that limited his playing time to just eight games and necessitated his retirement at the end of the season.

"The way that I kept my focus when I played was: my mom and dad always encouraged me when I was coming along. They helped me keep my focus. They would tell me to play 'like someone was trying to take food off your table.' I understood what they meant because we didn't have a lot coming up. And then when I had kids, that was another way to keep my focus. Life for me was sort of a struggle anyway. You have that struggle and you got that will to always do better and win, and then it's easy to keep your focus with all that you are trying to do or achieve."

—Fred Dean

The 49ers won four Super Bowl championships in the '80s (the fourth came in the first season after Walsh retired), played in five NFC Championship Games, and began a run of sixteen consecutive seasons with ten or more victories. With the West Coast offense, they became the vanguard of arguably the most significant strategic shift in the game's history.

As the decade ended, the old football philosophy—run to set up the pass—was out. A new football philosophy—pass to set up the run—was in. In the old game, the object of the offense was to overpower the defense, wearing it down physically with running plays and then throwing the ball later when the defense was tired. Walsh turned that strategy on its head.

In advance, he scripted his team's first fifteen plays for each game as a kind of laboratory to see how the defense would react in certain circumstances. The emphasis was on throwing short, simple passes with the aim of controlling the ball and spreading the defense out,

"From the first day I played I knew I was better than the other guys. As a kid, you sense you can run faster or catch a little better. You can sense it, but you don't think about it. You recognize some things are coming easier to you. I used to ask myself, 'Why?' Now I just accept it. I've been blessed, but my father always told me not to forget that there was someone out there better. So I worked really hard. I didn't take it for granted."

—Marcus Allen

forcing it to cover the entire field. Walsh, a boxing aficionado, likened it to a fighter throwing jabs to see how the opponent would react so that the next time he called the play, or one that looked similar, he knew what to expect from the defense.

Later in games, when the defense was looking for a short pass, Walsh's teams would attack down the field with longer passes or, with the defense wary of a pass, begin trying to pile up first downs by running the ball.

Walsh and the 49ers got a reputation as a "finesse" team because of this strategy, and many football purists decried it as not manly. Yet he took his team from a 2–14 record in 1979 to a Super Bowl championship two years later—and the 49ers generally were also successful at running the ball and, not coincidentally, playing physical defense.

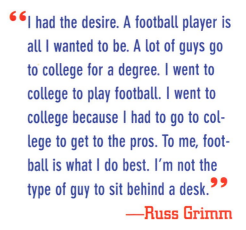

"I had the desire. A football player is all I wanted to be. A lot of guys go to college for a degree. I went to college to play football. I went to college because I had to go to college to get to the pros. To me, football is what I do best. I'm not the type of guy to sit behind a desk."

—Russ Grimm

RAIDER GREAT HOWIE LONG

Defensive end Howie Long joined the Oakland Raiders one year after the team won Super Bowl XV. Three years later, he was an integral part of the team that captured another Super Bowl title with a 38–9 win over the Washington Redskins. His five-tackle performance in Super Bowl XVIII capped off a season that saw him record a career-high 13 sacks, including five in one game against the Redskins. The following season Long recorded 58 tackles, 12 sacks, and nine passes defensed, for which he was named Defensive Lineman of the Year by the NFL Alumni Association. An eight-time Pro Bowl choice, Long was just the second Raider defensive lineman ever named to the postseason classic.

"I tend to be my own worst critic. I don't need a lot of criticism from other people because I get enough from myself."

—Howie Long

Right:

WALTER PAYTON'S RECORD UNIFORM

When he learned of his election to the Pro Football Hall of Fame, Walter Payton humbly remarked, "I'm thrilled but embarrassed. I got paid for playing a kid's game and I enjoyed it." This is the uniform that "Sweetness" wore on October 7, 1984, when he eclipsed Jim Brown as the game's all-time leading rusher.

Below:

WALTER PAYTON ON THE PHONE WITH THE PRESIDENT

There was no shortage of congratulations offered to running back Walter Payton when the popular running back broke Jim Brown's all-time career rushing yardage record in 1984. One fan who reached Payton on the phone in the locker room immediately after the game was President Ronald Reagan.

PHOTO: CARL SISSAC/
CHICAGO INDEPENDENT NEWS

Actually, they managed to develop championship teams only because Walsh married his offense with a dominant defensive team. Starting three rookies and a second-year player in the defensive backfield, Walsh's first championship team in 1981 ranked second in the league on defense but only thirteenth on offense.

The ultimate test of the Walsh strategy came in the NFC Championship Game between the 49ers and Chicago Bears in Chicago following the 1988 season. The Bears were built as a powerful defensive force in the image of coach Mike Ditka. Their offense was built around Payton's running, and the defense was for several years in a row among the strongest ever.

One of the coldest days in NFL history, a day when the wind chill at Soldier Field was minus 26 degrees, with winds gusting to 30 miles an hour, hardly seemed like the ideal laboratory for Walsh's warm-weather West Coast team to prove the value of his strategy. Bears players tried to intimidate the 49ers even before the game began, coming out for their warm-ups in short-sleeved uniform jerseys.

But once the game began, the so-called finesse team from California dominated from start to finish, winning the game 28–3, with Montana passing for 288 yards. The 49ers totaled more than 400 yards on offense and even gained more rushing yards than the Bears in winning their first playoff game on the road since 1970.

Suddenly, the West Coast offense was acknowledged as a strategy for all seasons, and the dramatic shift in offensive strategy was confirmed by the teams that won championships. During a three-year period beginning in 1976, the last two seasons before the liberalized rules and the first season after the change, the Super Bowl championship teams had run the ball on at least 58 percent of their plays during the season. A decade later, championship teams all were passing the ball on more than 50 percent of their plays.

> "I get stronger—and gain more yards—as the game goes on. It's like hitting two hammers together. After a while, one begins to dent."
>
> **—Walter Payton**

> "After you leave this game, what you want more than anything—what I want more than anything—is respect from my peers. That's what it is all about. I mean, from players, coaches, cousins, and reporters. I want people to say that I was an S.O.B. out there. That's what you want to leave the field with."
>
> **—Richard Dent**

TOM LANDRY'S ICONIC HAT
For twenty-nine seasons (1960–88), Tom Landry stoically paced the sidelines of NFL football fields as the head coach of the Dallas Cowboys. During that time he delivered thirteen division championships, five NFC titles, and five Super Bowl appearances, winning two.

JOHN HANNAH

Although 1985 was to be New England Patriots guard John Hannah's last season, he still played as if it were his first. Hannah, pictured here during a late-season game against the Indianapolis Colts, was the veteran leader of a Patriots team that captured the 1985 AFC title. Although the Patriots lost 46–10 to the Chicago Bears in Super Bowl XX, Hannah was named All-Pro for the tenth consecutive time.
PHOTO: TOM STRATTMAN

"I was born with a great measure of speed and talent. Probably the best one-on-one cover man in football. But I also was born with desire, the desire to go faster every year. I've set it as a personal goal, and by preparing harder and setting my goals higher, I've achieved that."

—Darrell Green

"I like stressful situations, things that other people would get nervous and uptight about. I think that's one reason why I'm a defensive captain, because I keep things in perspective, I keep guys calm."

—Harry Carson

Opposite:

CARSON'S GATORADE DUMP

New York Giants linebacker Harry Carson borrowed a sideline security member's jacket to help conceal his identity as he quietly snuck up on Giants coach Bill Parcells in the waning seconds of the Giants' 39–20 win over the Denver Broncos in Super Bowl XXI. Carson then dumped a bucket of ice-cold Gatorade on the unsuspecting coach. The celebratory Gatorade dump was a ritual started by Carson and teammate Jim Burt in 1985.
PHOTO: DAMIAN STROHMEYER/*DENVER POST*

"When it comes to linebackers, I'm the man. I've worked hard, and I believe that right now I'm the top linebacker in the league. When I came into the league I considered Lawrence Taylor and Hugh Green the best. They were where I wanted to be—the top—and I dedicated myself to getting there. By the beginning of last year I felt I had moved into the same category with Taylor at the top. Now I feel I'm ahead of them all. I don't want to sound bigheaded. I'm just being honest. I've done what's had to be done, making all the plays a linebacker has to make—stopping the run, making sacks, and other big plays."

—Andre Tippett

"I think the Steeler personality was set by my father; it's the people that mean something. To get very emotional, I would say it's love and that came from him, and we're trying to carry it on."

—Dan Rooney

BUD GRANT'S HEADSET AND SIDELINE JACKET

Bud Grant wore this sideline jacket and used this headset during the 1985 season, his last as head coach of the Minnesota Vikings. During his eighteen-year career, Grant led the Vikings to eleven divisional championships and represented the NFL/NFC in four Super Bowls.

"In coaching, I think you have to have a certain instinct. There has to be a constant awareness of the rules and how they are changing—what these changes allow you to do that you couldn't do before. I think the creative and innovative coaches are the ones who are introspective; ones who like to develop their ideas; ones who take a look at all the equations and want to find the right answers."

—Bill Walsh

JOE MONTANA'S SUPER BOWL XIX MVP JERSEY

Joe Montana was a master of late-game comebacks. During his fifteen-year career, spent mostly with the San Francisco 49ers, he directed thirty-one fourth-quarter come-from-behind wins, including a 92-yard drive in the closing seconds of Super Bowl XXIII. His uncanny ability to bring a team back from apparent defeat was so common that it simply became referred to as "Montana Magic." Eleven times he led his team to the playoffs, with victories in Super Bowls XVI, XIX, XXIII, and XXIV. He was MVP in Super Bowls XVI, XIX, and XXIV. This is the jersey he wore in Super Bowl XIX.

"What I have is recognition. The ability to see everything on the field. Position the other team to death. Keep the ball alive and keep it moving forward. Then, at the right moment, knock them on their ass."

—Joe Montana

THE DRIVE

In the 1986 AFC Championship Game between the Denver Broncos and the Cleveland Browns, Broncos quarterback John Elway led his team 98 yards to tie the game 20–20 with 37 seconds left in regulation. The nail-biting fifteen-play series that lasted just over five minutes is now known simply as "The Drive." On the Broncos' first possession in overtime Elway again worked his magic and drove 60 yards in nine plays to set up Rich Karlis's game-winning field goal. Elway wore this jersey during Denver's 1986 AFC championship season.

JERRY RICE RECORD PERFORMANCE ARTIFACTS

Jerry Rice is considered by many as the game's most prolific wide receiver. During his twenty-year career, primarily with the San Francisco 49ers, Rice broke nearly every major pass receiving record. This is the jersey he wore in 1987 when he set the NFL record for the most receiving touchdowns in a single season. He wore the helmet during the 1986 season and in the 1987 Pro Bowl. A molded replica of Rice's hands holds the football he caught when he tied the record for most career touchdown receptions. The other ball is the one he caught for a then-record 184 consecutive games with a reception.

> ❝What happens is that when you win a lot, you come in and you're more relieved than thrilled about winning.❞
>
> —**Joe Gibbs**

Yet in keeping with a cliché that nothing in football is ever truly brand-new, the fact was that the West Coast offense really had its roots in the American Football League, which was considered more progressive than the NFL. In the AFL's sixth year, 1965, the last season before the Super Bowl era, the champion Buffalo Bills ran on only 44.4 percent of their plays and the NFL champion Green Bay Packers ran on 55.3 percent of theirs. In 1961, the AFL's second year, Charley Hennigan of Houston averaged 124.7 pass receiving yards a game, a record that stood until San Diego's Wes Chandler topped it in 1982.

As the passing game evolved, as more coaches understood the dynamics and took advantage of the big-play opportunities the rule changes gave them, the shift became even more dramatic. The St. Louis Rams, the last NFL champion of the twentieth century, called running plays less than 43 percent of the time—on a par with the old AFL teams.

Walsh was hardly the only larger-than-life figure during this transformational decade. And he was just one of several figures in the league who began his pro football career in the AFC or even, in Walsh's case, the AFL, becoming significant figures only after settling in the NFC. He and his offense also were in the vanguard of a shift in the league's power structure.

Before the 1980s, the AFC had been the more dominant of the NFL's two conferences. In the '70s, when Pittsburgh won four Super Bowls and Miami produced the NFL's first perfect season, the AFC was clearly the stronger conference. Between the 1969 and 1980 seasons, AFC teams won ten of twelve Super Bowls. But Walsh and four other men groomed in the AFC took over three NFC franchises.

Starting with Walsh's 1981 team, this group produced nine Super Bowl champions in eleven seasons. Also during that eleven-year period, eight NFC teams compiled a regular-season record of at least 14–2, compared to only one in the AFC.

Here's a look at the leaders of this so-called brain drain:

WALSH. His first pro football job was as an assistant coach for the Oakland Raiders in the AFL. Later he served eight years as a top aide to the legendary Paul Brown with the Cincinnati Bengals, an AFL/AFC expansion team. Walsh knew the new team would have difficulty putting together a cohesive line and offense, so he devised a playbook full of short, ball-control passes, which some critics

> "Football is the reason for everything I've ever been able to have. That's why it's so important to me. It's everything for me."
>
> —Rickey Jackson

REGGIE WHITE'S RECORD SEASON JERSEY

Reggie White, the "Minister of Defense," made his NFL debut in Week 4 of the 1985 NFL season after two seasons with the ill-fated United States Football League (USFL). In his first game with the Philadelphia Eagles he recorded two and a half sacks and deflected a pass that was intercepted and returned for a touchdown. Despite playing just thirteen games, White was named Defensive Rookie of the Year. The following season he earned the first of thirteen consecutive Pro Bowl invitations. A three-time NFL Defensive Player of the Year, White recorded one of the finest seasons ever by a defensive lineman in the strike-shortened 1987 season. In just 12 games he recorded 21 sacks. This is the jersey he wore during that remarkable campaign.

> **"I think a lot of it** *[dealing with injury]* **has to do with just attitude. I have to think it's some type of insecurity. I really feel like I'm missing out if I'm not a part of playing on Sunday."**
>
> **—Dan Hampton**

DOUG WILLIAMS, POST–SUPER BOWL SIDELINE

A jubilant Doug Williams proved the Washington Redskins were indeed "number one" with a 42–10 win over the Denver Broncos in Super Bowl XXII. Down 10–0, Williams orchestrated an offensive explosion of 35 points in the second quarter, an NFL postseason record. The game MVP, Williams threw a record-tying four touchdown passes of 80, 27, 50, and eight yards.

PHOTO: CORKY TREWIN/SEATTLE SEAHAWKS

described as little more than long handoffs. Walsh's goal was to make 25 first downs a game.

He credited the basis for the offense to Sid Gillman, who taught it to Al Davis, Walsh's boss during his season with the Raiders, calling them "the biggest influence in my early career." The offense Walsh developed under Brown required a quarterback more accurate than powerful, and when he took over at San Francisco in the NFC in 1979, he found one in Montana, whom he drafted in the third round.

JOE GIBBS and BOBBY BEATHARD. Before he became Washington's coach in the NFC in 1981, Gibbs's job had been offensive coordinator at San Diego in the AFC for two years. There, he orchestrated an offense led by quarterback Dan Fouts, tight end Kellen Winslow, and wide receiver Charlie Joiner, all of whom are in the Hall of Fame.

Beathard, meanwhile, learned his trade as director of player personnel for Don Shula at Miami during the Dolphins' championship years. As general manager of the Redskins, he hired Gibbs and procured the players who helped Gibbs reach four Super Bowls in ten years, starting in 1982, and winning three of them. The first, following the 1983 season, began a run of unmatched conference dominance; NFC teams won fourteen consecutive Super Bowl titles.

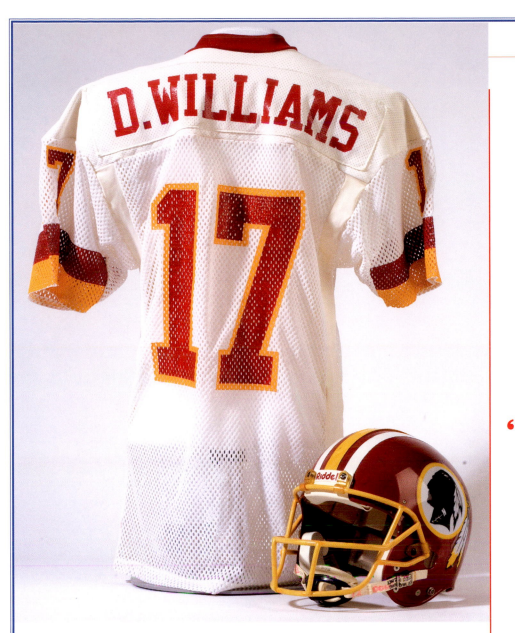

DOUG WILLIAMS'S REDSKINS HELMET AND JERSEY

The pressure for any Super Bowl quarterback is intense. But for Doug Williams, the first African American quarterback to start in a Super Bowl, it was immeasurable. Ignoring the pain of an early-game injury, the Washington Redskins signal caller passed for 340 yards and four touchdowns as he led his team to a 42–10 win over the Denver Broncos in Super Bowl XXII. Williams, the game's MVP, wore this jersey and helmet in that memorable game.

> **"You're always either bad or great. There are no in-betweens. I wish the public was more educated about defenses, but they're not....I've had some of my best games when I've completely shut out a guy and it goes unnoticed."**
>
> **—Mike Haynes**

Unlike Walsh, who had Montana at quarterback all the way, Gibbs won his three championships with three different starting quarterbacks. That he was able to do so was testimony to Beathard's eye for finding talent.

BILL PARCELLS and GEORGE YOUNG. Mostly a college coach (with a brief stop with the Giants) before going to the New England Patriots in 1980 as linebackers coach, Parcells later returned to the Giants and became their head coach in 1983. Unlike Walsh and Gibbs, he was known for his defensive tactics, not his offense, utilizing a 3–4 alignment that emphasized big, athletic linebackers.

Young, like Beathard, worked for Shula, starting as a volunteer coach while teaching high school in Baltimore. He became general manager of the Giants in 1979, hired Parcells, and was rewarded with two Super Bowl titles. Both of Parcells's New York championship teams ranked among the NFL's two best on defense while coming in no better than tenth on offense.

> **"I've already had every success you can have in this business. I'm a starter in the Pro Bowl. I was voted to some All-Pro teams. My team made the playoffs. What more is there?"** *[In 2012 he found out.]*
>
> **—Chris Doleman**

RONNIE LOTT

Ronnie Lott was the driving force on defense during the San Francisco 49ers' four Super Bowl seasons. During his fourteen-year career, he earned All-Pro honors at three different positions: cornerback, free safety, and strong safety.
PHOTO: MICKEY PFLEGER

"The way I play is important to me, because I know I'm not gifted with great athletic ability or speed. But God always gives you the ability to do one thing, and that's to try hard. That's my attitude. If that means going out and running into somebody who's bigger or faster or tougher than you, you just do it."

—Ronnie Lott

Then there were the players. Montana won the Super Bowl's MVP award three times. Taylor is considered by many the greatest defensive player in history. Payton retired as the league's all-time rushing leader. When a panel of NFL experts chose the league's 100 greatest players in 2010, all three were ranked among the top five. At least a portion of the West Coast offense tactics and, in many cases, Walsh's other innovations, such as a lightened load in training camp and practice, were adopted by just about every team in the league.

Meanwhile, the '80s also produced off-field turbulence that has helped to shape the NFL of the twenty-first century. The three most significant: two player strikes that led to free agency and a salary cap that made it considerably more difficult for teams to establish a dynasty; franchise movement that interrupted a long period of stability and led, ultimately, to a four-team expansion; and the retirement of Pete Rozelle as commissioner and selection of Paul Tagliabue as his successor, leading to changes in the long-term direction of the league.

In 1982, a players' strike wiped out nearly half the season. Another strike in 1987 led to three games played with "replacement players," but also served as the catalyst for an agreement bringing full free agency into pro football for the first time. Although strongly

"I don't think I could stress I'm either an offensive-minded coach or a defensive-minded coach. You have to have balance. I'm talking about three departments of play—offense, defense, and the kicking game. All three areas are important. It's an oversimplification, but the offense sells tickets, the defense wins games, and the kicking game wins championships."

—**Marv Levy**

opposed by the owners, the changes were a significant factor in increasing competitive balance throughout the league and decreasing the likelihood that any team could dominate for long.

During the last decade before free agency took hold, only ten different franchises played in the Super Bowl and only five won it. During the first decade under free agency, fifteen franchises played in the Super Bowl and eight won it.

Competitive balance is shown by another statistic: in the first three decades of the Super Bowl era, only five of the sixty teams that reached the final game were not division winners, and only one of these won the title. In the next fifteen years, eight teams reached the Super Bowl after having to begin play in the wild-card playoff round, and five of these won the championship.

Strikes by players were not the only challenge to the NFL's hegemony in the '80s: a well-financed rival league, the United States Football League, whose team owners included Donald Trump, began play in 1983. The USFL originally tried to position itself as a spring/summer league during the NFL's downtime, but began aggressively to expand both its membership and its reach, ultimately moving to a fall schedule, a mistake that led to mounting financial losses that caused the league to disband.

The USFL brought an antitrust suit against the NFL that ended in a pyrrhic victory for the upstart. A federal court ruled that the NFL was indeed a monopoly, but awarded the USFL just $1 in damages.

During its brief history, however, the USFL brought professional football to some cities that eventually would gain or regain NFL franchises, including Jacksonville and Phoenix, and also featured such future stars as defensive end Reggie White, offensive tackle Gary Zimmerman, and quarterbacks Jim Kelly and Steve Young, all of whom wound up in the Pro Football Hall of Fame after their NFL careers.

There were other notable performers during the decade, too.

Running back Eric Dickerson of the Rams became just the second player to rush for 2,000 yards in a single season. Walsh's West Coast offense enabled Roger Craig, a San Francisco running back, to become the first player in history to rush for 1,000 yards and catch passes for 1,000 yards in the same season (1985). Wide receiver Steve Largent of Seattle set a record (later broken) for catching passes in 177 consecutive games. Largent later was elected to the Pro Football Hall of Fame (and to the U.S. Congress).

"I'm not blazing fast, and I'm not quick like a guy who's 5'10", 5'11". I think what helps me is that I run well and when the ball's in the air I have enough gears where I can catch up to it and pull away from defenders. The reason I can do that is that I've run a lot, so I have good form and control."

—**James Lofton**

"Being an offensive lineman fits my personality because I don't like a lot of attention. You can't be looking for a lot of attention as an offensive lineman because that's not the nature of the position. Nobody sees us. Everybody's looking at who has the ball."

—**Dermontti Dawson**

Following spread:

JOHN TAYLOR SUPER BOWL CATCH

Trailing the Cincinnati Bengals 16–13 with 3:20 remaining in Super Bowl XXIII, the master of come-from-behind wins, San Francisco 49ers quarterback Joe Montana, began an 11-play drive that covered 92 yards and ended with this 10-yard touchdown pass to John Taylor with just 34 seconds remaining. The 20–16 win was the 49ers' third Super Bowl title.

PHOTO: SHAWNSPENCE.COM

JOE MONTANA

Joe Montana led the San Francisco 49ers to four Super Bowl victories and was named the game's MVP three times, including in Super Bowl XXIV, depicted here. Thought by some to be the game's greatest quarterback, Montana finished his career with 3,409 completions for 40,551 yards, 273 touchdowns, and four Super Bowl rings.

PHOTO: BOB ANDRES

Jerry Rice, who broke Largent's record and just about every other record for a receiver during a remarkable two-decade career, was drafted in the first round by the 49ers in 1985. Two years later, he scored 23 touchdowns in only twelve games. Gibbs's Redskins, while winning those three Super Bowls behind three different quarterbacks, became the first team renowned for its offensive linemen, known collectively as the "Hogs," even though within a few years their size would be dwarfed by every team in the league.

Defenses were led by Taylor, White, and Chicago's Mike Singletary and Dan Hampton. The 49ers had Ronnie Lott, who made the Pro Bowl at three different positions in the secondary—cornerback, free safety, and strong safety. And one of the most prolific kickers in history, Morten Andersen, began his run to the record book.

"Strength is important...you need a combination of strength, speed, and mobility or agility....I know I have good strength; but without the speed and agility to go with it, I would not be playing major league football."

—Randy White

"I'm not a very excitable person and I'm not intimidated very easily. I enjoy it when the situation gets tough, like when time is running out and we need something. The times I like the most are the times when everything is on the line."

—Art Monk

"I thrive on having everything put in my hands. I love being the guy who has to get it done. I've always been that way. Little League football, high school football, even high school basketball. Every game just seemed to wind up in my hands—if I made the big play, we were usually very successful; if I didn't, we usually lost. And that's what I like best about the no-huddle offense. Whether we score points or don't score points is in my hands."

—Jim Kelly

"I started wearing Number 1 in college because I always wanted to be the number one guy. I always want to remind my teammates that I'm the man who can get it done."

—Warren Moon

"It's just my personality to become mean when the game starts. My mean streak is just part of my desire to be competitive in everything I do. I get very wrapped up in the game and I tend to be very aggressive."

—Mike Munchak

"One thing we always worked on…was dominating our opponents. We called it finishing our blocks. We were taught to finish off our man until we heard the whistle."

—Anthony Muñoz

"Once the ball was in the air, I went after it. I think that was my biggest asset. Once the ball was in my area and I could get my hands on it, it belonged to me."

—Ozzie Newsome

"Hitting people has always been my style.…I'm not tall, but sometimes small things are the most dangerous. It's like a snake when it's coiled. You don't know when it'll strike, and whoosh, it's got you."

—Mike Singletary

"My overall goal was to become the best offensive tackle in the history of the game…and that's what I focused on.…I isolated myself completely, I was out here on a mission, and I chose to keep my world as small as I could. I was consumed by work."

—Jackie Slater

> "I don't want to ever get to the point where I think I'm a great player.... If I ever let my success get to me, I don't know what would happen to my game. There are a lot of good centers in this league. I'm just one of a large group."
>
> —Dwight Stephenson

> "Thirteen years of enjoyable times. I've done everything I can do. I've been to Super Bowls, I've been to playoffs, I've been a dominant force. I've earned the respect of players and people in general around the country. That's what you want to do in a good career."
>
> —Lawrence Taylor

The other major change that came from the '80s involved franchise stability, broken when the Oakland Raiders moved to Los Angeles before the 1982 season; they were to reverse that move thirteen years later. In 1984, the Colts were in Indianapolis, not Baltimore, and by the end of the decade the Cardinals had fled from St. Louis to Arizona.

Meanwhile, Rozelle, a former public relations man, the visionary who married pro football to television and spearheaded the NFL's merger with the AFL, retired after nearly thirty years as the league's commissioner. Tagliabue, an attorney by trade, later oversaw an explosion of new stadiums and a four-team expansion to create a thirty-two-team league by the early twenty-first century.

The '80s also saw a much lesser-known maneuver by Walsh that had a lasting effect for the league's inclusiveness. He originated a minority fellowship training program that helped African Americans move into NFL coaching positions. In its first two decades, more than a thousand coaches came through the program; at least five of them became NFL head coaches, and two, Mike Tomlin (Pittsburgh) and Lovie Smith (Chicago), took teams to the Super Bowl.

Further, one of Walsh's assistant coaches, Mike Holmgren, was the first to hire African Americans as both his offensive and defensive coordinators after he left the 49ers to become head coach at Green Bay. The first African American head coach in the modern NFL, however, was a star former player, Art Shell, who was hired by the Los Angeles Raiders in 1989. A year later, Shell was chosen as the NFL's coach of the year.

Within a decade and a half, the league had mandated a rule requiring teams to interview at least one minority candidate for every coaching vacancy, and shortly afterward the Indianapolis Colts defeated the Chicago Bears in a Super Bowl in which both coaches, Tony Dungy and Smith, were African American.

You can take any decade you wish to call the NFL's greatest; I'll take the '80s.

Opposite:

PETE ROZELLE'S FAREWELL LETTER TO STAFF

On March 22, 1989, NFL commissioner Rozelle sent this letter to his staff informing them of his planned retirement. The transfer of power to Commissioner Paul Tagliabue took place on November 5, 1989.

THE NATIONAL FOOTBALL LEAGUE

410 PARK AVENUE,   NEW YORK, N.Y. 10022 · 758-1500

22 March 1989

Dear Staff:

I regret this means of communicating with you but, unfortunately, it is the only feasible way of doing it.

Today I am announcing to the club presidents and the media that I intend to retire.

My decision was made last October, but I felt it important to keep it to myself. I did not wish to be a 'lame duck' commissioner during the course of the season.

I simply decided that while I was still in good health Carrie and I should have more stressless time to do many of the leisure activities that holding this position does not permit.

The conscientious efforts of the entire staff, many of you with the league for a considerable period of time, have certainly lessened the day-to-day burden on me. I will be eternally grateful for your constant devotion to the National Football League.

I would think it will be June or July before a transition can be fully implemented and we will be moving to California.

In the meantime, I will be looking forward to seeing all of you on my return.

Best,

PR:te

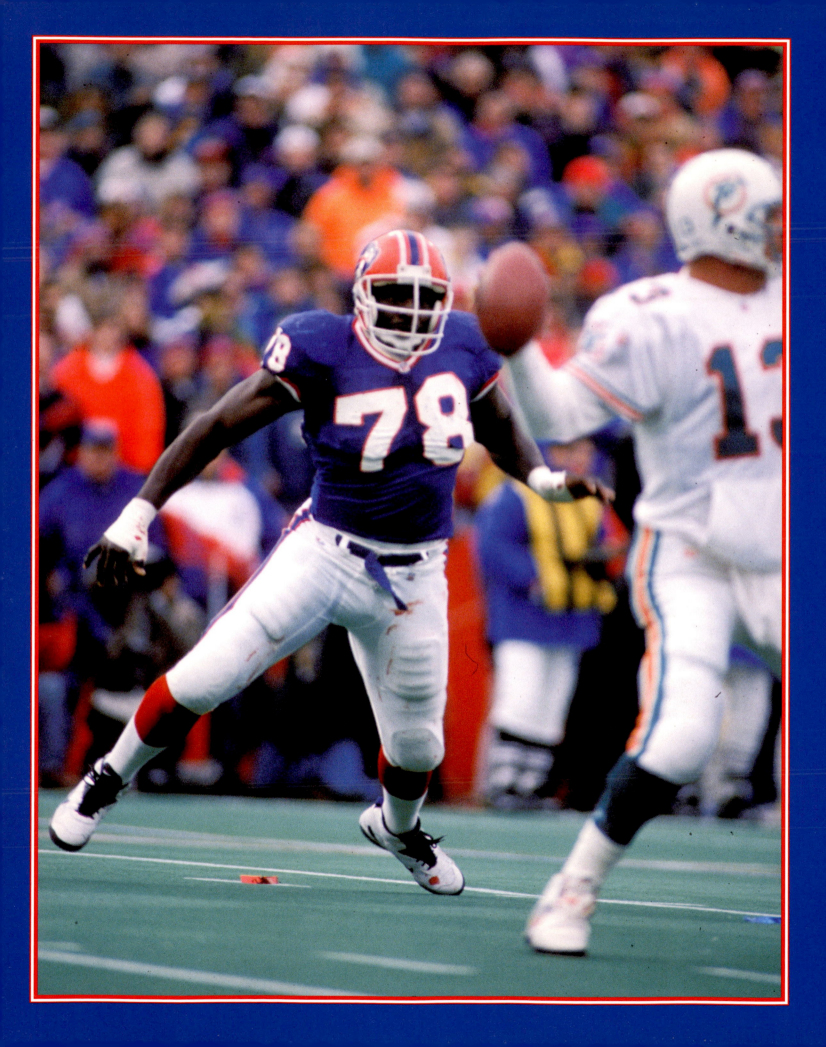

The 1990s
CONSTRUCTING A WINNER

PETER KING

Just after dawn on a late March morning in the spring of 1991, Dallas coach Jimmy Johnson and six Dallas Cowboys assistant coaches—including future NFL head men Butch Davis, Dave Wannstedt, and Norv Turner—boarded owner Jerry Jones's private jet. Destinations: Knoxville, Tennessee; Raleigh, North Carolina; South Bend, Indiana; and East Lansing, Michigan. They were off to see the top prospects work out prior to the NFL draft.

BUT IT WAS MORE than that.

"We're going to find out the real story with these players," Johnson said, settling into a seat in the rear of the plane, "not the story they want us to hear."

There are many reasons the Cowboys owned the '90s, winning three Super Bowls and proving you can dominate professional football in ways the traditionalists never imagined. But the biggest reason, I believe, is because Johnson and Jones brought new ideas to a league that often repelled original thinking. Bill Parcells saw it coming in his last year coaching the Giants, in 1990. "Watch out for them," he said late that season. "They're small, but they're fast. Real fast. This Jimmy Johnson knows what he's doing." Though Johnson brought team speed and an emphasis on a smaller and shiftier defense, he was a good schemer too. The NFL hadn't seen a four-across zone defensive secondary much before, but Johnson basically gave opposing quarterbacks this "quarters coverage" look that became a staple of his defense. He didn't need tremendous shutdown corners on passing downs, because there always seemed to be help coming from somewhere deep downfield.

But apart from the X-and-O stuff, Johnson came to the league with the very odd belief that you could build a great team in the NFL

Opposite:

BRUCE SMITH

Bruce Smith was a dominant player during his nineteen seasons with the Buffalo Bills (1985–99) and the Washington Redskins (2000–03). One of the most feared defensive ends in the modern game, he was routinely double- or even triple-teamed. Smith is the NFL's all-time career sack leader (200), and his thirteen seasons with 10 or more sacks is also an NFL record.

DUELING PLAYBOOKS

Quarterback Jim Kelly led his no-huddle Buffalo Bills offense to a 51–3 victory over the Los Angeles Raiders in the 1990 AFC Championship Game and advanced to the team's first Super Bowl appearance. In Super Bowl XXV the high-powered Bills faced a New York Giants ball-control offense and staunch defense. In one of the most exciting Super Bowls to date, the Giants squeaked out a 20–19 win when Buffalo kicker Scott Norwood's last-second field goal attempt sailed wide right. The strategies for those two games are found within the pages of these playbooks: Jim Kelly's 1990 AFC Championship Game playbook and Giants defensive coordinator Bill Belichick's Super Bowl XXV playbook.

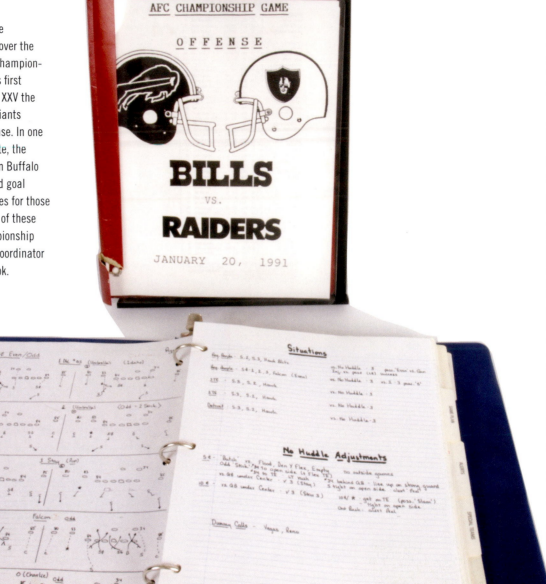

❝I'm afraid of not playing well. If I'm not at the top of my game each week, I will get my ass kicked by someone trying to make a name for himself, and I won't let that happen.**❞**

—Bruce Smith

Opposite:

WIDE RIGHT

After a grueling back-and-forth battle between the Buffalo Bills and New York Giants, Super Bowl XXV came down to a last-second 47-yard field goal attempt by Bills kicker Scott Norwood. With both sidelines standing in hopeful silence, Norwood's kick drifted just outside the right upright, preserving the Giants' 20–19 win. As a result, the term "wide right" became a permanent addition to the football lexicon, joining the likes of "The Drive," "The Catch," and the "Immaculate Reception."

PHOTO: JAMES McCOY/*BUFFALO NEWS*

SMITH AND SANDERS TOGETHER

Two of the game's greatest running backs, Barry Sanders and Emmitt Smith, were perennial 1,000-yard rushers. Sanders was the first player to gain more than 1,000 yards in each of his first ten seasons. Smith rushed for 1,000-plus yards in eleven seasons during his career, and each led the league in rushing four times.

PHOTO: RON JENKINS/*FT. WORTH STAR-TELEGRAM*

the way you built a great team in college. By stockpiling draft choices as if they were college letter-of-intent signees, you could get more players of your ilk—more guys you thought you could win with. And by massaging the coaches and trainers and campus insiders you knew from the college football wars, you could get the kind of information the average NFL scouts just wouldn't be able to acquire. Johnson saw the draft as a place he could win. He just thought he was smarter than everyone else—and, as importantly, he wasn't afraid of making a deal and having it backfire on him. If the kind of player Johnson liked could be had farther down the line in a draft, he figured he could trade down to get that player, and accumulate more picks along the way.

Keep those things in mind as you go on this recruiting trip with Johnson and his coaches, as they set out to build the best football team of the '90s.

AFTER A DAY LOOKING at video of Tennessee receiver Alvin Harper, a mid-first-round prospect, and interviewing Harper and nosing around the football facility with coaches and the medical staff about him, Johnson and his staff were invited out to coach Johnny Majors's home for a night of barbecue, longneck beers, and the singing of Joe Avezzano, who was quite a good amateur country crooner. Avezzano, the special teams coach of the Dolphins, had something in common with Majors and Johnson: they were all on the Iowa State coaching staff in 1969, with Majors being the head coach. Now, twenty-two years later, Johnson was the head coach of the Cowboys, and he needed information, and Majors was fine with giving it—privately. No other NFL coaches or scouts were up with Majors at midnight, on their fourth drink of the night.

Avezzano at one point began singing "Mamas, Don't Let Your Babies Grow Up to Be Cowboys." And the crowd of eight coaches howled with delight.

In one corner of the great room of Majors's house, Johnson got all the information he needed: Alvin Harper was a good kid, a kid who needed to be ridden hard sometimes but who'd give Johnson no trouble and would be the big receiver he needed opposite Michael Irvin. With that knowledge, the trip to Knoxville had paid dividends.

The next morning, the Cowboy plane left for the North Carolina State campus.

JIM KELLY, THURMAN THOMAS JERSEYS

Quarterback Jim Kelly and running back Thurman Thomas were the one-two punch of the Buffalo Bills' explosive no-huddle offense. Kelly, who called his own plays in the fast-paced offense, often used Thomas as a receiver out of the backfield. The strong-armed quarterback guided the Bills to eight postseason appearances and an unprecedented four consecutive Super Bowls. Thomas led the NFL in total yards from scrimmage a record four times and gained more than 1,000 yards in eight consecutive seasons.

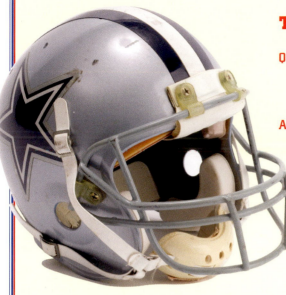

TROY AIKMAN

QUESTION: Statistics are often used to describe a quarterback's success. Is that fair… and how difficult is it for a quarterback, who may be judged by stats, to put team first, particularly when teammates are also often judged by their stats?

AIKMAN: You know, I think there are a lot of ways to go. First of all you tend to start comparing quarterbacks of different eras. It happens in other positions and it happens in other sports, but it seems like it happens more amongst quarterbacks—everybody wants to start talking about who were the greatest quarterbacks of all time. And in order to do that, inevitably statistics become a part of it and sometimes that's not entirely fair. One example: when Roger Staubach retired he was the highest-rated quarterback of all time with a quarterback rating of something like 84. Today, I'm not sure where he ranks, I think somewhere in the top twenty. But if you have a quarterback rating of 84 in today's game you're not going to be starting for very long. You know quarterback ratings today are 98, 99, well over 100 for the season. There was a time when Steve Young was about the only one who had ever done that. Just the last twenty years the game has changed dramatically and me having been, being a broadcaster, I understand why statistics play such a big part because I don't like using them. My career certainly wasn't established based on passing statistics because of the nature of the team I played on, yet I was very proud of the world championships and team accomplishments that we were able to have.

I have always believed that with the quarterback rating, some people scoff at it, some quarterbacks do. I don't—primarily because I think that it puts quarterbacks on a relatively level playing field regardless of the system in which they are playing. I was never going to have a passing title because we simply just didn't throw the ball enough. And so the quarterback rating for me at least gave me an opportunity to be measured against the other great quarterbacks of my era without having to throw the ball 35–40 times a game to win a passing title. So I felt that it was good, but I thought that within that formula there should be something to acknowledge winning and losing. There should be some barometer that measures that. For quarterbacks, even going back to college, when a quarterback loses a game in college that quarterback is pretty much eliminated from the Heisman Trophy candidacy. The year that I was a senior, Barry Sanders won the Heisman Trophy as a running back at Oklahoma State and I'm not sure exactly what their record was, 8–3 or 7–4, but a quarterback would never win the Heisman Trophy with a record like that. Winning certainly is a factor amongst quarterbacks and I think amongst historians and people who follow the game. I am a great example of that because without the championships, you know, the numbers of mine in and of themselves don't get me to Canton.

TROY AIKMAN, SUPER BOWL XXVII MVP QUARTERBACK

Troy Aikman wore this helmet during his 1992 breakout season with the Dallas Cowboys. That year the Cowboys went 13–3, swept through the playoffs, and clobbered the Buffalo Bills 52–17 in Super Bowl XXVII. His 22 of 30 for 273 yards passing and four touchdowns earned him Super Bowl MVP honors.

"I'd have to say that the Super Bowl was my greatest moment in sports, and it was also my most emotional moment. I tried all week to downplay the importance of the game, and I felt a real sense of peace during the week. And then they announced my name and I ran out onto the field at the Rose Bowl, and there was a tremendous rush, unlike anything I've ever known. I tried to tell myself to calm down, to just relax and play my game. But I was hyperventilating until the second quarter."

—**Troy Aikman**

THE END OF THE MIKE DITKA ERA IN CHICAGO

On December 13, 1992, Chicago Bears linebacker Mike Singletary waved a fond farewell to his fans after playing his final home game in Soldier Field. Singletary's retirement marked the end of the Mike Ditka–era teams that are best remembered for their 1985 Super Bowl XX–winning season. Singletary was the Bears' first- or second-leading tackler in each of his eleven seasons.

MIKE SINGLETARY AND THE CHICAGO BEARS' SUPER SEASON

Mike Singletary was the cornerstone of the Chicago Bears' innovative 46 defense. The NFL Defensive Player of the Year in 1985, Singletary led a Bears defense that allowed fewer than 11 points per game. In their 46–10 victory over the New England Patriots in Super Bowl XX, the Bears' league-leading defense held the Patriots to a record low seven yards rushing, while the hard-charging Singletary contributed with two fumble recoveries. This is Singletary's jersey from the 1985 season and a Super Bowl XX game ball.

ART MONK'S JERSEY AND FOOTBALL

Nine times during his sixteen-season career Art Monk exceeded 50 catches in a season. Five times he gained more than 1,000 receiving yards. He also set NFL records for most catches in a season (106), and consecutive games with at least one reception (183). On October 12, 1992, in a game against the Denver Broncos, he recorded his 820th career catch to become the NFL's all-time leading receiver. This is the jersey he wore that day and the football he caught for that then–NFL record. Monk finished his amazing career with 940 receptions.

> **I guess you could call me a football junkie. I'll look at anything, Arena, World League, anything. I love it. I am a student of the game. I try to see what is new, what a team is trying to do to stop an offense. I pick up new things. I never get tired of it. I'd play for nothing; I did for years.**
>
> **—Marshall Faulk**

When Johnson entered the NFL in 1989 from his successful tenure at the University of Miami and the Cowboys went a catastrophic 1–15, everyone said it proved the college guy couldn't adjust to life in the NFL. But he began making progress in 1990, winning seven games, and by the time he was on this trip, he started seeing light at the end of the tunnel. But he couldn't afford to make big mistakes high in the draft. And this trip to Raleigh would help him prove that—not just to his staff, but to Jones, and to those who still needed to see that the Johnson way was the right way.

Johnson believed that pro scouting was more like college recruiting than most people think. Looking at game tapes and conducting workouts is important, but almost as significant is what you can drag out of coaches and trainers and hangers-on after the VCR shuts off or while the player showers. "Do you think one of my friends in college coaching would sit down with a lot of these other NFL guys and tell them if a player's had drug problems?" Johnson said as the plane took off for Raleigh. "You might eliminate one mistake if you're out two weeks. But if you do, then you've saved your club a lot of money and a draft choice. The athletic ability you can see on film. The skeletons in the closet are going to have to come from a coach or trainer or teammate."

The Cowboy coaches called it "grinding," as in, "Hey, when we go to Michigan State, we've really got to start grinding [coach] George Perles about Dixon Edwards." Which they did. "We've got to be investigative reporters sometimes," said Davis, the Dallas defensive line coach.

It took a little Bob Woodward–style digging to get the truth at North Carolina State. Johnson demanded information from his staff on a defensive end who looked to be a good two-way prospect, playing the run and pass well, named Mike Jones. The Cowboys liked Jones's athleticism, but one thing puzzled them: he didn't play every play. They asked six Wolfpack staff members about this, and all of them said three defensive linemen alternated and that Jones was one of those. Strange, Davis thought, that such a highly touted prospect would be on the bench, especially with a game on the line. In fact, the Cowboys noticed one game when a healthy Jones was on the sideline for long stretches. It wasn't a disciplinary case, either; Davis was a good kid who kept his nose clean. Something was fishy. So before the Dallas staff left Raleigh, Davis found one last Wolfpack assistant away from the school's athletic facility. He told the guy he had to know the truth about Jones. And the staffer told Davis, "I don't know if he's tough enough. I question whether he wants to hit anybody."

The Dallas plane had to wait for Davis for maybe a half hour at the Raleigh airport. When he bounded aboard the plane, he said, "I got it!" And when he told Johnson the deal with Jones, Johnson looked like he'd just watched Troy Aikman throw a long touchdown pass.

> "The thing that gave me an edge was my work ethic. I was one of those guys who felt, the more you worked, the better you got. It was a confidence thing. I enjoy working. It's a psychological thing for me. Once you get emotional about it, you can get great at things, stronger, faster, whatever. Emotions take over. I tried to play that way and I tried to get my teammates to play that way. I wanted to be an emotional leader. I'm not the most talented guy in the world, not the fastest or strongest, just a guy who gave his all for his teammates and for the fans."
> —Michael Irvin

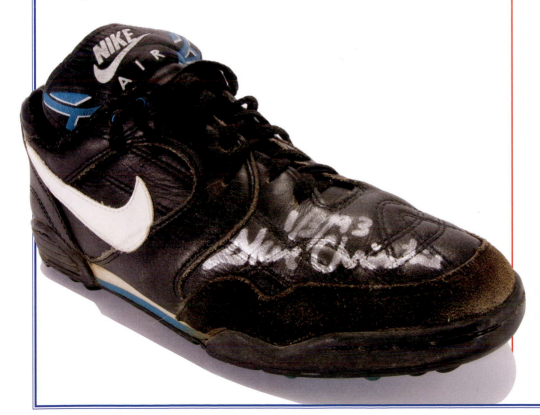

KICKER STEVE CHRISTIE'S SHOE

Down 35–3 in the third quarter of the 1992 AFC Wild-Card Game, the Buffalo Bills rallied to a seemingly impossible 38–35 lead over the Houston Oilers with less than three minutes to play. However, with seconds left in regulation, Oilers kicker Al Del Greco kicked a 26-yard field goal, sending the game into overtime. Early into the extra session, Bills defensive back Nate Odomes intercepted a Warren Moon pass that set the stage for kicker Steve Christie's 32-yard field goal that gave the Bills a dramatic 41–38 come-from-behind win. The 32-point deficit that the Bills overcame for a victory was the largest in NFL history.

SHULA'S RECORD

Miami Dolphins coach Don Shula was hoisted on the shoulders of his players after his Dolphins defeated the Philadelphia Eagles on November 14, 1993, to give him his record 325th career win, one more than George Halas. Shula's incredible overall record stands at 347–173–6.
PHOTO: JOE RIMKUS, JR./MIAMI HERALD

Dallas bypassed Jones, who was the thirty-second pick in the draft a month later. He went to the Cardinals for a disappointing three years before meandering to three teams for the last six years of a pedestrian NFL career. The Cowboys had found the skeleton in Jones's closet, and though he wouldn't have been a disastrous pick (Dallas had its share of those in Johnson's tenure), the Cowboys felt they could do much better. And usually they were right.

"I spent all my time with the players and coaches. The players used to call me 'Duke' because of my name. I watched game movies and sat in on team meetings and at that time knew every assignment on the team, offense and defense. I don't have time to do that anymore. And I'm not that close to the players either. They call me Mr. Mara now."

—Wellington Mara

DON SHULA'S RECORD WIN

On November 14, 1993, the Miami Dolphins defeated the Philadelphia Eagles and surpassed a onetime seemingly unbreakable pro football record. That day, Dolphins coach Don Shula registered his 325th career win and moved ahead of the legendary George Halas as the game's most successful coach. Shula provided the Hall of Fame with his coach's shirt he wore that day along with his game plan sheet.

JOHN ELWAY

Denver Broncos quarterback John Elway is the only player in NFL history to pass for more than 3,000 yards and rush for more than 200 yards in the same season seven consecutive times. He was only the second quarterback in NFL history to record more than 40,000 yards passing and 3,000 yards rushing during his career. At the time of his retirement, he ranked second all-time in three of the game's most significant passing categories: passing yards (51,475), attempts (7,250), and completions (4,123). Elway was named the NFL's MVP in 1987, AFC Offensive Player of the Year in 1993, and Super Bowl XXXIII MVP.

"I think probably the thing that I am most proud of is that I was able to hang in there long enough to win a couple of Super Bowls."

—John Elway

"I don't think I'm such a natural, I think what I'm doing is very hard work. I work hard to keep in shape, I work hard on the practice field, I work hard in a game. Cornerbacks are the best athletes on the team; they wouldn't be out there if they weren't. Those are the guys I have to beat. It isn't easy."

—Jerry Rice

Opposite:

JERRY RICE BREAKS JIM BROWN'S TOUCHDOWN RECORD

The San Francisco 49ers opened their 1994 season on September 5 in a Monday night matchup against the Los Angeles Raiders. Entering the game, Jerry Rice was just one touchdown behind Walter Payton and two behind Jim Brown on the career touchdown list. Rice put on a one-man show as he caught seven passes for 169 yards and scored three touchdowns (one of them rushing), passing both Payton and Brown on the career touchdown list. Rice's final catch of the game was this 38-yard scoring play.

PHOTO: MICKEY PFLEGER

Johnson and Jones made twenty-nine trades in the first twenty-six months of the new reign in Dallas. One of them spawned Dixon Edwards, the linebacker they investigated on the campus of Michigan State. Johnson wanted sideline-to-sideline playmakers at linebacker. Not just edge pass rushers, or big run stoppers behind the defensive line. At 6'1" and 228 pounds, Edwards was light for almost every team in the league. Johnson saw the speed and the playmaking, not the size.

One more interesting point about the 1991 draft for Dallas. The Cowboys traded up to get the first pick in the draft when it looked

BRUCE SMITH

QUESTION: Being the game's all-time sack leader is a great accomplishment. Do you feel that history fully appreciates the circumstances you faced—playing in a 3–4 defense and that you were more than just a pass rusher?

SMITH: During the course of my career, the fifteen years with Buffalo, I only had one teammate that ever had double digits in sacks. I want to phrase this the right way. Take, for example—and this is not a criticism of anyone or anything—but take, for example, Reggie White. Reggie played with Sean Jones and he played with Clyde Simmons. Both of those guys regularly had double digits in sacks each year. They had well over 100 sacks, I think one had 119, one had 111. Deacon Jones had Merlin Olsen. I didn't have any other defensive linemen that would require or would have double teams, and unfortunately they [opposing offenses] focused their attention on me.

I was a student of the game and I would try to beat that double team before it actually got to me. I knew where it was coming from, so if I put a quick move on the first guy I felt I could have a chance to at least have a single block on the second guy or, taking him around the corner, just flat-out beat those guys off the line of scrimmage and then they would have to chase me. I think I was quick enough and elusive enough to be able to break through and get to the quarterback.

The significance of being the all-time sack leader is that you had to stop the run before you put the opposing team into a passing situation. That was something that the teams I played for did very effectively. Consequently I was able to capitalize on teams having to pass the ball. But I did have to fight through double and triple teams because of the style of defense we played, which was the 3–4. It was pretty much unheard of and unprecedented to accomplish what I did, playing in a 3–4 defense. I can recall in 1990 where I was able to rack up 19 sacks while having 101 tackles. I think that combination (of sacks and tackles) is unheard of in any era of the game.

I think sacks are a part of the game that fans, even folks who play the game, tend to focus on and recognize. But to be quite honest, with me there was a great deal of balance. Not just rushing the quarterback and, in my opinion, being the best that's ever done it, but I was a student of the game and a complete player—against the run, against the pass, and on special teams. No one ever talks about this, but in 1996 I led the league in blocked field goals and extra points. These are things that go unnoticed or omitted. These are extremely important stats or facts that put your team in a position to win ball games.

"It is anonymous work all right. But in a way that's good. I watch guys like Barry Sanders and Jerry Rice. Everybody knows them. They can't go out and do the things they want to do without everybody recognizing them. I kind of like my way: the only time people recognize an offensive lineman is when some official throws a yellow flag and says we're holding or offsides. As long as my teammates and coaches know I am doing a good job, that's all that matters."

—**Randall McDaniel**

CRIS CARTER'S UNIFORM FROM RECORD-BREAKING SEASON

In 1994, Cris Carter shattered the NFL record for receptions in a season (112) held by Sterling Sharpe of the Green Bay Packers. Carter finished the '94 season with 122 catches for 1,256 yards and seven touchdowns. This is the jersey, helmet, and shoes he wore, and the football he caught when he set the then-single-season record.

like that pick might be dangerous receiver/returner Rocket Ismail. But Ismail took big money to go to Canada and play for the Bruce McNall/Wayne Gretzky/John Candy–owned Toronto Argonauts (remember that crazy football adventure?), and the Cowboys ended up taking a player who was panned by many in the football establishment: defensive tackle Russell Maryland. "Russell won't be a Hall of Fame football player," Johnson said the night before the draft. "But he'll be a perfect fit for our system, an athletic tackle. Play eight or ten years in the league. Probably make one Pro Bowl. Be a nice player. Show up every week and play. Great kid."

Maryland ended up playing ten solid seasons, missing six games due to injury, never getting in trouble with the coaches, and was the kind of quiet leader teams seek to build around. Oh—and he made one Pro Bowl.

Johnson and Jones heard the NFL chatter. *You picked Maryland*

After two seasons in the United States Football League (USFL), quarterback Steve Young joined the NFL's Tampa Bay Buccaneers through the 1984 supplemental draft. In 1987 he was traded to the San Francisco 49ers. After four years of limited action with the 49ers, Young stepped into the starter's role and recorded the first of his record-tying six league passing titles. His finest season came in 1994, when he guided the 49ers to a 13–3 regular-season record and a 49–26 victory over the San Diego Chargers in Super Bowl XXIX. Young, the game's MVP, passed for 325 yards and a Super Bowl record six touchdowns. This is the jersey he wore that day.

too high. It drives Johnson crazy to this day when people will criticize a team in the first round for picking a player too high. If he's the right player for your system, and he's going to be a valuable contributor but not a star, who cares? Great teams *need* valuable, humble contributors. Better taking Russell Maryland, particularly in a weak draft year like 1991 (no player except Brett Favre from that draft appears destined for the Pro Football Hall of Fame, and the first round was one of the worst in NFL history), than taking a risky guy who might be a star—but might be a washout.

"I'm from the business world," Jerry Jones said early in the Johnson tenure, when times were tough, "and deals I make can take up to five years before you know if they pan out. Here's an example: in 1986 I opened an oil and gas exploration business in Calgary. I knew with the overhead and start-up costs we wouldn't have positive cash flow for at least five years. We went in there prepared to spend between $15 million and $25 million a year to make it work. Today, we're drilling lots of holes up there and hitting some, but we still haven't recouped anywhere near our original investment. I don't know if we will. But if I let all the dry holes in my life get me down, I'd never have done it. You've just got to be tolerant of failure."

Director of player personnel Bob Ackles, a holdover from the Landry days, said, "Before, there was always a concern about getting screwed in a deal. So we didn't make them. In 1987 we traded with

"This is like being a kid, having fun and being animated. If I didn't do any of this, I would be too mechanical, too uptight. I want to be loose. I am at my best when I am rolling and throwing. I am different, but I am consistent."

—John Randle

"Fear...that's the thing that drives me...the fear of getting beat. It's not so much throwing a great block that springs a guy for a touchdown. It's more...don't get beat for a sack, don't be the guy who causes the running back to get blown up, don't be the guy who makes the mental error that causes Steve *[McNair]* to get blindsided."

—Bruce Matthews

"My goal as a football player was to be the best to ever play my position. I believe I've reached my goal."

—Reggie White

Opposite:

REGGIE WHITE WITH SUPER BOWL TROPHY

In 1987 Philadelphia Eagles defensive end Reggie White recorded one of the finest seasons ever posted by a defensive lineman. In just 12 games during the strike-shortened season he amassed 21 sacks. In 1993, after recording 124 sacks in 121 games over eight seasons in Philadelphia, White became the first big-name free agent to switch teams, joining the Green Bay Packers. In 1996, with White leading the Packers' top-ranked defense, the team recorded playoff and Super Bowl victories. In Super Bowl XXXI the "Minister of Defense," as he was known, recorded a record three sacks.
PHOTO: PATRICK J. FERRON

SHANNON SHARPE

If you remember when I came into the league they had the three amigos: Mark Jackson, Vance Johnson, Ricky Nattiel. Those were very small guys. Dan *[Reeves]* wanted to run the football, he wanted a more physical presence at the wide receiver position in the running game. My rookie year, all the tight ends got hurt: Clarence Kay, Orson Mobley, Chris Verhulst. I was the biggest receiver. Dan comes to me and asks would I be willing to try tight end and I said, "Am I going to get an opportunity to play?" He said, "Yeah," and the rest is, as they say, history.

The league was a running league back then. Everybody wanted to run the football. So you wanted a 270- to 280-pound guy that was really a third tackle that could dominate the line of scrimmage and if he caught ten balls, fifteen balls a year, okay, we're happy. If he caught ten passes and one touchdown and your running back rushed for 1,300 yards, he *[the tight end]* had a great year. Then, when Dan put me in at tight end, all of a sudden you started seeing matchup problems. Okay, *wow*—putting me in at the slot, putting me out wide, wide linebacker had to walk out and cover me, safety had to walk out and cover me, and then the next thing you know, everybody is like, "Hmmm, well, we can't get him, let's go find the next best thing. Let's go find the next him." Kansas City goes and drafts Tony Gonzalez. Seattle drafts Christian Fauria. Oakland drafts Rickey Dudley. San Diego drafts Freddie Jones. All these guys were high-round draft picks because they wanted someone that wasn't 280 and couldn't move.

That's where you see the transition—when they started putting more emphasis on throwing the ball down the field. The tight end is the best mismatch in the offensive passing game. The cornerback can run just as fast as or faster than the wide receiver. So now you get a tight end. Linebackers, they wanted to rush and hit the quarterback. They want to try and stop the run. You better find better running linebackers that can cover tight ends down the field. They are playing a nickel corner to do that now. Now if you stay base with your regular tight end on the field split him out wide or put him in the slot. Like Peyton Manning does with Dallas Clark. Like the New England Patriots take two tight ends in the first three or four rounds last year. And then you get what we have seen over the last five or six years. What we never thought would happen—a tight end customarily catching 100 balls, 90 balls, 12–13 touchdowns, when we thought we would never see that in the NFL.

"Blocking, running routes, speed—I think I'm the best tight end in the game. Can't nobody cover me. The other day a reporter asked me what I thought about my chances for the Hall of Fame *[in 1999]*. That knocked me out. I don't know. I know one thing, whatever you want to base it on, your numbers, your wins, your seasons played, your Pro Bowls, your Super Bowl appearances, your Super Bowl wins, I'll put mine against anybody's."
—Shannon Sharpe

the Seahawks for a tackle, Ron Essink. We gave them a fifth-round pick. Essink quit a couple of days after he got here. That just about ended trades for us. To Tom Landry, a fifth-round pick was so important. To Jimmy, he just figures he can get three of them on draft day if he really needs them."

The Cowboys had already been enriched by the Herschel Walker trade two years earlier, giving Dallas extra first- and second-round picks in this draft. On draft day 1991, Dallas took Maryland first overall and then Harper twelfth overall. That left them with one more first-round pick—the fourteenth overall. Next man up on the Dallas draft board was Edwards, but fourteenth was too high to take him.

BARRY SANDERS RUSHES FOR 2,000

Barry Sanders was one of pro football's most exciting runners. The Detroit Lions running back wore this jersey on December 21, 1997, when he joined O. J. Simpson and Eric Dickerson as the only players in NFL history to rush for more than 2,000 yards in a season. Sanders finished the season with 2,053 rushing yards. The elite club of 2,000-plus rushers stands at six as of this writing, with the addition of Terrell Davis in 1998, Jamal Lewis in 2003, and Chris Johnson in 2009.

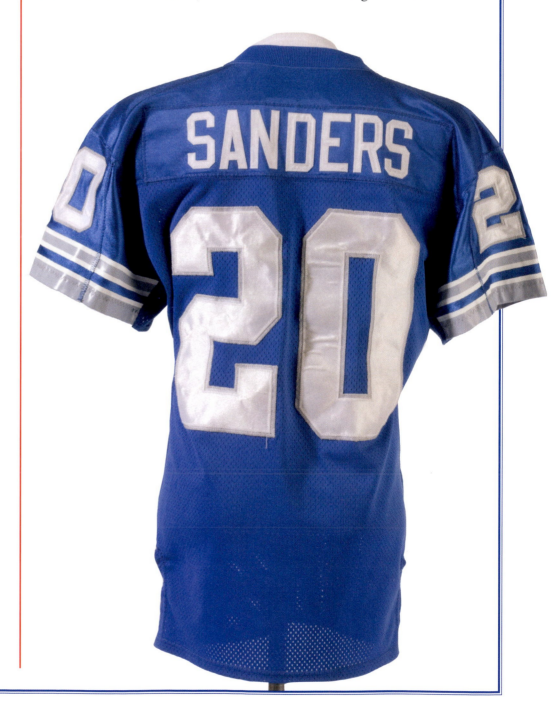

❝I never shared with anyone exactly how much that record meant to me. I valued it. It represented a real accomplishment and the kind of challenge that kept the blood circulating in my career....However, I never valued it so much that I thought it was worth my dignity or Walter's *[Payton]* dignity to pursue it amid so much media and marketing attention.**❞**

—**Barry Sanders**

"I think what got me to the top was that my last two years in college, I had to work really hard to get my game to where I wanted it to be because I had a guy behind me whose name was Barry Sanders. With him being behind me and not wanting him to take my job, if he ran ten 100-yard sprints, I had to run eleven. Just to keep that edge. I think that helped me once I got into the pros."

—**Thurman Thomas**

Johnson traded down to seventeenth, then to twentieth, and to thirty-seventh—in the second round. So for that fourteenth pick, Dallas acquired second-, third-, fourth-, fourth-, and fifth-round picks. And still got Edwards.

Dallas ended up making or receiving eighty-three phone calls in the first two rounds of this draft about trades, and took seventeen players in the twelve-round draft. The Cowboys got five Super Bowl starters, including Leon Lett and Erik Williams in the middle rounds, and they got quality if not stardom throughout.

The final pick of the draft for Dallas, in round twelve, the 320th player picked that year: cornerback Larry Brown, the Super Bowl XXX MVP for his two interceptions of Neil O'Donnell in the 27–17 win over Pittsburgh.

"A FEW YEARS AFTER I got out of coaching," Johnson said, "Bill Belichick came down to see me in Florida to ask me about the draft. He came down with all these notes in this big notebook, and he asked me about all the trades and my philosophy."

The volume of picks, Johnson said, was vital because it allowed you to make mistakes and still have a good draft. Picks are currency, Johnson said; use them like money. The Edwards example was a prime one. Don't overpick a player if you can get value for the pick and still get the player. With Edwards, Johnson still got his man, but he also got four additional draft picks while still getting the player he'd targeted all along.

"And," Johnson said, "I told Bill to make sure with all those picks, he picked guys *he* liked. *He* was going to have to be the one who coached those players, and those players were going to determine whether he won or lost. So don't go picking players other teams have rated high. Pick the players who fit your scheme, who do what you like, who have the characteristics you want."

Football is a copycat league. The same way teams began looking at the way Johnson won with speed and unique coverages to mask secondary deficiencies, teams began looking at his scouting and player-gathering. Belichick quotes Johnson on draft strategy, as does another

"I'm a big guy; people don't think I'm quick. They look at me and think I'm just another fat guy. But when we start playing and they see my first couple of plays, they know they have to take me seriously."

—**Cortez Kennedy**

"Hey, all my life I be the man. I mean, I've been in the spotlight at every level. It's just a bigger spotlight. I learned the system in college. How do you think defensive backs get attention? How do you think Jim McMahon made so many millions? They don't pay nobody to be humble. Some people will come out to see me do well. Some people will come out to see me get run over. But love me or hate me, they're going to come out. I'm a businessman now, and the product is me. Prime Time."

—**Deion Sanders**

DAN MARINO'S FOUR MAJOR NFL PASSING RECORDS

The Miami Dolphins were surprised when quarterback Dan Marino was still available when it came time to make their first pick in the 1983 NFL Draft. Five other quarterbacks, including future Hall of Famers Jim Kelly and John Elway, had been taken before the Dolphins' twenty-seventh overall pick. Marino earned the starting role early in his rookie season and for the next seventeen years the fortunes of the franchise rode on his shoulders. By the time he retired following the 1999 season, Marino had literally rewritten the passing section of the NFL's record book. These footballs were used by Marino in 1995 when he surpassed Fran Tarkenton as the career passing leader in attempts, completions, yards, and touchdowns.

"I remember my first start going back to 1983. It was against Buffalo. To be honest, I was a little nervous. I stood on the sidelines; I remember a veteran, a veteran safety coming up to me, Lyle Blackwood. He came up to me with a serious look and he shook my hand and he said, 'Dan, good luck today. And I don't want you to feel any pressure, but remember this one thing: if you play bad, we'll lose.' Now *that's* pressure on a rookie."

—Dan Marino

draft-pick hoarder, Andy Reid of the Eagles. His lessons haven't always been the most valuable. In 1995, the Eagles were desperate to match Dallas's defensive speed, and traded up with Tampa Bay to pick a superhero from the Scouting Combine that year, speedy defensive end Mike Mamula. The Bucs picked Warren Sapp with Philly's first-round choice, and added two second-round picks in the deal—one of the most lopsided trades in recent NFL history, as it turns out. Mamula had 31 NFL sacks, and his underachieving play eventually helped get coach Ray Rhodes, who pushed for the deal, fired.

Belichick used Johnson's lessons wisely, following in a long line of coaches who learned from those who came before them. Paul Brown begat Don Shula and Bill Walsh. Vince Lombardi spawned a generation of tough teachers. Chuck Noll taught Tony Dungy well. Jimmy Johnson lasted only five years in Dallas—he eventually got divorced from Jones in a split the E! Channel should have covered live—but he made three Super Bowl titles possible, and he left a legacy of how a modern football team is not only coached, but constructed.

"I was a hothead early. Now I still get upset, but it takes a lot more to get me upset. Once you're in this game for a while, you understand the biggest key is playing from your shoulders up. I wish I would've known that when I first came in the league."

—Rod Woodson

"Outside stuff never did affect me very much because I'm basically driven from within. I don't like to compete against others. For me, it's about self-improvement and being better than I was the day before."

—Steve Young

"Winning the ring, doing what nobody thought we could do, that's what I'll always remember. That's what you play the game for."

—Gary Zimmerman

"I've become more consistent, especially in rush and pass defense as well as rushing the passer. My first couple of years I had a great deal of success that came from playing with athletic ability and emotion. But at some point you have to increase your knowledge of the game. I really think I'm a better student of the game now *[said in 1995]*."

—Derrick Thomas

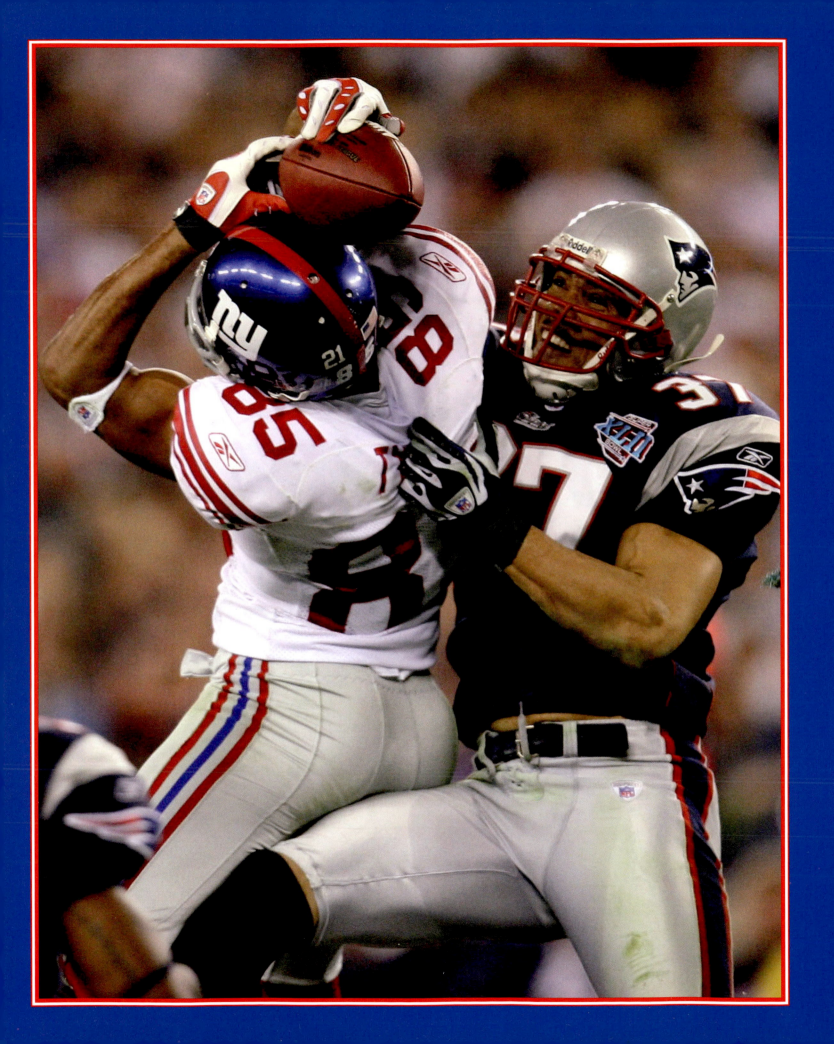

The 2000s

PROSPERING IN THE AGE OF THE SALARY CAP

RON BORGES

The creation of the salary cap was supposed to be the final leveler for a league obsessed with the importance of parity. It was, many insisted, an accounting tool as revolutionary to the game as the forward pass, the West Coast offense, or the zone blitz—and as lethal to the idea of sustained dominance in the NFL as anything any coaching mind ever created.

"**THE DYNASTIES HAVE GONE** the way of the dinosaurs," former Cleveland Browns and Baltimore Ravens owner Art Modell lamented ten years after the salary cap was first introduced in 1994. "You'll never see [one] again. The system has changed to preclude that. Lombardi would not be the Vince Lombardi of yesterday in this climate. The rules have changed so much. Vinny would not be able to cope with free agency, having [Paul] Hornung or [Bart] Starr jump elsewhere. I don't think he'd be able to maintain his supremacy in this system."

Prior to the dawning of the new millennium, each decade had its alpha team: the Chicago Bears of the 1940s, the Cleveland Browns of the 1950s, the Green Bay Packers of the 1960s, the Pittsburgh Steelers of the 1970s, the San Francisco 49ers of the 1980s, and the Dallas Cowboys of the 1990s. Without fail, and despite all the efforts of the league's owners to create a level playing field, some team always emerged above the rest.

But in the early years of the new century the consensus was that dominance had been replaced by an alteration in the old saying of former NFL commissioner Bert Bell that "on any given Sunday" any team could beat another. Now the saying was that "in any given season" any team could emerge after a 1–15 debacle or a 5–11 collapse and win the Super Bowl.

Opposite:

DAVID TYREE CATCH

Late in the fourth quarter of Super Bowl XLII, New York Giants quarterback Eli Manning somehow escaped the grasp of New England Patriots defenders to throw the ball downfield. Giants wide receiver David Tyree made a spectacular catch as he managed to control the ball by pinning it to his helmet. The 32-yard completion on third-and-five kept the Giants' game-winning drive alive. Four plays later, Manning connected with Plaxico Burress for the winning score.
PHOTO: JOHN DAVID MERCER/US PRESSWIRE

SUPER BOWL MVP KURT WARNER'S GAME JERSEY

Quarterback Kurt Warner played three seasons with the Arena Football League's Iowa Barnstormers (1995–97) and another with NFL Europe's Amsterdam Admirals (1998) before finally getting a chance to play in the NFL. Warner appeared in only one game in 1998 as a backup quarterback for the St. Louis Rams and attempted only 11 passes. But in 1999 he put together one of the best seasons by a quarterback in NFL history. That season Warner passed for 4,353 yards and 41 touchdowns, was named NFL MVP, won a Super Bowl championship, and was named Super Bowl MVP. This is the jersey Warner wore in Super Bowl XXXIV when he completed his rags-to-riches pro football story.

RAY LEWIS JERSEY WORN IN SUPER BOWL XXXV

In 2000 the Baltimore Ravens led the NFL in six defensive categories and set a sixteen-game single-season record for fewest points allowed (165) and fewest rushing yards allowed (970). The leader of the Ravens defense was linebacker Ray Lewis, who was selected as the 2000 Defensive Player of the Year. Lewis finished the season with an outstanding performance in Super Bowl XXXV, in which he recorded 11 tackles (five solo) and was credited with four passes defended, earning him game MVP honors. This is Lewis's Super Bowl XXXV jersey.

MARVIN HARRISON

In 2002 Marvin Harrison set a new record for receptions in a season with 143. Paired with one of the all-time great quarterbacks in Peyton Manning, Harrison holds the NFL record for most receptions between a wide receiver and a quarterback with 943.

> " I take a lot of pride in what I do, and I don't get beat—period. I take things very personally, especially when our quarterback is getting hit. "
>
> —Willie Roaf

MICHAEL STRAHAN'S UNIFORM

New York Giants defensive end Michael Strahan wore this uniform on January 6, 2002, when in a game against the Green Bay Packers he set the single-season record for sacks. The record sack came when Packers quarterback Brett Favre faked a handoff and attempted to run to Strahan's side of the field. With Strahan running free toward him, Favre chose to avoid the inevitable collision and slid down, conceding the record sack. Strahan's record total is 22.5.

EMMITT SMITH RECORD WITH MARCUS ALLEN

A pyrotechnic display on October 27, 2002, honoring Number 22, Emmitt Smith, exploded as the Dallas Cowboys honored their running back when he became the NFL's all-time leading rusher, surpassing Hall of Fame great Walter Payton (16,726 yards). Smith's children seem to be taking all the excitement in stride as their father is congratulated by another Hall of Fame running back, Marcus Allen.

PHOTO: LOUIS DELUCA/
DALLAS MORNING NEWS

EMMITT SMITH'S JERSEY AND HELMET

Chicago Bears running back great Walter Payton was Emmitt Smith's boyhood hero. So as Emmitt approached the legendary Payton's career rushing record in 2002, he may have felt an even greater sense of awe. Smith broke Payton's record on October 27 in a game against the Seattle Seahawks. His record carry— for 11 yards—came in the game's fourth quarter. Anticipating he'd break Payton's record that day, Smith wore a different jersey in each quarter. He presented this jersey, worn during the third quarter, to the Hall of Fame along with the helmet he wore when he set the record. Smith's career rushing record stands at 18,355 yards.

SHANNON SHARPE'S JERSEY

Shannon Sharpe wore this jersey on November 18, 2001, in a game against the Cleveland Browns when he broke the career record for most receptions by a tight end. Former Browns tight end Ozzie Newsome, whose record Sharpe broke, was on hand for the performance and added his autograph to the milestone jersey.

JERRY RICE AND TIM BROWN

Two "titans" of the game, wide receivers Jerry Rice and Tim Brown, celebrated in the end zone after Brown caught a fourth-quarter touchdown pass as the Oakland Raiders defeated the Tennessee Titans 52–25 early in the 2002 season. Both teams finished the season with 11–5 records and met in the AFC Championship Game, which Oakland won 41–24. One week later, the Raiders were defeated by the Tampa Bay Buccaneers 48–21 in Super Bowl XXXVII.
PHOTO: BRYAN PATRICK/
THE SACRAMENTO BEE

COWHER SCREAMING

Pittsburgh Steelers coach Bill Cowher had plenty to shout about during the 2002 AFC Wild-Card Game. Pittsburgh quarterback Tommy Maddox, the NFL's Comeback Player of the Year, led Cowher's Steelers to 29 points in the final 19 minutes to overcome a 17-point deficit, defeating the Cleveland Browns 36–33.
PHOTO: DILIP VISHWANAT

The Denver Broncos had won back-to-back Lombardi Trophies in 1998–99, when the cap was still in its infancy and how to operate under it was still being ironed out. Only a year later, however, when the St. Louis Rams won the Super Bowl one season after going 4–12—and then saw their "Greatest Show on Turf" upset the following year by a New England Patriots team that was coming off a 5–11 record—Modell was far from alone in his assessment. Despite having beaten the number one seed in the AFC playoffs and the number one seed in the NFC, New England, a fourteen-and-a-half-point underdog the day it beat the Rams on Adam Vinatieri's 48-yard field goal as time expired, was labeled by then–Packers general manager Ron Wolf as a team that "won the Super Bowl with a waiver-wire team. No one has done anything like that before."

It all seemed to point to a revolving door of champions, a decade where no one would last long at the top or be long mired at the bottom. NFL dynasties had become like the Ming Dynasty. They were long gone and unlikely to return.

The experts, it turned out, could not have been more wrong. The way the first decade of the new millennium played, the advent

Right:

MARVIN HARRISON'S SINGLE-SEASON RECORD

Indianapolis Colts wide receiver Marvin Harrison set a new NFL record in 2002 for receptions in a single season. His 143 receptions eclipsed by 20 the old record held by Detroit Lions wide receiver Herman Moore. Harrison wore this jersey on December 15, 2002, when in a game against the Cleveland Browns he caught his 124th pass, breaking Moore's record.

Above:

TOM BRADY'S SUPER BOWL XXXVI JERSEY

Drafted in the sixth round of the 2000 NFL Draft, New England Patriots quarterback Tom Brady led his team to five Super Bowl appearances, earning game MVP honors in Super Bowls XXXVI and XXXVIII. This is the jersey he wore in Super Bowl XXXVI.

Right:

LaDAINIAN TOMLINSON'S SHOES AND GLOVES FROM 100/1000 SEASON

LaDainian Tomlinson was the first running back in NFL history to rush for 1,000 yards and have 100 receptions in the same season. These are the shoes and gloves the San Diego Chargers back wore on December 28, 2003, when in a game against the Oakland Raiders he made history by reaching the 100-reception mark. Tomlinson added to his record résumé in 2006 when he broke two NFL records, most touchdowns (31) and points (186) in a season.

TEDY BRUSCHI

Linebacker Tedy Bruschi's pro football career appeared to be over in 2005 after he suffered a mild stroke caused by a congenital heart defect. Determined to play again, the nine-year veteran completed an extensive rehabilitation program and, after sitting out the 2005 season, returned to his starter's role in 2006. At Bruschi's August 31, 2009, retirement press conference, an emotional Patriots coach Bill Belichick called him "the perfect player."

PHOTO: JIM DAVIS/*BOSTON GLOBE*

of the salary cap allowed the NFL to become more competitive from top to bottom, and more popular than any sport in American history, but only altered—not destroyed—the way a dynasty would be built.

Unlike in the past, when profligate spending could save a well-heeled team from its mistakes, today's dynasty had to be created on the solid footing of sound, long-term economic thinking and a firm grasp of the NFL's new economic realities. However, core policy continued to consist of two principles—stable, creative coaching and management; and stable, creative quarterbacking. With those in place all things were possible. Without them, well, you relied on the hope that on any given Sunday Bert Bell was right.

Beginning in 2000 and throughout the decade, the Patriots had not only stable management, coaching, and quarterbacking, but arguably some of the greatest examples of each in league history. Along with them came three Lombardi Trophies in four years, four Super Bowl appearances, a record-breaking 16–0 season in 2007 in which Tom Brady threw 50 touchdown passes, a stunning twenty-one straight victories at one point, and eight division titles in ten years.

MARSHALL FAULK SET CAREER RECEIVING MARK BY A RUNNING BACK

Marshall Faulk wore these shoes, gloves, and jersey on December 11, 2005, when he established an NFL record for career receiving yardage by a running back. The St. Louis Rams runner broke the old mark when he caught five passes for 25 yards in a game against the Minnesota Vikings. Faulk finished his career with 6,875 yards on 767 receptions and is one of only two players in NFL history to eclipse 1,000 yards rushing and receiving in the same season (1999).

The Patriots' head coach, Bill Belichick, once reviled as a hapless loser in Cleveland, became the architect of the first dynasty of the salary cap era, going 135–43 overall and 15–6 in the playoffs, the best winning percentages of his time and nearly the best in league history, while becoming the first NFL coach to win fourteen or more games in a season four times.

"I really don't think you can find too many people who can argue he's not the best coach in football," said Mike Ditka, who is one of only five NFL coaches to win fourteen or more games at least twice. "It speaks not only to his coaching ability but to the stability of the organization and their personnel and the way they do things. That's unbelievable when you think about fourteen wins in a sixteen-game season. Doing it four times? That's truly amazing.

"Sure you can say he's got the quarterback, but would the quarterback be greater in another system? I don't know that. Nobody knows that. They just play so well as a team and it all goes back to the coach. The record speaks for itself."

The Patriots' ascendance as the first dynasty of the salary cap era came utterly without warning. Few teams had as little success as the Patriots over the first forty-two years of their existence, and even

TIKI BARBER GOES OUT ON TOP

New York Giants running back Tiki Barber wore this jersey in what he declared to be his final regular-season game. That day, against the Washington Redskins, Barber rushed for 234 yards on 23 carries, the most yards gained by a running back in his final regular-season game. The old record was 165 yards and was established in 1937 by Redskins Hall of Fame running back Cliff Battles. Barber's career totals include 10,449 rushing yards and 5,183 receiving yards, and he joins Marshall Faulk and Marcus Allen as the only other running backs to gain more than 10,000 rushing yards and 5,000 receiving yards in a career.

HINES WARD SUPER BOWL XL

It took three big plays on offense for the Pittsburgh Steelers to defeat the Seattle Seahawks and win their record-tying fifth Super Bowl. The biggest play was a 43-yard fourth-quarter touchdown pass. The play began as a handoff from quarterback Ben Roethlisberger to running back Willie Parker, who handed off to wide receiver Antwaan Randle El on a reverse. Rolling to his right, Randle El then fired a picture-perfect pass to Hines Ward for the Steelers' game-clinching touchdown. The Steelers defeated Seattle 21–10.

PHOTO: DAN POWERS/*THE POST-CRESCENT*

[Martin talking about his elusiveness]

"*[It's been there]* all my life, back to my childhood days, when I was five, six, seven, eight, playing tag, I'd stand right in front of them and make them miss. On the football field, that's the way I envision it—like I'm still playing tag."

—Curtis Martin

BEARDED PATRIOTS LINEMEN

In a show of unity, New England Patriots linemen Matt Light (72), Logan Mankins (70), Dan Koppen (67), and Stephen Neal (61) all shunned razors during the 2006 season. Although the bearded linemen performed well, the 12–4 Patriots "missed by a hair" in the AFC Championship Game, losing to the Indianapolis Colts 38–34. Indianapolis defeated the Chicago Bears 29–17 in Super Bowl XLI.
PHOTO: JOHN BIEVER/*SPORTS ILLUSTRATED*

when they did briefly win, it was followed by two of the worst championship game losses in history, a 51–10 shellacking in the 1963 AFL Championship Game, after which they didn't make the playoffs again for twelve years, and a 46–10 loss in Super Bowl XX to Ditka's Bears that was at the time the worst loss in Super Bowl history.

After Robert Kraft purchased the team, for $172 million in 1994, the team improved, but something always seemed to go wrong. A dynasty they were not when the grim news of 9/11 hit with the stunning revelation that a terrorist attack had felled the World Trade Center in Manhattan.

At that moment, Kraft had what he terms a "blue steel moment." Earlier in the year, without having the financing in place, he had ordered $64 million worth of custom-made blue steel to begin construction of one of the first privately funded stadiums in league history. With the attacks in New York no one knew what the future held or what the economic status of the country would be.

At that moment, Kraft, whose team would soon lose its $100 million starting quarterback, Drew Bledsoe, to the injury that would

ADRIAN PETERSON'S UNIFORM FROM SINGLE-GAME RUSHING RECORD

Minnesota Vikings rookie running back Adrian Peterson wore this uniform on November 4, 2007, when he rushed for an NFL record 296 yards against the San Diego Chargers. Amazingly, Peterson gained 253 of those yards in the game's second half.

ANTONIO CROMARTIE'S 109-YARD RETURN OF A MISSED FIELD GOAL

A missed 57-yard field goal is normally not a historically significant event. But on November 4, 2007, when Minnesota Vikings kicker Ryan Longwell's 57-yard attempt came up short, history was made. That's because standing deep in the end zone was San Diego Chargers defensive back Antonio Cromartie, who hauled in the errant kick and bolted 109 yards for a touchdown. This is the ball he carried and the gloves he wore when he set the never-to-be-broken record.

Following page:

REGGIE BUSH

New Orleans Saints rookie running back Reggie Bush (25) dived into the end zone for his first touchdown from scrimmage during a November 12, 2006, game against the Pittsburgh Steelers at Heinz Field.

PHOTO: MIKE EHRMANN

BRETT FAVRE'S CAREER RECORDS

In his final season in Green Bay, quarterback Brett Favre surpassed Dan Marino as the NFL's all-time leader in all four major passing categories—touchdowns (442), completions (5,377), attempts (8,758), and yards (61,655). He added to those totals in 2008 with the New York Jets and in 2009–10 with the Minnesota Vikings. Favre wore this uniform on December 16, 2007, against the St. Louis Rams when he bettered Marino's career passing yardage total. The football is the one he threw on September 30, 2007, against the Minnesota Vikings for his record-setting 421st career touchdown.

SUPER BOWL XLII GAME BALL AND TOM COUGHLIN'S PLAYSHEET

In Super Bowl XLII, the NFC Wild Card New York Giants scored with 35 seconds remaining to defeat the New England Patriots 17–14. The Giants' upset win ended the Patriots' shot at a "perfect season," as they had gone 16–0 in the regular season and 2–0 in the playoffs.

free Brady from obscurity, had to make a choice. "I wrote a personal letter to guarantee the money," he recalled. "It's not like it was a roll of paper you could send back. It was custom designed. Seven years earlier I'd paid nearly $57 million more than my financial people told me I should to buy a team that was twenty-eighth in won-lost record and twenty-eighth in revenue. Those things they don't teach you at Harvard Business School."

In the end, it would work out. Brady would become the best quarterback of his era, Belichick would become its best coach, and Gillette Stadium would become a monument to the organization Kraft created. Yet as imposing as the standards set by the Patriots were after they won three Super Bowls in four years in 2001–04, they were not alone. By the end of the decade the Steelers and Colts had put up nearly as imposing victory totals and among them the three had reached nine of the twelve Super Bowls since 2000, with the Steelers making a loud case of their own for first dynasty of the new millennium.

Each had done it in its own way, yet all had done it the same way—by managing a mathematical formula without forgetting that the needs of team-building in this new environment must not ignore that football dominance was still rooted where it had always been.

"The teams that have had the most success since the salary cap came into being are the football-oriented organizations that never succumbed to the idea you could financially engineer your way to success," said Colts president Bill Polian, a five-time NFL Executive of the Year who was one of the architects of the salary cap. "With the cap we felt things would go in four-year cycles. In reality that's what's happened, so teams that are able to maintain coaching continuity and quarterback continuity prosper. Pittsburgh has had two coaches since this began and [Ben] Roethlisberger at quarterback for some time.

"New England has had two coaches since the salary cap was instituted, Bill Parcells and Bill Belichick, and Belichick and Tom Brady for the entire decade. We've been in Indianapolis thirteen years with three coaches (Jim Mora Sr., Tony Dungy, and Jim Caldwell) and really one quarterback (Peyton Manning). I would include the Eagles and the Packers in that group as well. The common denominator? The Super Bowl drives the train in those places."

Clearly, the best-run teams in the decade of the salary cap have been in the AFC. Between 2001 and 2010, the NFC crowned ten different conference champions while New England (four), Pittsburgh (three), and Indianapolis (two) won nine of ten AFC titles. What did the Patriots and Steelers

TIGHT END TONY GONZALEZ SETS RECORDS

Kansas City Chiefs tight end Tony Gonzalez caught two touchdown passes on October 14, 2007, in a 27–20 win over the Cincinnati Bengals. The first touchdown reception moved him past Shannon Sharpe into sole possession of the NFL record for touchdown receptions by a tight end. This is the jersey he wore that day.

MVP PEYTON MANNING UNIFORM

Following the 2008 season, quarterback Peyton Manning was honored for a record third time with NFL MVP honors. He had previously earned MVP recognition in 2003 (shared with Tennessee Titans quarterback Steve McNair), and in 2004. His 2008 honors did not come easily. Prior to the start of the season, the Colts' all-time leading passer had two knee operations that affected his early-season performance. After starting 3–4, Manning and the Colts posted nine consecutive wins, ending with a 23–17 wild-card playoff loss to the San Diego Chargers. The following season, Manning earned MVP honors for a fourth time. This is the uniform he wore during his 2008 campaign.

in particular do that allowed them to emerge as the alpha teams of a decade designed to prevent such a thing?

"For us to dominate now, when everything is geared to be 8–8, was the hardest thing," Kraft said. "It's a much more difficult job than it used to be.

"For the Patriots to win in 2001, with all that had gone on in the country, with 9/11 and the uncertainty of trying to build a new stadium, was a tremendous feat. When Tommy spiked the ball and caught it in his left hand and handed it to the referee and Adam came on and made the kick, it was red, white, and blue. We were all Patriots that night.

"That we went on to three more Super Bowls in the next six years happened because we realized to be consistently successful today you needed not just strong football people who understood personnel and strategy but also people who understood economics and value. You need football people who understand where the breaking point is

when a contract could hurt you. If you don't understand economics and value in today's NFL you won't succeed.

"Bill has an understanding of finances as well as football. You can't stockpile guys. You have limits on what you can spend. You must know if you make bad decisions you will be penalized for many years, not just for a few quarters. Bill understood value."

The cap prevents situations like the Cowboys had with both Roger Staubach and Craig Morton as quarterbacks at the same time. The same is true of the 49ers' years with Joe Montana and Steve Young on their roster. Economics preclude it because it would prevent the kind of top-to-bottom team-building and flexibility now necessary to win.

Former Dallas Cowboys personnel director Gil Brandt was in the middle of the Dallas dynasty of the Tom Landry era and admits what the Patriots, Steelers, Colts, and to a lesser extent Packers and Eagles accomplished in the new millennium was a far more delicate balancing act than in his day.

"It is a lot harder to win consistently today than it was when

NFL INTERNATIONAL

Even though running back LaDainian Tomlinson rushed for 105 yards, the New Orleans Saints still managed to pull out a 37–32 victory over the San Diego Chargers on October 26, 2008, at London's Wembley Stadium, in the NFL's second regular-season game played outside North America. The New York Giants had defeated the Miami Dolphins 13–10 a year earlier at Wembley. "Playing a limited number of regular-season games internationally will help build and grow an already passionate international fan base," proclaimed NFL commissioner Roger Goodell in 2008. The NFL's International Series of regular-season games is now an annual event.
PHOTO: K.C. ALFRED

ED REED BREAKS HIS OWN RECORD

On November 23, 2008, Baltimore Ravens safety Ed Reed intercepted this football and returned it 107 yards for a touchdown. The scoring play is the longest interception return in NFL history, surpassing the 106-yard record he had established in 2004. These are the shoes he wore that day and the jersey he wore when he broke his own record in 2008.

we did it," Brandt concedes. "The competitive balance is closer and closer all the time. It's hard to get an edge.

"We might have drafted our fiftieth-ranked player in the sixth round then because half the teams were drafting out of comic books. At quarterback we always tried to have a pair and a spare. You can't do that today, so drafting is more important than ever because it's not only young talent, it's cheap talent.

"Some people understand the cap better and know how to use it better. Some coaches know how to deploy their people better. Those things became more important after the cap came into the league."

One thing the salary cap did was prevent teams with a superior financial situation from stockpiling talent, but there was more to it than that. It also put an end to sentimentality in personnel decisions.

No longer could a veteran player in decline be retained in recognition of past contributions. Either he goes or you go, a decision younger coaches and personnel men seemed more able to make without sentimentality. This meant teams tended to favor cheaper but less experienced prospects with growth potential who might quickly enter their prime while still being cheaper.

This meant more mistakes on the field from less experienced players and a premium being placed on versatility by a coach like Belichick, whose motto quickly became, "The more you can do…"

Just as there is an art to running an offense or creating a defensive plan, there has always been an art to building a roster that wins consistently. Today it is art produced with a carving knife as well as a checkbook.

"There's much more to this today than a financial formula," Polian said. "Building a team that can win consistently still involves 80 percent football planning and strategy and 20 percent financial engineering.

"The history of free agency in all sports is you always overpay. We overpaid Peyton Manning, but he was a unique talent vital to our system. We had to balance the payroll elsewhere. We all read *Moneyball* [the bestselling book on how the Oakland A's built contending

CURTIS MARTIN

Curtis Martin, seen here running out of the grasp of Pittsburgh Steelers linebacker Kendrell Bell, joined fellow Hall of Fame running back Barry Sanders as the only runners to start their careers with ten straight 1,000-yard seasons. Martin led his teams in rushing each of his eleven seasons with the New York Jets and New England Patriots. In 2012 he was named to the Hall of Fame.
PHOTO: EZRA SHAW/GETTY IMAGES

DAVID TYREE'S HELMET

New York Giants wide receiver David Tyree wore this helmet in Super Bowl XLII. He made a spectacular fourth-quarter catch of an Eli Manning pass by pinning it against his helmet as he was pulled to the ground by a New England Patriots defender.

baseball teams with limited budgets]. Where can we find players who fit our system and cost us less?

"Tony [Dungy] said in our defense we could play with a different type of linebacker and corner. They're fungible for us. I hate that word because it takes the human element away, but that's what the game became. Where can you save?

"You cannot prosper within the salary cap system unless you're willing and able to make those hard decisions. I do think the younger personnel guys like my son Chris, Mike Tannenbaum with the Jets, Scott Pioli with New England and now the Chiefs, [Thomas] Dimitroff in Atlanta, are less troubled by it. It's the only system they've known. In my era, a guy was with your team his whole career most of the time.

"It's different building a team today and, I must say, not quite as much fun. Leave-taking is never much fun or as sentimental as it once was. But you can't pay more for production than it's worth to your system or you're doomed....System football has become a much more critical factor in how you acquire players. You never heard the phrase 'system football' before the salary cap. Linebackers are not critical to our system. Other positions are not critical to Bill Belichick's. Everyone on the personnel side needs to understand your system. In the ideal, the position a guy plays and the money outlay ought not to factor into who you draft. You should always draft the best player, but you can't today. In our economic model we couldn't draft Lawrence Taylor with a high first-round pick unless we projected him as a defensive end.

"That's why very few teams trade up anymore. It's tempting if you need a left tackle but you can't pay him. It's worse yet if I need a right tackle or a nose tackle. The risk/reward ratio drafting high is too great so you don't go up...very often. You blow a high first-round pick today, you lose a four-year cycle. You do it on a quarterback, you end up with $35–$40 million in dead money and it's three or four years before you begin to cover that."

Many of these changes in philosophy on how a team is built grew from the Patriot way, which, simply put, values roster flexibility (how many ways can I use you?) and a sense of team over self. As Pioli has often said, "It's not about collecting talent. It's about assembling a team."

What acquiring talent is not about is preserving that team for a ten-year run. It's about being forced, as the Steelers were, to trade top receiver and Super Bowl XLIII MVP hero Santonio Holmes to the Jets and still get back to the Super Bowl two years later with two rookie wideouts. It's about choices, and no one made better ones than Pittsburgh this decade, with eight of its previous ten first-round picks starting in Super Bowl XLV, the absent Holmes a ninth.

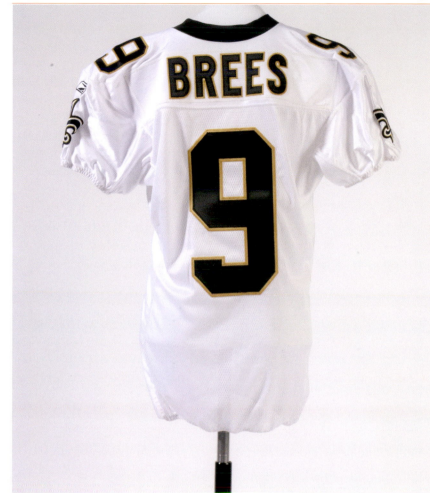

DREW BREES'S SUPER BOWL MVP JERSEY

Quarterback Drew Brees's MVP performance in Super Bowl XLIV put the exclamation point on the New Orleans Saints' storybook 2009 season. Wearing this jersey, Brees completed 32 of 39 passes for 288 yards and two touchdowns in the Saints' 31–17 win over the Indianapolis Colts. His 32 completions tied a Super Bowl record set by Tom Brady in Super Bowl XXXVIII.

SUPER BOWL XLIII RING

The term "sixcess" was coined after the Pittsburgh Steelers captured their record sixth Super Bowl ring after defeating the Arizona Cardinals in Super Bowl XLIII. The history-making victory came in dramatic come-from-behind fashion when quarterback Ben Roethlisberger found Santonio Holmes in the corner of the end zone in the waning seconds of the game. The Steelers have earned the most division titles and wins in the regular season and postseason since the 1970 AFL-NFL merger.

"Panic doesn't seem to work, let's put it that way," said Steelers President Art Rooney II. "There are enough people that seem to have gone through that mode, so our feeling is you pick good people and try to stick with them. We've always believed building through the draft was the right way to do it. The cap enhanced that feeling."

But difficult decisions must be made too—decisions like Belichick's to cut safety Lawyer Milloy after he refused to take a pay cut just before the 2003 season began. Milloy was a backbone of the defense and long one of Belichick's favorite players, so much so that Belichick gave Milloy his suite before Super Bowl XXXVI after he complained about his cramped quarters.

Giving up a suite was one thing. Giving up roster flexibility in the age of the salary cap is quite another. If you do the latter too often, you won't be in the former for very long.

Following page:

RAVENS AND PATRIOTS IN THE MUD

Defensive lineman Jarvis Green did his best to overcome a double-team and bad footing in this throwback-looking game between the New England Patriots and Baltimore Ravens at Gillette Stadium.

PHOTO: JIM DAVIS/*BOSTON GLOBE*

The Eleven Greatest Moments

PETE FIERLE

Opposite (detail) and below (full frame):

SQUARING OFF IN SUPER BOWL XLV

Two great champions, the Green Bay Packers and the Pittsburgh Steelers, went head to head in Super Bowl XLV. The Packers emerged victorious by a score of 31–25.

A *Harris Poll in 1965 determined, for the first time, that professional football was the favorite sport of fans across the United States of America. Pro football not only remains the country's top sport but continues to grow in popularity worldwide.*

HELPING SHAPE THE GAME'S appeal are countless exciting moments that have helped define the National Football League. But which of these great events truly have had a long-lasting effect on the game? The list, though long, gets smaller when one assigns "enduring impact" to the criteria. The challenge of determining the most significant of the NFL's memorable moments was put forth to a panel of experts that included the Pro Football Hall of Fame's Senior Selection Committee along with the editors and contributing writers of this book.

The list could have easily been fifty to coincide with the present theme of fifty years of the Pro Football Hall of Fame. But that might have produced a candidate list ten times that number, making consensus difficult if not impossible. Because the official rules of American football have long stipulated that the game shall be played with eleven players on either side of the line of scrimmage, it seemed like eleven was the perfect "football number" and would focus the selectors' attention on the undeniable landmarks of the game.

A preliminary list was prepared by the Pro Football Hall of Fame and distributed to the panel. The only criterion for inclusion was that the moment had an influence on the game larger than the event itself. No ranking was requested; just eleven moments the panelists felt stood the test of time. Here are the results; each of the great moments is highlighted in red.

1. THE 1958 CHAMPIONSHIP GAME

Football fans could relive the excitement of the 1958 NFL Championship Game by listening to this 45-RPM recording of the game's play-by-play broadcast.

2. THE FORMATION OF THE AMERICAN FOOTBALL LEAGUE

The team owners of the upstart American Football League lightheartedly referred to themselves as "The Foolish Club."

A THREE-YEAR PERIOD THAT bridged the 1950s and '60s garnered significant support. Three of the eleven moments that made the cut occurred during this time. Interestingly, one centered on an individual, another involved off-the-field negotiations, and the third was one of the most spectacular games in league annals.

Labeled the "Greatest Game Ever Played," the 1958 NFL Championship Game pitted the Baltimore Colts against the New York Giants. A sell-out crowd at New York's Yankee Stadium and a national television audience witnessed one of the most memorable come-from-behind victories in league history. Down 17–14 in the fourth quarter, Colts quarterback Johnny Unitas calmly orchestrated 73- and 80-yard drives for a last-second game-tying field goal and overtime touchdown run. An eerie photo of the now-famous Alan Ameche touchdown run was captured by an Associated Press photographer as the workhorse back plowed through the right side of the Colts line for the win. It was the first time in history that the NFL championship was determined in sudden death. More significant than the game needing overtime to determine a winner was that the dramatic finish drew the attention of a national television and radio audience. It marked the beginning of an era; soon thereafter, pro football would explode in popularity across the nation.

On August 14, 1959, a twenty-six-year-old Texas oilman named Lamar Hunt announced plans for a new professional football league to begin play in 1960. Hunt's plan for a rival league came after NFL owners rejected his proposal to secure an NFL franchise. Convinced that the sport was primed for expansion, Hunt contacted other sportsmen, including Bud Adams, who like Hunt had been rejected by NFL owners. Shortly thereafter the Hunt-led group announced the formation of the American Football League (AFL). The AFL operated for ten seasons before merging with the older NFL. During its decade of play, the AFL succeeded in spreading the game into new markets such as Houston, Oakland, and Denver, and placing teams in cities that had previously held NFL franchises like Buffalo, Boston, and Dallas. It also created opportunity for more players, especially African Americans. Several of the AFL clubs began scouting small black colleges, helping to tear down the racial barrier in the sport. The AFL also introduced a number of innovations to the game such as the two-point conversion and the addition of names on the back of uniforms.

At the same time that Hunt and others were consumed with creating a new league, NFL owners were faced with the difficult decision of finding a new leader for theirs. Longtime NFL commissioner Bert Bell died suddenly after suffering a heart attack in the closing minutes of the Philadelphia Eagles' game against the Pittsburgh Steelers on October 11, 1959. Mired in debate about who would succeed Bell, the NFL owners shocked the sports world when they selected the comparatively unknown thirty-three-year-old general manager of the Los Angeles Rams as their next leader. On January 26, 1960, **Pete Rozelle was named NFL commissioner**. Surely, the group of owners could never have imagined that their pick would be so influential in growing the game into the country's most popular sport. But that's exactly what Rozelle accomplished during his twenty-nine years as NFL commissioner. Widely regarded as the finest commissioner of any sports league, he secured the NFL's first league-wide television contract. He was pivotal in negotiating the merger between the NFL and AFL and the subsequent realignment of the new combined leagues. Perhaps his term as commissioner can be best defined by his vision for the Super Bowl. Rozelle transformed the league's championship game into the international extravaganza it is today.

It goes without saying that the **formation meeting of the National Football League**, held on September 17, 1920, in Canton, Ohio, has to be among the eleven most significant moments in NFL history. Representatives of the league's ten charter members crammed into the tiny showroom of Canton Bulldogs owner Ralph Hay's Hupmobile dealership and created the American Professional Football Association, which was renamed the National Football League in 1922. Interestingly, the impetus behind forming the league was to combat three major issues plaguing the game at that time: rising salaries, college eligibility, and players jumping from team to team. The organization of the league brought structure to a previously ungoverned sport. Regular meetings among the team owners created rules and bylaws to allow for fair and stable play on the pro level for the first time.

As could be expected, the league experienced growing pains in the early years as teams came and went. With each new season the league struggled just to keep going while pursuing the vision set forth during the 1920 meeting in Canton. Now this country's most successful sports league, the NFL survived forty-eight failed franchises, the majority of which occurred during its first decade. Just two franchises represented at the league's founding meeting remain in existence. The Decatur Staleys are today the Chicago Bears, while the Racine Cardinals (from Chicago, not Racine, Wisconsin) operate as the Arizona Cardinals.

A defining moment by the Bears in 1925 was pivotal to the NFL as the league gained great notoriety and, perhaps more importantly, respect. Playing in the shadow of pro baseball and college football, the NFL received a huge boost when late that season Chicago **signed Harold "Red" Grange**, the nation's most heralded college star, to a pro contract. The Illinois halfback made his pro debut on Thanksgiving Day just five days after playing his final college game. A capacity crowd of 36,000 fans filled Cubs Park in Chicago to see Grange and the Bears battle the crosstown rival Cardinals.

3. PETE ROZELLE NAMED COMMISSIONER

After 23 ballots failed to produce a new leader, NFL owners at their 1960 annual meeting made a surprise decision and named thirty-three-year-old Pete Rozelle commissioner.

4. THE FORMATION OF THE NFL

Canton Bulldogs owner Ralph Hay hosted the NFL's organizational meeting in Canton on September 17, 1920. Pictured here is his Jordan and Hupmobile service garage. The meeting was held in his nearby auto showroom.

5. RED GRANGE TURNS PRO

Chicago Bears co-owners Dutch Sternaman and George Halas look on as Red Grange and his manager, C. C. Pyle, examine Red's contract to play pro football.

6

DRAFT 2000

ROUND #   6   NEW ENGLAND

CHOICE FROM: Compensatory Selection

NAME: Brady, Tom
        (Last)   (First)

POSITION: QB

SCHOOL: Michigan

OVERALL #: #199

Patriots

6. THE NFL DRAFT

Started in 1936, the NFL draft is where dreams come true for a lucky few, including some "long-shots" like the 199th player chosen in the 2000 draft, quarterback Tom Brady.

7

7. THE REINTEGRATION OF PRO FOOTBALL

Marion Motley and Bill Willis went on to have Hall of Fame careers after breaking pro football's color barrier in 1946.

Ten days later 70,000 spectators packed the Polo Grounds in New York City to watch Grange's Bears take on the hometown Giants. The showing convinced Giants owner Tim Mara to continue to operate his club in the NFL's largest market, rather than fold the team as he had considered doing. After the season, Grange and the Bears embarked on a cross-country barnstorming tour. Grange, pro football's first big gate attraction, not only helped spread the game to tens of thousands of new fans, but his signing also provided much-needed credibility to the financial prospects of the sport.

By the mid-1930s the NFL was an established league but not without its issues. A growing problem was a competitive imbalance that resulted in a few teams—most notably the Giants, Bears, and Packers—monopolizing the top spot in the league, while other less fortunate clubs constantly struggled at the bottom of the standings.

An innovative idea was introduced by Eagles owner and future NFL commissioner Bert Bell, whereby teams could select college players in inverse order of their finish the prior season. Bell's proposal of a system to help weaker teams improve was widely accepted by his fellow owners, and the first NFL draft was held on February 8, 1936. The group of owners liked the idea so much that after they picked five players as prescribed, Bell made a motion to continue and pick four additional players. His suggestion was approved unanimously.

Today, Bell's idea has morphed into a huge spectacle that compels teams to invest people, time, and resources into sophisticated scouting procedures, the result of which can confirm or change the fate of a club almost immediately. The NFL draft has also been transformed into a huge fan celebration as each team's faithful eagerly await the annual infusion of talent into their team's roster.

Every major sport has iconic figures whose contributions have left an indelible mark. Sometimes the contribution is well known, but the contributor or contributors may not be as well remembered. Nearly any sports fan can cite Jackie Robinson as the player who broke modern Major League Baseball's "color barrier." Yet the names of four African American pioneers who made possible the permanent reintegration of pro football are lesser known. Furthermore, the fact that Marion Motley, Bill Willis, Woody Strode, and Kenny Washington signed pro football contracts one year before Robinson's debut in the majors is even less familiar to most sports fans.

Although there were a handful of African American players in pro football between 1904 and 1933, pro football, like baseball, had its own color barrier from 1934 until 1946, when the Los Angeles Rams signed Strode and Washington, and the Cleveland Browns of the new rival All-America Football Conference inked Motley and Willis. While the Rams tandem (due primarily to injury and

age) had limited success, both Motley and Willis turned in careers that earned them election to the Pro Football Hall of Fame. However, the true legacy of these four pioneers is the path they created for future generations of players. As a result of their courage and determination, pro football quickly started to reintegrate, and by the mid-1960s every pro football roster included African American players.

The impact of the foursome's appearance on football fields not only laid the groundwork for those who followed, but Brooklyn Dodgers owner Branch Rickey once shared that it influenced his decision to bring Robinson up to the majors. He felt that if Motley, Willis, Strode, and Washington could play a bruising contact sport like pro football without a major incident, then the time was right to integrate baseball.

Sundays have long been synonymous with NFL football. But in 1970, a new weekly tradition that included one featured game on Monday night forever changed the landscape of the game. Few could imagine the enduring impact of ABC's telecast of the NFL during prime time on a weeknight. Doubters were prevalent when the Cleveland Browns faced the New York Jets in the *Monday Night Football* debut on September 21, 1970. Yet the tradition became a nationwide phenomenon that captured huge ratings and in turn was a major reason for the NFL's dramatic rise in popularity in the years that followed.

At the same time the league began a regular-season schedule under lights, the spotlight shined brightly on the Jets and their star quarterback, Joe Namath. The former All-America at Alabama was the media darling of New York. His signature moment came in the days leading up to **Super Bowl III** following the 1968 season. The confident passer was preparing to lead his Jets team against the heavily favored Baltimore Colts. After all, the NFL had dominated the AFL in the two Super Bowls to date. Namath, when questioned by reporters about the upcoming game, brashly predicted that not only would the Jets win the game but he "guaranteed" it. In one of the greatest upsets in sports history, Namath guided the Jets to a stunning 16–7 victory. American Football League fans on hand at Miami's Orange Bowl for the game cheered wildly with chants of "AFL, AFL, AFL!" as the clock clicked down to the final gun.

Aside from making Namath a sports hero, the Jets' win "guaranteed" the AFL's place as a credible league worthy of competition with the older NFL. The AFL win also fueled the Super Bowl rivalry between the two leagues that continues today, less heatedly, between the AFC and the NFC.

One game, perhaps more than any other, cemented the legacy of one of the finest coaches ever to roam an NFL sideline. The Green

8. *MONDAY NIGHT FOOTBALL*
Monday Night Football debuted on ABC-TV on September 21, 1970.

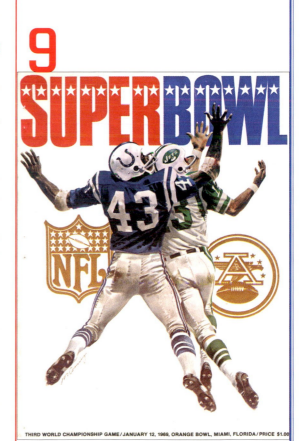

THIRD WORLD CHAMPIONSHIP GAME/JANUARY 12, 1969, ORANGE BOWL, MIAMI, FLORIDA/PRICE $1.00

9. SUPER BOWL III
Joe Namath "guaranteed" a win for his New York Jets in Super Bowl III.

10

10. THE ICE BOWL

Green Bay Packers defensive end Willie Davis surely hoped that Lambeau's "electrified" field would prevent the playing surface from freezing. It didn't.

11

11. THE AFL/NFL MERGER

Dallas Cowboys president/general manager Tex Schramm, NFL Commissioner Pete Rozelle, and AFL founder Lamar Hunt addressed the media on June 8, 1966, to announce the merger of the two rival leagues.

Bay Packers hosted the Dallas Cowboys at Lambeau Field for the NFL championship on New Year's Eve 1967. The two teams fought for the league title in unbearably frigid conditions. Earning the moniker the Ice Bowl, the game remains one of the NFL's all-time classics. When quarterback Bart Starr dove over the goal line on a quarterback sneak in the closing seconds to give Green Bay the 21–17 victory, it put the exclamation point on the Vince Lombardi era of the Green Bay Packers.

Lombardi, whose name now adorns the Super Bowl trophy given to the NFL's champions each season, led the Packers as they developed into one of the greatest dynasties the league has ever seen. He guided Green Bay to five NFL titles during the 1960s, including victories in the first two Super Bowls.

As it turned out, the Ice Bowl also marked the last time that Lombardi coached the Packers at Lambeau Field. He and the Packers followed the championship win with a second straight Super Bowl victory. Lombardi then resigned, only to resurface as the coach and executive vice president of the Washington Redskins before his untimely death at age fifty-seven on September 3, 1970.

Pro football was growing on all levels in the 1960s. Perhaps the only major diversion was the escalating "war" between the NFL and the AFL. A rival league was nothing new to the NFL, as other pro leagues had challenged the senior circuit in every decade since the league was born in 1920. But the AFL of the 1960s was different. Its brand of football was on par with what was being played in the NFL. So the two leagues fought for new talent, battled for supremacy in similar markets, and ultimately decided to raid each other's rosters.

It became apparent that for the betterment of the sport, peace needed to be drawn. Several secret meetings were held between leaders of both leagues that resulted in the June 8, 1966, announcement of the AFL-NFL merger. The first phase called for an annual world championship game (later named the Super Bowl), preseason games between league teams, and a joint college player draft starting in 1967. The final piece of the merger came in 1970 when the two leagues became one. Clearly, had the battle stayed the course and rational minds not prevailed in working toward a merger, the game's growth would have been stunted.

Nearly a hundred years after the NFL was founded in Canton, Ohio, it continues to thrive. Huge revenue and television ratings that dwarf those of any other sports league continue as the NFL moves toward a greater worldwide presence. Week in and week out throughout the year, there are many great moments on the field and off. Eventually one or more of these eleven iconic pro football moments will succumb to progress.

Opposite:
REGGIE WHITE

Reggie White, the "Minister of Defense," was named to the NFL's All-Decade Teams of the 1980s and 1990s, the NFL's 75th Anniversary Team, was voted first-team All-Pro ten times in his fifteen-year career, and was elected to the Pro Football Hall of Fame in 2006.

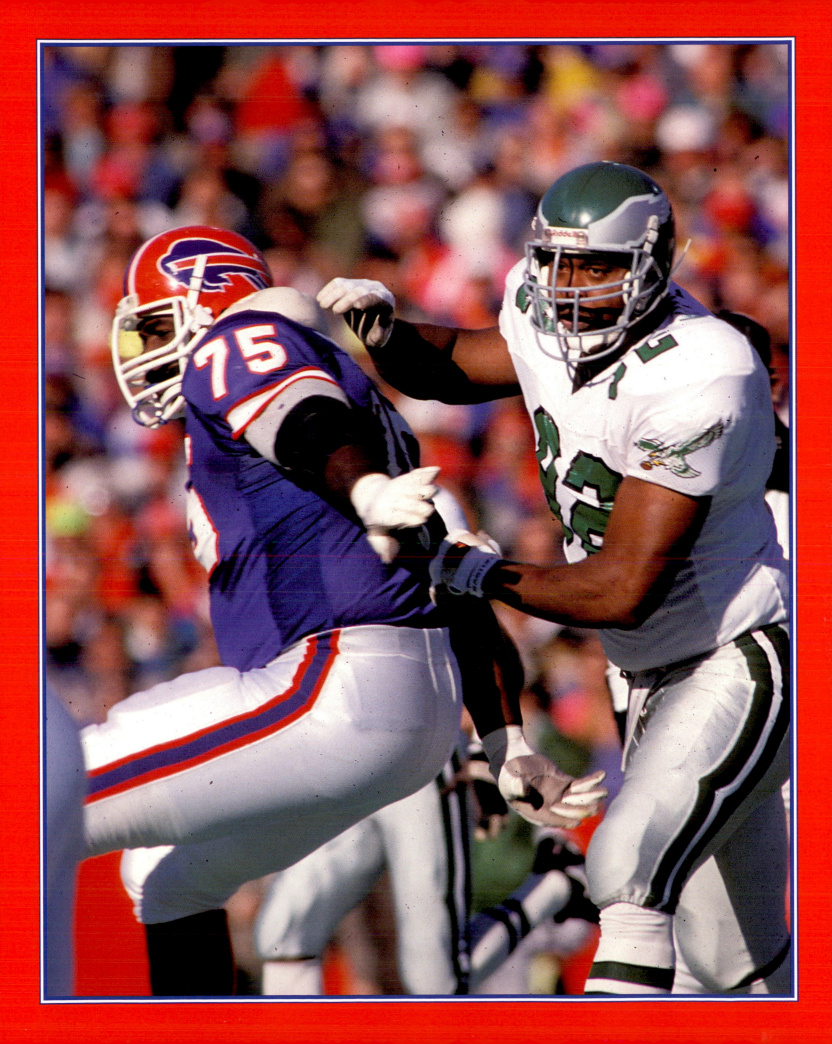

About the Essayists

DAVE ANDERSON, a *New York Times* sports columnist since 1971, was awarded a Pulitzer Prize for distinguished commentary in 1981 and the Pro Football Hall of Fame's Dick McCann Award in 1998. In addition to his *Times* columns, he has written nearly four hundred magazine articles and twenty-two books, including four in collaboration with Hall of Fame coach John Madden, and *Countdown to Super Bowl*, a 1969 day-by-day chronicle leading to the Jets' 16–7 upset of the Baltimore Colts. A past member of the Pro Football Hall of Fame Selection Committee, he has written about the NFL since 1956. He is a member of the National Sportscasters and Sportswriters Hall of Fame. He lives in Tenafly, New Jersey, with his wife, Maureen.

JARRETT BELL has been an NFL beat writer for *USA Today* since 1993. He previously covered the San Francisco 49ers for the *Marin* (County) *Independent Journal* for three years (1990–92) and served as editor of the *Dallas Cowboys Weekly*. He began a nine-year association with the Cowboys in 1981, shortly after graduating from Michigan State University. After four years as a contributing writer for the team-owned *Cowboys Weekly*, he joined the staff full-time in 1985 as an assistant editor. He was promoted to editor in 1989. Bell is the recipient of multiple writing awards from the Pro Football Writers of America and has been a member of the Pro Football Hall of Fame Selection Committee since 1997. He has also served on the media panel that selects the Super Bowl MVP.

RON BORGES has been a sportswriter since 1974, beginning his career at the smallest weekly newspaper in Massachusetts before traveling to California, where he covered the Oakland Raiders, Golden State Warriors, boxing—and at one point the Senate campaign of Tom Hayden—for the *Sacramento Observer, Sacramento Union,* and *Oakland Tribune*. Returning east in 1982, he covered the Baltimore Orioles for the *Baltimore News-American* and the New England Patriots for the *Boston Globe,* for whom he wrote a national football column from 1983 to 2000. Next he moved on to become general sports columnist at the *Boston Herald*. Borges has also contributed work to HBO Sports, *Pro Football Weekly, The Ring,* and MSNBC, as well as local radio and television. He has been honored to serve as a member of the Pro Football Hall of Fame Selection Committee and the senior selection committee since 2003. His only real achievement, he states, is raising two happy children, which is fine by him.

Opposite:

JOHN MADDEN

"I believe that the busts talk to each other," John Madden proclaimed during his enshrinement speech. "I can't wait for that conversation, I really can't. Vince Lombardi, Reggie [White], Walter Payton, all my ex-players, we'll be there forever and ever and ever talking about whatever. That's what I believe. That's what I think is going to happen, and no one's ever going to talk me out of that."

BOB CARROLL, a talented researcher, writer, and sports historian, was the author of more than twenty books, most notably *Pro Football: When the Grass Was Real* and *Baseball Between the Lies*. He was also the founder and executive director of the Professional Football Researchers Association, and edited the group's newsletter, *The Coffin Corner*, until his death in 2009. He was a retired art and English teacher at McKeesport High School in McKeesport, Pennsylvania. Carroll was coauthor of *The Hidden Game of Football* (with John Thorn and Pete Palmer), as well as *Total Football: The Official Encyclopedia of the National Football League*, the ultimate football reference book. His non-sports books included *The Importance of Napoleon* and *The Battle of Stalingrad*.

PETE FIERLE joined the Pro Football Hall of Fame in 1988 and today serves as manager of digital media/communications. A member of the Hall of Fame's management team, he directs all aspects of the hall's website—programming, promotion, and development. He serves as the site's editor and primary writer, manages the Hall of Fame's social media platforms, and is editor of the *Official Pro Football Hall of Fame Yearbook*. He is also responsible for the day-to-day management of the Hall of Fame's research department that assists the NFL, the thirty-two teams, the media, members of the academic community, students, and fans. A graduate of Ithaca College, Fierle lives with his wife, Debbie, and two children in Jackson Township, Ohio.

RICK GOSSELIN worked for United Press International for two years in Detroit before transferring to New York City in 1975 to cover the New York Giants and coordinate NFC coverage for the wire service. He transferred to Kansas City in 1977, spending nine years as UPI's Midlands sports editor, before moving to the *Kansas City Star* in 1986. He moved to the

Dallas Morning News in 1990 and covered the Cowboys in 1990–91, then served as the newspaper's NFL columnist from 1992 to 2010 before his appointment as a general sports columnist in 2011. The recipient of several writing awards, including the Dick McCann Memorial Award in 2004 for "long and distinguished reporting in the field of professional football," Gosselin is a member of the Pro Football Hall of Fame Selection Committee.

JOE HORRIGAN is a thirty-five-year employee of the Pro Football Hall of Fame. Currently the Hall of Fame's vice president of communications/exhibits, he previously served as its curator/director of research information. A recognized historian of the sport, Horrigan has written extensively on pro football and is the author of *The Pro Football Hall of Fame Answer Book* and *Football Legends of All Time* (with Bob Carroll). A charter member and past president of the Pro Football Researchers Association, he was the 1991 recipient of that organization's Ralph Hay Award. Among his Hall of Fame responsibilities, Horrigan administers the Pro Football Hall of Fame's annual enshrinee selection process and the production of the nationally televised Pro Football Hall of Fame Enshrinement Ceremony. He and his wife, Mary Ann, live in Green, Ohio.

PETER KING has written six books, the most recent of which is *Monday Morning Quarterback: A Fully Caffeinated Guide to Everything You Need to Know About the NFL*. His Monday Morning Quarterback column on SI.com has become a must-read for fans and league insiders. Prior to joining *Sports Illustrated* as a staff writer in 1989, he covered the NFL for *Newsday* (1985–89) and the *Cincinnati Enquirer* (1980–85). King has won several awards throughout his career, including two AP Sports Editors Awards for excellence in sports journalism. Most recently, he was named 2010 National Sportswriter of the Year by the National Sportscasters and Sportswriters Association. For the past six years King has served as a reporter for NBC's *Football Night in America* studio show. He lives in Boston with his wife, Ann.

IRA MILLER, who covered the NFL for the *San Francisco Chronicle* from 1977 through 2005, is a past president of the Pro Football Writers of America. He also has contributed to *Sporting News*, NFL.com, and other media outlets. He won three first-place awards in the PFWA's annual writing competition, and in 1997 was honored by the Press Club of the (San Francisco) East Bay with the award for "best sports news story," chronicling the departure of former 49ers coach George Seifert. In 1993, he won the Dick McCann Memorial Award, presented by the PFWA for "long and distinguished coverage of pro football." Miller is a member of the Pro Football Hall of Fame Selection Committee.

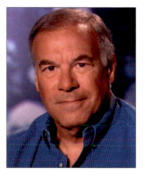

STEVE SABOL, president of NFL Films, began his career in 1964 as a cinematographer working for his father and founder of NFL Films, Ed Sabol. He has been awarded thirty-four Emmys for writing, cinematography, editing, directing, and producing. No one has earned as many Emmys in as many different categories. In 2002 Sabol was named Sports Executive of the Year by *Sporting News*. In 2003 he and his father were honored with the Lifetime Achievement Emmy from the National Academy of Television Arts and Sciences. Sabol is also the recipient of the Pete Rozelle Award, as well as the Pro Football Hall of Fame's Dan Reeves Pioneer Award. Sabol is one of only eight people to have attended every Super Bowl.

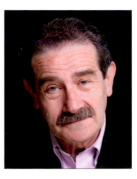

JOHN THORN is a sports historian of long standing. He is the author of *Pro Football's Ten Greatest Games* and the anthologist of *The Armchair Quarterback*, to which his current coeditor, Joe Horrigan, contributed an article more than thirty years ago. With Pete Palmer and Bob Carroll he cowrote *The Hidden Game of Football*, and with Carroll, David Neft, and Mike Gershman he created *Total Football: The Official Encyclopedia of the National Football League*. He is a past president of the Professional Football Researchers Association. When not wearing his football helmet, Thorn writes a regular column for *Voices*, the publication of the New York Folklore Society, and he writes about baseball, New York City, and the Hudson Valley. He appears irregularly in the *Boston Globe*, *New York Times,* and *New York Times Book Review*. The official historian of Major League Baseball, Thorn lives in Catskill, New York, with his wife, Erica.

Appendix

50 YEARS OF HALL OF FAMERS

HERB ADDERLEY Enshrined in 1980
(Michigan State) / CORNERBACK 6-0, 205
1961–69 Green Bay Packers,
1970–72 Dallas Cowboys

TROY AIKMAN Enshrined in 2006
(Oklahoma, UCLA) / QUARTERBACK 6-4, 219
1989–2000 Dallas Cowboys

GEORGE ALLEN Enshrined in 2002
(Alma, Eastern Michigan, Marquette, Michigan) /
COACH
1966–1970 Los Angeles Rams,
1971–77 Washington Redskins

MARCUS ALLEN Enshrined in 2003
(Southern California) / RUNNING BACK 6-2, 210
1982–1992 Los Angeles Raiders,
1993–97 Kansas City Chiefs

LANCE ALWORTH Enshrined in 1978
(Arkansas) / FLANKER 6-0, 184
1962–1970 San Diego Chargers,
1971–72 Dallas Cowboys

DOUG ATKINS Enshrined in 1982
(Tennessee) / DEFENSIVE END 6-8, 257
1953–54 Cleveland Browns, 1955–1966 Chicago
Bears, 1967–69 New Orleans Saints

MORRIS (RED) BADGRO Enshrined in 1981
(Southern California) / END 6-0, 191
1927–28 New York Yankees, 1930–35 New York
Giants, 1936 Brooklyn Dodgers

LEM BARNEY Enshrined in 1992
(Jackson State) / CORNERBACK 6-0, 188
1967–1977 Detroit Lions

CLIFF BATTLES Enshrined in 1968
(West Virginia Wesleyan) / HALFBACK 6-1, 195
1932–37 Boston Braves/Boston Redskins,
1937 Washington Redskins

SAMMY BAUGH Charter Enshrinee, 1963
(Texas Christian) / QUARTERBACK 6-2, 182
1937–1952 Washington Redskins

CHUCK BEDNARIK Enshrined in 1967
(Pennsylvania) / CENTER / LINEBACKER 6-3, 233
1949–1962 Philadelphia Eagles

BERT BELL Charter Enshrinee, 1963
(Pennsylvania) / LEAGUE ADMINISTRATOR / OWNER
1933–1940 Philadelphia Eagles,
1941–46 Pittsburgh Steelers,
1946–1959 National Football League

BOBBY BELL Enshrined in 1983
(Minnesota) / LINEBACKER / DEFENSIVE END
6-4, 228
1963–1974 Kansas City Chiefs

RAYMOND BERRY Enshrined in 1973
(Southern Methodist) / END 6-2, 187
1955–1967 Baltimore Colts

ELVIN BETHEA Enshrined in 2003
(North Carolina A&I) / DEFENSIVE END 6-2, 260
1968–1983 Houston Oilers

CHARLES BIDWILL, SR. Enshrined in 1967
(Loyola of Chicago) / OWNER
1933–1946 Chicago Cardinals

FRED BILETNIKOFF Enshrined in 1988
(Florida State) / WIDE RECEIVER 6-1, 190
1965–1978 Oakland Raiders

GEORGE BLANDA Enshrined in 1981
(Kentucky) / QUARTERBACK / KICKER 6-2, 215
1949 Chicago Bears, 1950 Baltimore Colts,
1950–58 Chicago Bears, 1960–66 Houston Oilers,
1967–1975 Oakland Raiders

MEL BLOUNT Enshrined in 1989
(Southern University) / CORNERBACK 6-3, 205
1970–1983 Pittsburgh Steelers

TERRY BRADSHAW Enshrined in 1989
(Louisiana Tech) / QUARTERBACK 6-3, 215
1970–1983 Pittsburgh Steelers

BOB (THE BOOMER) BROWN Enshrined
in 2004
(Nebraska) / TACKLE 6-4, 280
1964–68 Philadelphia Eagles, 1969–1970
Los Angeles Rams, 1971–73 Oakland Raiders

JIM BROWN Enshrined in 1971
(Syracuse) / FULLBACK 6-2, 232
1957–1965 Cleveland Browns

PAUL BROWN Enshrined in 1967
(Miami–OH) / COACH
1946–1962 Cleveland Browns (AAFC/NFL)

ROOSEVELT BROWN Enshrined in 1975
(Morgan State) / TACKLE 6-3, 255
1953–1965 New York Giants

WILLIE BROWN Enshrined in 1984
(Grambling) / CORNERBACK 6-1, 195
1963–66 Denver Broncos,
1967–1978 Oakland Raiders

JUNIOUS (BUCK) BUCHANAN Enshrined
in 1990
(Grambling) / DEFENSIVE TACKLE 6-7, 270
1963–1975 Kansas City Chiefs

Opposite:

DAN MARINO

"I'll remember this day for the rest of my life," an emotional Dan Marino told the thousands
of Miami Dolphins fans in attendance at his 2005 enshrinement ceremony.

NICK BUONICONTI Enshrined in 2001
(Notre Dame) / LINEBACKER 5-11, 220
1962–68 Boston Patriots;
1969–1974, 1976 Miami Dolphins

DICK BUTKUS Enshrined in 1979
(Illinois) / MIDDLE LINEBACKER 6-3, 245
1965–1973 Chicago Bears

JACK BUTLER Enshrined in 2012
(St. Bonaventure) / CORNERBACK 6-1, 200
1951–59 Pittsburgh Steelers

EARL CAMPBELL Enshrined in 1991
(Texas) / RUNNING BACK 5-11, 232
1978–1984 Houston Oilers,
1984–85 New Orleans Saints

TONY CANADEO Enshrined in 1974
(Gonzaga) / HALFBACK 5-11, 190
1941–44, 1946–1952 Green Bay Packers

JOE CARR Charter Enshrinee, 1963
(No College) / LEAGUE ADMINISTRATOR
1921–1939 National Football League

HARRY CARSON Enshrined in 2006
(South Carolina State) / LINEBACKER 6-2, 237
1976–1988 New York Giants

DAVE CASPER Enshrined in 2002
(Notre Dame) / TIGHT END 6-4, 240
1974–1980, 1984 Oakland/Los Angeles Raiders,
1980–83 Houston Oilers, 1983 Minnesota Vikings

GUY CHAMBERLIN Enshrined in 1965
(Nebraska) / END 6-2, 196; COACH
1919 Canton Bulldogs (pre-NFL), 1920–21
Decatur/Chicago Staleys, 1922–23 Canton
Bulldogs, 1924 Cleveland Bulldogs,
1925–26 Frankford Yellow Jackets,
1927–28 Chicago Cardinals

JACK CHRISTIANSEN Enshrined in 1970
(Colorado State) / SAFETY 6-1, 205
1951–58 Detroit Lions

EARL (DUTCH) CLARK Charter Enshrinee,
1963
(Colorado College) / QUARTERBACK 6-0, 185
1931–32/1934–38 Portsmouth Spartans/
Detroit Lions

GEORGE CONNOR Enshrined in 1975
(Holy Cross, Notre Dame) / TACKLE / LINEBACKER
6-3, 240
1948–1955 Chicago Bears

JIMMY CONZELMAN Enshrined in 1964
(Washington of St. Louis) / QUARTERBACK 6-0,
175; COACH / OWNER
1920 Decatur Staleys, 1921–22 Rock Island
Independents, 1922–24 Milwaukee Badgers,
1925–26 Detroit Panthers,
1927–1930 Providence Steam Roller,
1940–42, 1946–48 Chicago Cardinals

LOU CREEKMUR Enshrined in 1996
(William & Mary) / TACKLE / GUARD 6-4, 246
1950–59 Detroit Lions

LARRY CSONKA Enshrined in 1987
(Syracuse) / FULLBACK 6-3, 237
1968–1974, 1979 Miami Dolphins,
1976–78 New York Giants

AL DAVIS Enshrined in 1992
(Wittenberg, Syracuse) / COACH /
COMMISSIONER / OWNER
1963–65 Oakland Raiders,
1966 American Football League, 1966–2011
Oakland/Los Angeles Raiders

WILLIE DAVIS Enshrined in 1981
(Grambling) / DEFENSIVE END 6-3, 243
1958–59 Cleveland Browns,
1960–69 Green Bay Packers

DERMONTTI DAWSON Enshrined in 2012
(Kentucky) / CENTER 6-2, 288
1988–2000 Pittsburgh Steelers

LEN DAWSON Enshrined in 1987
(Purdue) / QUARTERBACK 6-0, 190
1957–59 Pittsburgh Steelers,
1960–61 Cleveland Browns, 1962/1963–1975
Dallas Texans/Kansas City Chiefs

FRED DEAN Enshrined in 2008
(Louisiana Tech) / DEFENSIVE END 6-3, 230
1975–1981 San Diego Chargers,
1981–85 San Francisco 49ers

JOE DeLAMIELLEURE Enshrined in 2003
(Michigan State) / GUARD 6-3, 254
1973–79, 1985 Buffalo Bills,
1980–84 Cleveland Browns

RICHARD DENT Enshrined in 2011
(Tennessee State) / DEFENSIVE END 6-5, 265
1983–1993, 1995 Chicago Bears, 1994 San
Francisco 49ers, 1996 Indianapolis Colts,
1997 Philadelphia Eagles

ERIC DICKERSON Enshrined in 1999
(Southern Methodist) / RUNNING BACK 6-3, 220
1983–87 Los Angeles Rams, 1987–1991
Indianapolis Colts, 1992 Los Angeles Raiders,
1993 Atlanta Falcons

DAN DIERDORF Enshrined in 1996
(Michigan) / TACKLE 6-3, 275
1971–1983 St. Louis Cardinals

MIKE DITKA Enshrined in 1988
(Pittsburgh) / TIGHT END 6-3, 228
1961–66 Chicago Bears, 1967–68 Philadelphia
Eagles, 1969–1972 Dallas Cowboys

CHRIS DOLEMAN Enshrined in 2012
(Pittsburgh) / DEFENSIVE END / LINEBACKER
6-5, 270
1985–1993, 1999 Minnesota Vikings, 1994–95
Atlanta Falcons, 1996–98 San Francisco 49ers

ART DONOVAN Enshrined in 1968
(Boston College) / DEFENSIVE TACKLE 6-2, 263
1950 Baltimore Colts, 1951 New York Yanks,
1952 Dallas Texans, 1953–1961 Baltimore Colts

TONY DORSETT Enshrined in 1994
(Pittsburgh) / RUNNING BACK 5-11, 192
1977–1987 Dallas Cowboys, 1988 Denver Broncos

JOHN (PADDY) DRISCOLL Enshrined in 1965
(Northwestern) / QUARTERBACK 5-11, 160
1919 Hammond Pros (pre-NFL), 1920 Decatur
Staleys, 1920–25 Chicago Cardinals,
1926–29 Chicago Bears

BILL DUDLEY Enshrined in 1966
(Virginia) / HALFBACK 5-10, 182
1942, 1945–46 Pittsburgh Steelers;
1947–49 Detroit Lions; 1950–51,
1953 Washington Redskins

ALBERT GLEN (TURK) EDWARDS
Enshrined in 1969
(Washington State) / TACKLE 6-2, 255
1932/1933–36/1937–1940 Boston Braves/Boston
Redskins/Washington Redskins

CARL ELLER Enshrined in 2004
(Minnesota) / DEFENSIVE END 6-6, 247
1964–1978 Minnesota Vikings,
1979 Seattle Seahawks

JOHN ELWAY Enshrined in 2004
(Stanford) / QUARTERBACK 6-3, 215
1983–1998 Denver Broncos

WEEB EWBANK Enshrined in 1978
(Miami–OH) / COACH
1954–1962 Baltimore Colts,
1963–1973 New York Jets

MARSHALL FAULK Enshrined in 2011
(San Diego State) / RUNNING BACK 5-10, 208
1994–98 Indianapolis Colts,
1999–2005 St. Louis Rams

TOM FEARS Enshrined in 1970
(Santa Clara, UCLA) / END 6-2, 216
1948–1956 Los Angeles Rams

JIM FINKS Enshrined in 1995
(Tulsa) / ADMINISTRATOR
1964–1973 Minnesota Vikings, 1974–1982
Chicago Bears, 1986–1992 New Orleans Saints

RAY FLAHERTY Enshrined in 1976
(Gonzaga) / COACH
1936–1942 Boston/Washington Redskins,
1946–48 New York Yankees (AAFC),
1949 Chicago Hornets (AAFC)

LEN FORD Enshrined in 1976
(Morgan State, Michigan) / DEFENSIVE END
6-4, 245
1948–49 Los Angeles Dons (AAFC), 1950–57
Cleveland Browns, 1958 Green Bay Packers

DAN FORTMANN Enshrined in 1965
(Colgate) / GUARD 6-0, 210
1936–1943 Chicago Bears

DAN FOUTS Enshrined in 1993
(Oregon) / QUARTERBACK 6-3, 204
1973–1987 San Diego Chargers

BENNY FRIEDMAN Enshrined in 2005
(Michigan) / QUARTERBACK 5-10, 183
1927 Cleveland Bulldogs,
1928 Detroit Wolverines, 1929 1931 New York
Giants, 1932–34 Brooklyn Dodgers

FRANK GATSKI Enshrined in 1985
(Marshall, Auburn) / CENTER 6-3, 233
1946–1956 Cleveland Browns (AAFC/NFL),
1957 Detroit Lions

BILL GEORGE Enshrined in 1974
(Wake Forest) / LINEBACKER 6-2, 237
1952–1965 Chicago Bears,
1966 Los Angeles Rams

JOE GIBBS Enshrined in 1996
(Cerritos Junior College, San Diego State) / COACH
1981–1992 Washington Redskins

FRANK GIFFORD Enshrined in 1977
(Southern California) / HALFBACK / FLANKER
6-1, 197
1952–1960, 1962–64 New York Giants

SID GILLMAN Enshrined in 1983
(Ohio State) / COACH
1955–59 Los Angeles Rams; 1960–69,
1971 Los Angeles/San Diego Chargers;
1973–74 Houston Oilers

OTTO GRAHAM Enshrined in 1965
(Northwestern) / QUARTERBACK 6-1, 196
1946–1955 Cleveland Browns (AAFC/NFL)

HAROLD (RED) GRANGE Charter
Enshrinee, 1963
(Illinois) / HALFBACK 6-0, 180
1925, 1929–1934 Chicago Bears, 1926 New York
Yankees (AFL), 1927 New York Yankees (NFL)

BUD GRANT Enshrined in 1994
(Minnesota) / COACH
1967–1983, 1985 Minnesota Vikings

DARRELL GREEN Enshrined in 2008
(Texas A&I) / CORNERBACK 5-8, 176
1983–2002 Washington Redskins

JOE GREENE Enshrined in 1987
(North Texas State) / DEFENSIVE TACKLE 6-4, 275
1969–1981 Pittsburgh Steelers

FORREST GREGG Enshrined in 1977
(Southern Methodist) / TACKLE / GUARD 6-4, 249
1956, 1958–1970 Green Bay Packers,
1971 Dallas Cowboys

BOB GRIESE Enshrined in 1990
(Purdue) / QUARTERBACK 6-1, 190
1967–1980 Miami Dolphins

RUSS GRIMM Enshrined in 2010
(Pittsburgh) / GUARD 6-3, 273
1981–1991 Washington Redskins

LOU GROZA Enshrined in 1974
(Ohio State) / OFFENSIVE TACKLE / PLACEKICKER
6-3, 240
1946–1959, 1961–67 Cleveland Browns
(AAFC/NFL)

JOE GUYON Enshrined in 1966
(Carlisle, Georgia Tech) / HALFBACK 5-10, 195
1919–1920 Canton Bulldogs, 1921 Cleveland
Indians, 1922–23 Oorang Indians, 1924 Rock
Island Independents, 1924–25 Kansas City
Cowboys, 1927 New York Giants

GEORGE HALAS Charter Enshrinee, 1963
(Illinois) / FOUNDER / OWNER / COACH
1920–1983 Decatur/Chicago Staleys,
Chicago Bears

JACK HAM Enshrined in 1988
(Penn State) / LINEBACKER 6-1, 225
1971–1982 Pittsburgh Steelers

DAN HAMPTON Enshrined in 2002
(Arkansas) / DEFENSIVE TACKLE / DEFENSIVE END
6-5, 264
1979–1990 Chicago Bears

CHRIS HANBURGER Enshrined in 2011
(North Carolina) / LINEBACKER 6-2, 218
1965–1978 Washington Redskins

JOHN HANNAH Enshrined in 1991
(Alabama) / GUARD 6-2, 265
1973–1985 New England Patriots

FRANCO HARRIS Enshrined in 1990
(Penn State) / RUNNING BACK 6-2, 230
1972–1983 Pittsburgh Steelers,
1984 Seattle Seahawks

BOB HAYES Enshrined in 2009
(Florida A&M) / WIDE RECEIVER 5-11, 185
1965–1974 Dallas Cowboys,
1975 San Francisco 49ers

MIKE HAYNES Enshrined in 1997
(Arizona State) / CORNERBACK 6-2, 192
1976–1982 New England Patriots,
1983–89 Los Angeles Raiders

ED HEALEY Enshrined in 1964
(Dartmouth) / TACKLE 6-0, 207
1920–22 Rock Island Independents,
1922–27 Chicago Bears

MEL HEIN Charter Enshrinee, 1963
(Washington State) / CENTER 6-2, 225
1931–1945 New York Giants

TED HENDRICKS Enshrined in 1990
(Miami–FL) / LINEBACKER 6-7, 220
1969–1973 Baltimore Colts, 1974 Green Bay
Packers, 1975–1983 Oakland/Los Angeles Raiders

WILBUR (PETE) HENRY Charter Enshrinee,
1963
(Washington & Jefferson) / TACKLE 5-11, 245
1920–23, 1925–26 Canton Bulldogs,
1927 New York Giants,
1927–28 Pottsville Maroons

ARNIE HERBER Enshrined in 1966
(Wisconsin, Regis) / QUARTERBACK 5-11, 203
1930–1940 Green Bay Packers,
1944–45 New York Giants

BILL HEWITT Enshrined in 1971
(Michigan) / END 5-9, 190
1932–36 Chicago Bears, 1937–39
Philadelphia Eagles, 1943 Phil–Pitt

GENE HICKERSON Enshrined in 2007
(Mississippi) / GUARD 6-3, 248
1958–1973 Cleveland Browns

CLARKE HINKLE Enshrined in 1964
(Bucknell) / FULLBACK 5-11, 202
1932–1941 Green Bay Packers

ELROY (CRAZY LEGS) HIRSCH Enshrined
in 1968
(Wisconsin, Michigan) / HALFBACK / END 6-2, 190
1946–48 Chicago Rockets (AAFC),
1949–1957 Los Angeles Rams

PAUL HORNUNG Enshrined in 1986
(Notre Dame) / HALFBACK 6-2, 215
1957–1962, 1964–66 Green Bay Packers

KEN HOUSTON Enshrined in 1986
(Prairie View A&M) / STRONG SAFETY 6-3, 197
1967–1972 Houston Oilers, 1973–1980
Washington Redskins

ROBERT (CAL) HUBBARD Charter Enshrinee,
1963
(Centenary, Geneva) / TACKLE 6-2, 253
1927–28, 1936 New York Giants; 1929–1933,
1935 Green Bay Packers; 1936 Pittsburgh Pirates

SAM HUFF Enshrined in 1982
(West Virginia) / LINEBACKER 6-1, 230
1956–1963 New York Giants; 1964–67,
1969 Washington Redskins

LAMAR HUNT Enshrined in 1972
(Southern Methodist) / LEAGUE FOUNDER / OWNER
1960–2006 Dallas Texans/Kansas City Chiefs

DON HUTSON Charter Enshrinee, 1963
(Alabama) / END 6-1, 183
1935–1945 Green Bay Packers

MICHAEL IRVIN Enshrined in 2007
(Miami–FL) / WIDE RECEIVER 6-2, 207
1988–1999 Dallas Cowboys

RICKEY JACKSON Enshrined in 2010
(Pittsburgh) / LINEBACKER 6-2, 243
1981–1993 New Orleans Saints,
1994–95 San Francisco 49ers

JIMMY JOHNSON Enshrined in 1994
(UCLA) / CORNERBACK 6-2, 187
1961–1976 San Francisco 49ers

JOHN HENRY JOHNSON Enshrined in 1987
(St. Mary's, Arizona State) / FULLBACK 6-2, 210
1954–56 San Francisco 49ers,
1957–59 Detroit Lions, 1960–65 Pittsburgh
Steelers, 1966 Houston Oilers

CHARLIE JOINER Enshrined in 1996
(Grambling) / WIDE RECEIVER 5-11, 188
1969–1972 Houston Oilers, 1972–75 Cincinnati
Bengals, 1976–1986 San Diego Chargers

DAVID (DEACON) JONES Enshrined in 1980
(South Carolina State, Mississippi Vocational) /
DEFENSIVE END 6-5, 272
1961–1971 Los Angeles Rams, 1972–73 San
Diego Chargers, 1974 Washington Redskins

STAN JONES Enshrined in 1991
(Maryland) / GUARD / DEFENSIVE TACKLE 6-1, 252
1954–1965 Chicago Bears,
1966 Washington Redskins

HENRY JORDAN Enshrined in 1995
(Virginia) / DEFENSIVE TACKLE 6-2, 248
1957–58 Cleveland Browns,
1959–1969 Green Bay Packers

SONNY JURGENSEN Enshrined in 1983
(Duke) / QUARTERBACK 5-11, 202
1957–1963 Philadelphia Eagles, 1964–1974
Washington Redskins

JIM KELLY Enshrined in 2002
(Miami–FL) / QUARTERBACK 6-3, 225
1986–1996 Buffalo Bills

LEROY KELLY Enshrined in 1994
(Morgan State) / RUNNING BACK 6-0, 202
1964–1973 Cleveland Browns

CORTEZ KENNEDY Enshrined in 2012
(Northwest Mississippi Community College,
Miami–FL) / DEFENSIVE TACKLE 6-3, 298
1990–2000 Seattle Seahawks

WALT KIESLING Enshrined in 1966
(St. Thomas of Minnesota) / GUARD 6-2, 249;
COACH
1926–27 Duluth Eskimos; 1928 Pottsville
Maroons; 1929–1933 Chicago Cardinals;
1934 Chicago Bears; 1935–36 Green Bay Packers;
1937–39 Pittsburgh Pirates; 1940–42,
1954–56 Pittsburgh Steelers (coach);
1943 Phil–Pitt; 1944 Card–Pitt

FRANK (BRUISER) KINARD Enshrined
in 1971
(Mississippi) / TACKLE 6-1, 216
1938–1944 Brooklyn Dodgers/Tigers,
1946–47 New York Yankees (AAFC)

PAUL KRAUSE Enshrined in 1998
(Iowa) / SAFETY 6-3, 200
1964–67 Washington Redskins, 1968–1979
Minnesota Vikings

EARL (CURLY) LAMBEAU Charter
Enshrinee, 1963
(Notre Dame) / FOUNDER / COACH
1919–1949 Green Bay Packers, 1950–51 Chicago
Cardinals, 1952–53 Washington Redskins

JACK LAMBERT Enshrined in 1990
(Kent State) / LINEBACKER 6-4, 220
1974–1984 Pittsburgh Steelers

TOM LANDRY Enshrined in 1990
(Texas) / COACH
1960–1988 Dallas Cowboys

DICK (NIGHT TRAIN) LANE Enshrined in
1974
(Scottsbluff Junior College) / CORNERBACK
6-1, 194
1952–53 Los Angeles Rams, 1954–59 Chicago
Cardinals, 1960–65 Detroit Lions

JIM LANGER Enshrined in 1987
(South Dakota State) / CENTER 6-2, 250
1970–79 Miami Dolphins,
1980–81 Minnesota Vikings

WILLIE LANIER Enshrined in 1986
(Morgan State) / LINEBACKER 6-1, 245
1967–1977 Kansas City Chiefs

STEVE LARGENT Enshrined in 1995
(Tulsa) / WIDE RECEIVER 5-11, 187
1976–1989 Seattle Seahawks

YALE LARY Enshrined in 1979
(Texas A&M) / SAFETY 5-11, 185
1952–53, 1956–1964 Detroit Lions

DANTE LAVELLI Enshrined in 1975
(Ohio State) / END 6-0, 191
1946–1956 Cleveland Browns (AAFC/NFL)

BOBBY LAYNE Enshrined in 1967
(Texas) / QUARTERBACK 6-1, 201
1948 Chicago Bears, 1949 New York Bulldogs,
1950–58 Detroit Lions,
1958–1962 Pittsburgh Steelers

DICK LeBEAU Enshrined in 2010
(Ohio State) / CORNERBACK 6-1, 185
1959–1972 Detroit Lions

ALPHONSE (TUFFY) LEEMANS Enshrined
in 1978
(Oregon, George Washington) / HALFBACK /
FULLBACK 6-0, 195
1936–1943 New York Giants

MARV LEVY Enshrined in 2001
(Wyoming, Coe, Harvard) / COACH
1978–1982 Kansas City Chiefs,
1986–1997 Buffalo Bills

BOB LILLY Enshrined in 1980
(Texas Christian) / DEFENSIVE TACKLE 6-5, 260
1961–1974 Dallas Cowboys

FLOYD LITTLE Enshrined in 2010
(Syracuse) / RUNNING BACK 5-10, 196
1967–1975 Denver Broncos

LARRY LITTLE Enshrined in 1993
(Bethune–Cookman) / GUARD 6-1, 265
1967–68 San Diego Chargers,
1969–1980 Miami Dolphins

JAMES LOFTON Enshrined in 2003
(Stanford) / WIDE RECEIVER 6-3, 192
1978–1986 Green Bay Packers, 1987–88
Los Angeles Raiders, 1989–1992 Buffalo Bills,
1993 Los Angeles Rams, 1993 Philadelphia Eagles

VINCE LOMBARDI Enshrined in 1971
(Fordham) / COACH
1959–1967 Green Bay Packers,
1969 Washington Redskins

HOWIE LONG Enshrined in 2000
(Villanova) / DEFENSIVE END 6-5, 268
1981–1993 Oakland/Los Angeles Raiders

RONNIE LOTT Enshrined in 2000
(Southern California) / CORNERBACK / SAFETY
6-0, 203
1981–1990 San Francisco 49ers, 1991–92
Los Angeles Raiders, 1993–94 New York Jets

SID LUCKMAN Enshrined in 1965
(Columbia) / QUARTERBACK 6-0, 197
1939–1950 Chicago Bears

WILLIAM ROY (LINK) LYMAN Enshrined
in 1964
(Nebraska) / TACKLE 6-2, 233
1922–23; 1925 Canton Bulldogs; 1924 Cleveland
Bulldogs; 1925 Frankford Yellow Jackets;
1926–28, 1930–31, 1933–34 Chicago Bears

TOM MACK Enshrined in 1999
(Michigan) / GUARD 6-3, 250
1966–1978 Los Angeles Rams

JOHN MACKEY Enshrined in 1992
(Syracuse) / TIGHT END 6-2, 224
1963–1971 Baltimore Colts,
1972 San Diego Chargers

JOHN MADDEN Enshrined in 2006
(San Mateo Junior College, California
Polytechnic) / COACH
1969–1978 Oakland Raiders

TIM MARA Charter Enshrinee, 1963
(No College) / FOUNDER / OWNER
1925–1959 New York Giants

WELLINGTON MARA Enshrined in 1997
(Fordham) / OWNER / ADMINISTRATOR
1937–2005 New York Giants

GINO MARCHETTI Enshrined in 1972
(San Francisco) / DEFENSIVE END 6-4, 244
1952 Dallas Texans; 1953–1964,
1966 Baltimore Colts

DAN MARINO Enshrined in 2005
(Pittsburgh) / QUARTERBACK 6-4, 218
1983–1999 Miami Dolphins

GEORGE PRESTON MARSHALL Charter
Enshrinee, 1963
(Randolph–Macon) / FOUNDER / OWNER
1932/1933–36/1937–1969 Boston Braves/
Boston Redskins /Washington Redskins

CURTIS MARTIN Enshrined in 2012
(Pittsburgh) / RUNNING BACK 5-11, 207
1995–97 New England Patriots,
1998–2005 New York Jets

OLLIE MATSON Enshrined in 1972
(San Francisco) / HALFBACK 6-2, 220
1952, 1954–58 Chicago Cardinals,
1959–1962 Los Angeles Rams,
1963 Detroit Lions, 1964–66 Philadelphia Eagles

BRUCE MATTHEWS Enshrined in 2007
(Southern California) / GUARD / TACKLE / CENTER
6-5, 289
1983–2001 Houston Oilers,
Tennessee Oilers/Titans

DON MAYNARD Enshrined in 1987
(Texas Western) / WIDE RECEIVER 6-0, 180
1958 New York Giants, 1960–1972 New York
Titans/Jets, 1973 St. Louis Cardinals

GEORGE McAFEE Enshrined in 1966
(Duke) / HALFBACK 6-0, 178
1940–41, 1945–1950 Chicago Bears

MIKE McCORMACK Enshrined in 1984
(Kansas) / TACKLE 6-4, 246
1951 New York Yanks,
1954–1962 Cleveland Browns

RANDALL McDANIEL Enshrined in 2009
(Arizona State) / GUARD 6-3, 276
1988–1999 Minnesota Vikings,
2000–01 Tampa Bay Buccaneers

TOMMY McDONALD Enshrined in 1998
(Oklahoma) / WIDE RECEIVER 5-9, 176
1957–1963 Philadelphia Eagles, 1964 Dallas
Cowboys, 1965–66 Los Angeles Rams,
1967 Atlanta Falcons, 1968 Cleveland Browns

HUGH McELHENNY Enshrined in 1970
(Washington, Compton Junior College) / HALFBACK
6-1, 195
1952–1960 San Francisco 49ers,
1961–62 Minnesota Vikings,
1963 New York Giants, 1964 Detroit Lions

JOHN (BLOOD) McNALLY Charter Enshrinee,
1963
(Notre Dame, St. John's of Minnesota) / HALFBACK
6-1, 188
1925–26 Milwaukee Badgers; 1926–27 Duluth
Eskimos; 1928 Pottsville Maroons; 1929–1933,
1935–36 Green Bay Packers; 1934,
1937–38 Pittsburgh Pirates

MIKE MICHALSKE Enshrined in 1964
(Penn State) / GUARD 6-0, 210
1926 New York Yankees (AFL); 1927–28 New York
Yankees (NFL); 1929–1935,
1937 Green Bay Packers

WAYNE MILLNER Enshrined in 1968
(Notre Dame) / END 6-1, 189
1936–1941, 1945 Boston/Washington Redskins

BOBBY MITCHELL Enshrined in 1983
(Illinois) / WIDE RECEIVER / HALFBACK 6-0, 192
1958–1961 Cleveland Browns,
1962–68 Washington Redskins

RON MIX Enshrined in 1979
(Southern California) / TACKLE 6-4, 250
1960–69 Los Angeles/San Diego Chargers,
1971 Oakland Raiders

ART MONK Enshrined in 2008
(Syracuse) / WIDE RECEIVER 6-3, 210
1980–1993 Washington Redskins,
1994 New York Jets, 1995 Philadelphia Eagles

JOE MONTANA Enshrined in 2000
(Notre Dame) / QUARTERBACK 6-2, 200
1979–1992 San Francisco 49ers,
1993–94 Kansas City Chiefs

WARREN MOON Enshrined in 2006
(West Los Angeles Junior College, Washington) /
QUARTERBACK 6-3, 212
1984–1993 Houston Oilers, 1994–96 Minnesota
Vikings, 1997–98 Seattle Seahawks,
1999–2000 Kansas City Chiefs

LENNY MOORE Enshrined in 1975
(Penn State) / FLANKER / RUNNING BACK 6-1, 191
1956–1967 Baltimore Colts

MARION MOTLEY Enshrined in 1968
(South Carolina State, Nevada) / FULLBACK 6-1,
232
1946–1953 Cleveland Browns (AAFC/NFL),
1955 Pittsburgh Steelers

MIKE MUNCHAK Enshrined in 2001
(Penn State) / GUARD 6-3, 281
1982–1993 Houston Oilers

ANTHONY MUÑOZ Enshrined in 1998
(Southern California) / TACKLE 6-6, 278
1980–1992 Cincinnati Bengals

GEORGE MUSSO Enshrined in 1982
(Millikin) / TACKLE / GUARD 6-2, 262
1933–1944 Chicago Bears

BRONKO NAGURSKI Charter Enshrinee, 1963
(Minnesota) / FULLBACK 6-2, 226
1930–37, 1943 Chicago Bears

JOE NAMATH Enshrined in 1985
(Alabama) / QUARTERBACK 6-2, 200
1965–1976 New York Jets, 1977 Los Angeles Rams

EARLE (GREASY) NEALE Enshrined in 1969
(West Virginia Wesleyan) / COACH
1941–1950 Philadelphia Eagles

ERNIE NEVERS Charter Enshrinee, 1963
(Stanford) / FULLBACK 6-0, 204
1926–27 Duluth Eskimos,
1929–1931 Chicago Cardinals

OZZIE NEWSOME Enshrined in 1999
(Alabama) / TIGHT END 6-2, 232
1978–1990 Cleveland Browns

RAY NITSCHKE Enshrined in 1978
(Illinois) / MIDDLE LINEBACKER 6-3, 235
1958–1972 Green Bay Packers

CHUCK NOLL Enshrined in 1993
(Dayton) / COACH
1969–1991 Pittsburgh Steelers

LEO NOMELLINI Enshrined in 1969
(Minnesota) / DEFENSIVE TACKLE 6-3, 259
1950–1963 San Francisco 49ers

MERLIN OLSEN Enshrined in 1982
(Utah State) / DEFENSIVE TACKLE 6-5, 270
1962–1976 Los Angeles Rams

JIM OTTO Enshrined in 1980
(Miami—FL) / CENTER 6-2, 255
1960–1974 Oakland Raiders

STEVE OWEN Enshrined in 1966
(Phillips) / TACKLE 6-2, 215; COACH
1924–25 Kansas City Cowboys, 1925 Cleveland
Bulldogs, 1926–1953 New York Giants

ALAN PAGE Enshrined in 1988
(Notre Dame) / DEFENSIVE TACKLE 6-4, 245
1967–1978 Minnesota Vikings, 1978–1981
Chicago Bears

CLARENCE (ACE) PARKER Enshrined
in 1972
(Duke) / QUARTERBACK 5-10, 178
1937–1941 Brooklyn Dodgers, 1945 Boston Yanks,
1946 New York Yankees (AAFC)

JIM PARKER Enshrined in 1973
(Ohio State) / GUARD / TACKLE 6-3, 273
1957–1967 Baltimore Colts

WALTER PAYTON Enshrined in 1993
(Jackson State) / RUNNING BACK 5-10, 200
1975–1987 Chicago Bears

JOE PERRY Enshrined in 1969
(Compton Junior College) / FULLBACK 6-0, 200
1948–1960, 1963 San Francisco 49ers (AAFC/
NFL), 1961–62 Baltimore Colts

PETE PIHOS Enshrined in 1970
(Indiana) / END 6-1, 210
1947–1955 Philadelphia Eagles

FRITZ POLLARD Enshrined in 2005
(Brown) / HALFBACK 5-9, 165; COACH
1919–1921, 1925–1926 Akron Pros/Indians;
1922 Milwaukee Badgers; 1923–24 Gilberton
Cadamounts (independent pro team); 1923, 1925
Hammond Pros; 1925 Providence Steam Roller

JOHN RANDLE Enshrined in 2010
(Trinity Valley Community College, Texas A&I) /
DEFENSIVE TACKLE 6-1, 278
1990–2000 Minnesota Vikings,
2001–03 Seattle Seahawks

HUGH (SHORTY) RAY Enshrined in 1966
(Illinois) / TECHNICAL ADVISOR ON RULES /
SUPERVISOR OF OFFICIALS
1938–1952 National Football League

DAN REEVES Enshrined in 1967
(Georgetown) / OWNER
1941–1971 Cleveland / Los Angeles Rams

MEL RENFRO Enshrined in 1996
(Oregon) / CORNERBACK / SAFETY 6-0, 190
1964–1977 Dallas Cowboys

JERRY RICE Enshrined in 2010
(Mississippi Valley State) /
WIDE RECEIVER 6-2, 200
1985–2000 San Francisco 49ers, 2001–04
Oakland Raiders, 2004 Seattle Seahawks

LES RICHTER Enshrined in 2011
(California) / LINEBACKER 6-3, 238
1954–1962 Los Angeles Rams

JOHN RIGGINS Enshrined in 1992
(Kansas) / RUNNING BACK 6-2, 230
1971–75 New York Jets; 1976–79, 1981–85
Washington Redskins

JIM RINGO Enshrined in 1981
(Syracuse) / CENTER 6-2, 232
1953–1963 Green Bay Packers, 1964–67
Philadelphia Eagles

WILLIE ROAF Enshrined in 2012
(Louisiana Tech) / TACKLE 6-5, 300
1993–2001 New Orleans Saints,
2002–05 Kansas City Chiefs

ANDY ROBUSTELLI Enshrined in 1971
(Arnold) / DEFENSIVE END 6-1, 230
1951–55 Los Angeles Rams,
1956–1964 New York Giants

ART ROONEY Enshrined in 1964
(Georgetown, Duquesne) / FOUNDER / OWNER
1933–1988 Pittsburgh Pirates/Steelers

DAN ROONEY Enshrined in 2000
(Duquesne) / ADMINISTRATOR / OWNER
1955–Present Pittsburgh Steelers

PETE ROZELLE Enshrined in 1985
(Compton Junior College, San Francisco) /
COMMISSIONER
1960–1989 National Football League

ED SABOL Enshrined in 2011
(Ohio State) / FOUNDER / PRESIDENT / CHAIRMAN
1964–1995 NFL Films

BARRY SANDERS Enshrined in 2004
(Oklahoma State) / RUNNING BACK 5-8, 203
1989–1998 Detroit Lions

CHARLIE SANDERS Enshrined in 2007
(Minnesota) / TIGHT END 6-4, 230
1968–1977 Detroit Lions

DEION SANDERS Enshrined in 2011
(Florida State) / CORNERBACK / KICK RETURNER /
PUNT RETURNER 6-1, 195
1989–1993 Atlanta Falcons, 1994 San Francisco
49ers, 1995–99 Dallas Cowboys, 2000
Washington Redskins, 2004–05 Baltimore Ravens

GALE SAYERS Enshrined in 1977
(Kansas) / HALFBACK 6-0, 198
1965–1971 Chicago Bears

JOE SCHMIDT Enshrined in 1973
(Pittsburgh) / LINEBACKER 6-0, 220
1953–1965 Detroit Lions

TEX SCHRAMM Enshrined in 1991
(Texas) / ADMINISTRATOR
1947–1956 Los Angeles Rams,
1960–1989 Dallas Cowboys,
1989–1990 World League of American Football

LEE ROY SELMON Enshrined in 1995
(Oklahoma) / DEFENSIVE END 6-3, 256
1976–1984 Tampa Bay Buccaneers

SHANNON SHARPE Enshrined in 2011
(Savannah State) / TIGHT END 6-2, 230
1990–99, 2002–03 Denver Broncos,
2000–01 Baltimore Ravens

BILLY SHAW Enshrined in 1999
(Georgia Tech) / GUARD 6-2, 258
1961–69 Buffalo Bills

ART SHELL Enshrined in 1989
(Maryland State–Eastern Shore) / TACKLE 6-5, 265
1968–1982 Oakland/Los Angeles Raiders

DON SHULA Enshrined in 1997
(John Carroll) / COACH
1963–69 Baltimore Colts,
1970–1995 Miami Dolphins

O. J. SIMPSON Enshrined in 1985
(City College–San Francisco, Southern California) /
RUNNING BACK 6-1, 212
1969–1977 Buffalo Bills,
1978–79 San Francisco 49ers

MIKE SINGLETARY Enshrined in 1998
(Baylor) / LINEBACKER 6-0, 230
1981–1992 Chicago Bears

JACKIE SLATER Enshrined in 2001
(Jackson State) / TACKLE 6-4, 277
1976–1995 Los Angeles/St. Louis Rams

BRUCE SMITH Enshrined in 2009
(Virginia Tech) / DEFENSIVE END 6-4, 280
1985–1999 Buffalo Bills,
2000–03 Washington Redskins

EMMITT SMITH Enshrined in 2010
(Florida) / RUNNING BACK 5-9, 207
1990–2002 Dallas Cowboys,
2003–04 Arizona Cardinals

JACKIE SMITH Enshrined in 1994
(Northwestern Louisiana) / TIGHT END 6-4, 235
1963–1977 St. Louis Cardinals,
1978 Dallas Cowboys

JOHN STALLWORTH Enshrined in 2002
(Alabama A&M) / WIDE RECEIVER 6-2, 191
1974–1987 Pittsburgh Steelers

BART STARR Enshrined in 1977
(Alabama) / QUARTERBACK 6-1, 197
1956–1971 Green Bay Packers

ROGER STAUBACH Enshrined in 1985
(New Mexico Military Institute, Navy) /
QUARTERBACK 6-3, 197
1969–1979 Dallas Cowboys

ERNIE STAUTNER Enshrined in 1969
(Boston College) / DEFENSIVE TACKLE 6-1, 230
1950–1963 Pittsburgh Steelers

BOB ST. CLAIR Enshrined in 1990
(San Francisco, Tulsa) / TACKLE 6-9, 263
1953–1963 San Francisco 49ers

JAN STENERUD Enshrined in 1991
(Montana State) / PLACEKICKER 6-2, 187
1967–1979 Kansas City Chiefs, 1980–83 Green
Bay Packers, 1984–85 Minnesota Vikings

DWIGHT STEPHENSON Enshrined in 1998
(Alabama) / CENTER 6-2, 255
1980–87 Miami Dolphins

HANK STRAM Enshrined in 2003
(Purdue) / COACH
1960–1974 Dallas Texans/Kansas City Chiefs,
1976–77 New Orleans Saints

KEN STRONG Enshrined in 1967
(New York) / HALFBACK 6-0, 206
1929–1932 Staten Island Stapletons;
1933–35, 1939, 1944–47 New York Giants;
1936–37 New York Yanks (AFL)

JOE STYDAHAR Enshrined in 1967
(West Virginia) / TACKLE 6-4, 233
1936–1942, 1945–46 Chicago Bears

LYNN SWANN Enshrined in 2001
(Southern California) / WIDE RECEIVER 5-11, 180
1974–1982 Pittsburgh Steelers

FRAN TARKENTON Enshrined in 1986
(Georgia) / QUARTERBACK 6-0, 190
1961–66, 1972–78 Minnesota Vikings,
1967–1971 New York Giants

CHARLEY TAYLOR Enshrined in 1984
(Arizona State) / WIDE RECEIVER 6-3, 210
1964–1975, 1977 Washington Redskins

JIM TAYLOR Enshrined in 1976
(Hinds [MS] Junior College, Louisiana State) /
FULLBACK 6-0, 214
1958–1966 Green Bay Packers,
1967 New Orleans Saints

LAWRENCE TAYLOR Enshrined in 1999
(North Carolina) / LINEBACKER 6-3, 237
1981–1993 New York Giants

DERRICK THOMAS Enshrined in 2009
(Alabama) / LINEBACKER 6-3, 243
1989–1999 Kansas City Chiefs

EMMITT THOMAS Enshrined in 2008
(Bishop) / CORNERBACK 6-2, 192
1966–1978 Kansas City Chiefs

THURMAN THOMAS Enshrined in 2007
(Oklahoma State) / RUNNING BACK 5-10, 198
1988–1999 Buffalo Bills, 2000 Miami Dolphins

JIM THORPE Charter Enshrinee, 1963
(Carlisle) / HALFBACK 6-1, 202
1915–17, 1919–1920, 1926 Canton Bulldogs,
1921 Cleveland Indians, 1922–23 Oorang
Indians, 1924 Rock Island Independents,
1925 New York Giants, 1928 Chicago Cardinals

ANDRE TIPPETT Enshrined in 2008
(Iowa, Ellsworth [IA] Junior College) /
LINEBACKER 6-3, 240
1982–1993 New England Patriots

Y. A. TITTLE Enshrined in 1971
(Louisiana State) / QUARTERBACK 6-0, 192
1948–49 Baltimore Colts (AAFC), 1950 Baltimore
Colts (NFL), 1951–1960 San Francisco 49ers,
1961–64 New York Giants

GEORGE TRAFTON Enshrined in 1964
(Notre Dame) / CENTER 6-2, 230
1920/21, 1923–1932 Decatur/Chicago Staleys/
Chicago Bears

CHARLEY TRIPPI Enshrined in 1968
(Georgia) / HALFBACK / QUARTERBACK 6-0, 186
1947–1955 Chicago Cardinals

EMLEN TUNNELL Enshrined in 1967
(Toledo, Iowa) / DEFENSIVE BACK 6-1, 187
1948–1958 New York Giants, 1959–1961 Green
Bay Packers

CLYDE (BULLDOG) TURNER Enshrined
in 1966
(Hardin–Simmons) / CENTER /
LINEBACKER 6-1, 237
1940–1952 Chicago Bears

JOHNNY UNITAS Enshrined in 1979
(Louisville) / QUARTERBACK 6-1, 194
1956–1972 Baltimore Colts,
1973 San Diego Chargers

GENE UPSHAW Enshrined in 1987
(Texas A&I) / GUARD 6-5, 255
1967–1981 Oakland Raiders

NORM VAN BROCKLIN Enshrined in 1971
(Oregon) / QUARTERBACK 6-1, 190
1949–1957 Los Angeles Rams,
1958–1960 Philadelphia Eagles

STEVE VAN BUREN Enshrined in 1965
(Louisiana State) / HALFBACK 6-0, 200
1944–1951 Philadelphia Eagles

DOAK WALKER Enshrined in 1986
(Southern Methodist) / HALFBACK 5-11, 173
1950–55 Detroit Lions

BILL WALSH Enshrined in 1993
(San Mateo Junior College,
San Jose State) / COACH
1979–1988 San Francisco 49ers

PAUL WARFIELD Enshrined in 1983
(Ohio State) / WIDE RECEIVER 6-0, 188
1964–69, 1976–77 Cleveland Browns,
1970–74 Miami Dolphins

BOB WATERFIELD Enshrined in 1965
(UCLA) / QUARTERBACK 6-1, 200
1945–1952 Cleveland/Los Angeles Rams

MIKE WEBSTER Enshrined in 1997
(Wisconsin) / CENTER 6-1, 255
1974–1988 Pittsburgh Steelers, 1989–1990
Kansas City Chiefs

ROGER WEHRLI Enshrined in 2007
(Missouri) / CORNERBACK 6-0, 190
1969–1982 St. Louis Cardinals

ARNIE WEINMEISTER Enshrined in 1984
(Washington) / DEFENSIVE TACKLE 6-4, 235
1948 New York Yankees (AAFC),
1949 Brooklyn–New York Yankees (AAFC),
1950–53 New York Giants

RANDY WHITE Enshrined in 1994
(Maryland) / DEFENSIVE TACKLE 6-4, 257
1975–1988 Dallas Cowboys

REGGIE WHITE Enshrined in 2006
(Tennessee) / DEFENSIVE END 6-5, 291
1985–1992 Philadelphia Eagles, 1993–98
Green Bay Packers, 2000 Carolina Panthers

DAVE WILCOX Enshrined in 2000
(Boise Junior College, Oregon) /
LINEBACKER 6-3, 241
1964–1974 San Francisco 49ers

BILL WILLIS Enshrined in 1977
(Ohio State) / MIDDLE GUARD 6-2, 213
1946–1953 Cleveland Browns (AAFC/NFL)

LARRY WILSON Enshrined in 1978
(Utah) / FREE SAFETY 6-0, 190
1960–1972 St. Louis Cardinals

RALPH WILSON, JR. Enshrined in 2009
(Virginia, Michigan) / FOUNDER / OWNER
1960–Present Buffalo Bills

KELLEN WINSLOW Enshrined in 1995
(Missouri) / TIGHT END 6-5, 251
1979–1987 San Diego Chargers

ALEX WOJCIECHOWICZ Enshrined in 1968
(Fordham) / CENTER / LINEBACKER 5-11, 217
1938–1946 Detroit Lions,
1946–1950 Philadelphia Eagles

WILLIE WOOD Enshrined in 1989
(Southern California) / SAFETY 5-10, 190
1960–1971 Green Bay Packers

ROD WOODSON Enshrined in 2009
(Purdue) / CORNERBACK / SAFETY 6-0, 200
1987–1996 Pittsburgh Steelers,
1997 San Francisco 49ers, 1998–2001
Baltimore Ravens, 2002–03 Oakland Raiders

RAYFIELD WRIGHT Enshrined in 2006
(Fort Valley State) / TACKLE 6-6, 255
1967–1979 Dallas Cowboys

RON YARY Enshrined in 2001
(Cerritos Junior College, Southern California) /
TACKLE 6-5, 255
1968–1981 Minnesota Vikings,
1982 Los Angeles Rams

STEVE YOUNG Enshrined in 2005
(Brigham Young) / QUARTERBACK 6-2, 205
1985–86 Tampa Bay Buccaneers,
1987–1999 San Francisco 49ers

JACK YOUNGBLOOD Enshrined in 2001
(Florida) / DEFENSIVE END 6-4, 247
1971–1984 Los Angeles Rams

GARY ZIMMERMAN Enshrined in 2008
(Oregon) / TACKLE 6-6, 294
1986–1992 Minnesota Vikings,
1993–97 Denver Broncos

A GENEALOGY OF NFL TEAMS
(Through 2012)

TEAM NAME	DATE OF FOUNDING	YEARS IN OPERATION
Akron Pros/Indians	8/20/20	1920–22/1923–26
Arizona Cardinals	*(see Chicago Cardinals)*	
Atlanta Falcons	6/30/65	1966–present
Baltimore Colts	12/28/46 (AAFC)	1947–49 (AAFC), 1950 (NFL)
Baltimore/Indianapolis Colts	1/23/53	1953–1983/1984–present
Moved to Indianapolis, 3/28/84.		
Baltimore Ravens	2/9/96	1996–present
Boston Braves/Redskins/ Washington Redskins	7/9/32	1932/1933–36/1937–present
Boston Bulldogs	*(see Pottsville Maroons)*	
Boston/New England Patriots	11/22/59 (AFL)	1960–69 (AFL), 1970 (NFL)/1971–present (NFL)
Boston Yanks	6/19/43	1944–48
Brooklyn Dodgers/Tigers	7/12/30 (purchased Dayton Triangles franchise)	1930–1943/1944
Merged with Boston Yanks, 1945.		
Brooklyn Lions	7/10/26	1926
Buffalo All-Americans/Bisons/Rangers/Bisons	8/20/20	1920–23/1924–25/1926/1927, 1929
Buffalo Bills	10/28/59 (AFL)	1960–69 (AFL), 1970–present (NFL)
Canton Bulldogs	8/20/20	1920–23, 1925–26
Carolina Panthers	10/26/93	1995–present
Chicago Bears	*(see Decatur Staleys)*	
Chicago Cardinals/St. Louis/Phoenix/Arizona	9/17/20	1920–1959/1960–1987/ 1988–1993/1994–present
Chicago Tigers	1920	1920
Cincinnati Bengals	5/23/67 (AFL)	1968–69 (AFL), 1970–present (NFL)
Cincinnati Celts	1921	1921
Cincinnati Reds	7/8/33	1933–34
Merged with St. Louis Gunners for the last half of 1934.		
Cleveland Browns	6/4/44 (AAFC)	1946–49 (AAFC), 1950–present (NFL)
Inactive, 1996–1998.		
Cleveland Tigers/Indians	8/20/20	1920/1921
Cleveland Indians/Bulldogs	7/8/23	1923/1924–25, 1927
Cleveland Indians	7/12/31	1931

TEAM NAME	DATE OF FOUNDING	YEARS IN OPERATION
Cleveland/Los Angeles/St. Louis Rams	2/12/37	1937–42, 1944–45/1946–1994/1995–present
Columbus Panhandles/Tigers	1920	1920–22/1923–26
Dallas Cowboys	1/28/60	1960–present
Dallas Texans	1/24/52	1952
Franchise was awarded after Dallas purchased assets of New York Yanks from the NFL.		
Dallas Texans/Kansas City Chiefs	8/14/59 (AFL)	1960–62/1963–69 (AFL), 1970–present (NFL)
Dayton Triangles	8/20/20	1920–29
Brooklyn purchased the Dayton franchise, 1930.		
Decatur Staleys/Chicago Staleys/Chicago Bears	9/17/20	1920/1921/1922–present
Denver Broncos	8/14/59 (AFL)	1960–69 (AFL), 1970–present (NFL)
Detroit Heralds	1920	1920
Detroit Lions	*(see Portsmouth Spartans)*	
Detroit Panthers	8/1/25	1925–26
Detroit Tigers	6/18/21	1921
Detroit Wolverines	8/17/28	1928
Duluth Kelleys/Eskimos	7/28/23	1923–25/1926–27
The Duluth franchise was transferred to Orange, 7/27/29.		
Evansville Crimson-Giants	8/27/21	1921–22
Frankford Yellow Jackets	7/25/24	1924–31
Green Bay Packers	8/27/21	1921–present
Hammond Pros	8/20/20	1920–26
Hartford Blues	7/10/26	1926
Houston/Tennessee Oilers/Tennessee Titans	8/14/59 (AFL)	1960–69 (AFL), 1970–1996 /1997–1998/1999–present (NFL)
Houston Texans	10/6/99	2002–present
Indianapolis Colts	*(see Baltimore Colts)*	
Jacksonville Jaguars	11/30/93	1995–present
Kansas City Blues/Cowboys	1/27/24	1924/1925–26
Kansas City Chiefs	*(see Dallas Texans)*	
Kenosha Maroons	1924	1924
Los Angeles Buccaneers	7/11/26	1926
Los Angeles/San Diego Chargers	8/14/59 (AFL)	1960/1961–69 (AFL), 1970–present (NFL)
Los Angeles Raiders	*(see Oakland Raiders)*	
Los Angeles Rams	*(see Cleveland Rams)*	
Louisville Brecks/Colonels	1921	1921–23/1926
Miami Dolphins	8/16/65 (AFL)	1966–69 (AFL), 1970–present (NFL)
Milwaukee Badgers	6/24/22	1922–26
Minneapolis Marines/Redjackets	8/27/21	1921–24/1929–30
Minnesota Vikings	1/28/60	1961–present
Muncie Flyers	9/17/20	1920–21
New England Patriots	*(see Boston Patriots)*	
Newark Tornadoes	*(see Orange Tornadoes)*	

TEAM NAME	DATE OF FOUNDING	YEARS IN OPERATION
New Orleans Saints	11/1/66	1967–present
New York Bulldogs/Yanks	1/21/49	1949/1950–51
New York Giants	1921	1921
New York Giants	8/1/25	1925–present
New York Jets	*(see New York Titans)*	
New York Yankees	9/4/27	1927–28
New York Titans/Jets	8/14/59 (AFL)	1960–62/1963–69 (AFL), 1970–present
Oakland/Los Angeles/Oakland Raiders	1/30/60 (AFL)	1960–69 (AFL), 1970–1981/1982–1994/1995–present (NFL)
Oorang Indians	6/24/22	1922–23
Orange/Newark Tornadoes	7/27/29	1929/1930
The Duluth franchise was sold and transferred to Orange, and one year later to Newark.		
Philadelphia Eagles	7/8/33	1933–present
Pittsburgh Pirates/Steelers	7/8/33	1933–39/1940–present
Portsmouth Spartans/Detroit Lions	7/12/30	1930–33/1934–present
The Portsmouth franchise was sold and moved to Detroit, 6/30/34.		
Pottsville Maroons/Boston Bulldogs	8/1/25	1925–28/1929
The Pottsville team relocated to Boston, 7/28/29.		
Providence Steam Roller	8/1/25	1925–31
Racine Legion/Tornadoes	6/24/22	1922–24/1926
Rochester Jeffersons	8/20/20	1920–25
Rock Island Independents	9/17/20	1920–25
San Diego Chargers	*(see Los Angeles Chargers)*	
San Francisco 49ers	6/4/44 (AAFC)	1946–49 (AAFC), 1950–present (NFL)
Seattle Seahawks	6/4/74	1976–present
St. Louis All-Stars	7/28/23	1923
St. Louis Cardinals	*(see Chicago Cardinals)*	
St. Louis Gunners	11/6/34	1934 (partial season)
Purchased Cincinnati franchise.		
St. Louis Rams	*(see Cleveland Rams)*	
Staten Island Stapletons/Stapes	7/27/29	1929–30/1931–32
The Brooklyn franchise was transferred to Staten Island.		
Tampa Bay Buccaneers	4/24/74	1976–present
Tennessee Oilers	*(see Houston Oilers)*	
Tennessee Titans	*(see Houston Oilers)*	
Toledo Maroons	8/20/22	1922–23
Tonawanda Kardex	8/27/21	1921
Washington Redskins	*(see Boston Braves)*	
Washington Senators	1921	1921

INDEX

NOTE: *Italic page references* indicate photographs

Opposite:

RANDALL McDANIEL

Guard Randall McDaniel blocked for six 1,000 yard rushers during his 14-year Hall of Fame career with the Minnesota Vikings (1998–1999) and Tampa Bay Buccaneers (2000–2001).

I

J

K

Kansas City Chiefs, 280
    Super Bowl I, 141, *141,*
        142, *142–43*
    Super Bowl IV, 150, 153–54,
        156, 178
Kapp, Joe, 154
Karlis, Rich, 195
Karr, Bill, 62–63, *63*
Karras, Alex, 126, 127
Kay, Clarence, 227
Kelly, Jim, 201, 205, 210, 213,
    230, 274
    jersey, *213*
Kelly, Leroy, 147, 274
Kemp, Jack, 129
Kennedy, Cortez, 229, 274
Kennedy, John F., 123, 127
Kiesling, Walt, 59, 274
Kinard, Frank "Bruiser," 76, 274
King, Peter, 209–31, 268
Koppen, Dan, *244*
Kraft, Robert, 244, 249–51
Kramer, Jerry, 124, 148–49
Krause, Paul, 171, 174, 274
    jersey, *174*
Kuehner, Oscar, 13

L

Lambeau, Earl "Curly," 39, 41, 62,
    122, 128, 274
Lambeau Field, 139, 145, 264
Lambert, Jack, 163, 164, 188, 274
    shoes, *188*
Landry, Tom, 99, 169, *169,* 182, 191,
    228, 251, 274
    hat, *191*
Lane, Dick "Night Train," 114, 274
Langer, Jim, 178, 274
Lanier, Willie, 150, 156, 178, 274
    helmet, 146, *146*
Largent, Steve, 182, 201, 274
Lary, Yale, 114, 274
Latone, Tony, 38
Latrobe Athletic Club, 7
Lavelli, Dante, 97, 99, 274
Layden, Elmer, letter to Ward Cuff,
    77, *77*
Layne, Bobby, 103–4, 110, 274
Lebeau, Dick, 148, 275
Leemans, Alphonse "Tuffy,"
    62, 66, 75, 275
Leggett, Earl, ix–x
Lett, Leon, 229
Levy, Marv, 201, 275
Lewis, Jamal, 228
Lewis, Ray, 234
    jersey, *234*
Light, Matt, *244*
Lilly, Bob, 147, 150, 163, 167, 275
Lingo, Walter, 28
Little, Floyd, 156, 159, 275

Little, Larry, 156, 169, 275
Lofton, James, 201, 275
Lombardi, Vince, 121–50, 154,
    231, 233, 264, 275
Lombardi Trophy, 150
Long, Howie, *ix,* ix–xi, 189, 275
    uniform, *x, 189*
Longwell, Ryan, 245
Los Angeles Raiders, 206, 280
Los Angeles Rams, 82, 116, 156, 280
    Fearsome Foursome,
        122, 123, *123*
    1950 NFL Championship Game,
        98, *98*
Lott, Ronnie, 200, *200,* 204, 275
Luckman, Sid, 74, *74,* 84, *84,* 85, 275
Lummus, Jack, 75
Lundy, Lamar, 122, 123
Lyman, William Roy "Link," 42, 275
Lynch, Jim, 178
Lyons, Leo, 16–17

M

Mack, Connie, 9, 17
Mack, Tom, 175, 275
Mackey, John, 175, 275
Madden, John, 160, 161, *266,*
    267, 275
Maddox, Tommy, 238
Majors, Johnny, 213
Manders, Jack, 62
Mankins, Logan, *244*

O

P

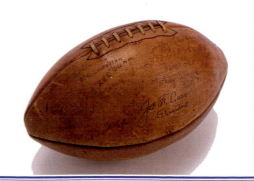